THE ARCHAEOLOGY OF
MEDIEVAL BRITAIN

Series Editor: Dr Helen Clarke

Medieval Monasteries

MEDIEVAL MONASTERIES

—— J. PATRICK GREENE ——

LEICESTER UNIVERSITY PRESS
Leicester, London and New York

*Distributed in the United States and Canada
by St. Martin's Press, New York*

To my children – Jenny, Laura, Andrew and Christopher
– for their patience, interest and companionship
on visits to many of the monasteries that appear
in this book

© J. Patrick Greene, 1992

First published in Great Britain in 1992 by Leicester University Press

Editorial offices
Fielding Johnson Building, University of Leicester,
University Road, Leicester, LE1 7RH, England

Trade and other enquiries
25 Floral Street, London, WC2E 9DS, England
and Room 400, 175 Fifth Avenue, New York, NY10010, USA

British Library Cataloguing in Publication Data
A CIP cataloguing record for this book is available
from the British Library

ISBN 0–7185–1296–0

Library of Congress Cataloging in Publication Data
A CIP cataloging record for this book is available from the
Library of Congress

Typeset by Mayhew Typesetting, Rhayader, Powys
Printed and bound in Great Britain by
Biddles Ltd, Guildford and King's Lynn

Contents

Foreword

This is the second publication in the series *The Archaeology of Medieval Britain*, initiated in 1990 with John R. Kenyon's work, *Medieval Fortifications*. The aim of the books in the series is to present up-to-date surveys of the archaeological evidence for specific aspects of Britain in the Middle Ages. The core period to be covered in depth is from the Norman Conquest of 1066 to the Reformation, but there are no hard-and-fast chronological boundaries and examples are drawn from before and after the period where appropriate. The books are not narrowly site- or object-orientated, emphasising rather the social and economic aspects of the subjects in question, and pursuing the most recent thoughts and research in the field. Although primarily devoted to knowledge gained from archaeological excavation and research, they also refer to written, cartographic, and pictorial evidence and are of interest to archaeologists and historians alike. Their style of presentation and their lavish illustrations also make them attractive to general readers interested in their medieval heritage.

Each topic is covered by an expert in that field, whose depth and breadth of knowledge will throw new and exciting light on the Middle Ages. Archaeological excavations in recent decades are used as the basis for wide-ranging conclusions and synthesis.

J. Patrick Greene, the author of the present volume, is well known for his pioneering work at Norton Priory, Runcorn, Cheshire, where he directed the large-scale and meticulous excavation of an Augustinian priory. He was also responsible for the establishment of the site museum, and the presentation of the site to the public in an innovatory and exciting manner. This experience, together with his wider researches into medieval monastic houses in Britain, make him the ideal author for this book which deals not only with the details of medieval monastic life and buildings but also with the place of the monastery in social and economic development in the Middle Ages. A gazetteer of sites to visit and comments on the way in which they are displayed to the public will also help the general reader to discover the delights of visiting some of the most spectacular remains which survive from the Britain of the Middle Ages.

Helen Clarke
January 1992

Preface

There are numerous books about medieval monasteries, but none that tackles the subject from an archaeological standpoint for the whole of the British Isles. This volume attempts to give an overview of the archaeology of monasteries in Britain, and it forms part of a series that is intended to provide a particularly wide-ranging survey of medieval archaeology. Some of the topics covered in this volume will therefore emerge in subsequent books in the series, such as the volume on medieval towns and the volume devoted to religious houses for women.

There are two main strands to my text. The first is methodological, examining how the techniques of archaeology can be applied to monastic houses and their estates. The second strand is an account of the types of information that archaeology has produced, drawing particularly on work carried out during the last two decades, arranged on a thematic basis. Underlying the entire subject is the sheer breadth of sources of information, ranging from contemporary historical sources to modern scientific and computer-based techniques.

Chapter 1 provides a background to post-Conquest monasticism, including the emergence of different types of monastic organisation in North Africa and Europe from the fourth century. The proliferation of orders of religious can be daunting to anyone new to the subject (and even for people with some familiarity with it). An understanding of the major monastic movements is, however, an essential prerequisite for appreciating the ways in which they were adopted within the British Isles. Chapter 1 also examines the theory and practice of the planning of monasteries, and looks at a number of case studies which illustrate the diversity of variations on the 'standard' layout of buildings. Throughout the book, I have tried to avoid obscure terminology, using, for example, 'latrines' instead of 'reredorter' (the latter was, in any case, a euphemism coined in the nineteenth century; it would have meant nothing to a medieval monk).

The way in which archaeology has been used in the investigation of monastic sites is the subject of Chapter 2. The limited objectives and methods of nineteenth-century excavators are contrasted with the breadth of archaeological techniques applied today. Chapter 3 describes the methods used by medieval masons and other craftsmen to construct monastic buildings, including temporary accommodation for the inmates and the building workers. The growth and elaboration of monasteries, and rebuildings as deliberate policy or as a result of disaster, are examined in Chapter 4.

Chapter 5 discusses an outstanding feature of monastic planning: the use of water for a multitude of purposes including drinking, sanitation, fish-rearing, and as a source of power for mills. Other aspects of water management include drainage and flood protection of monastic lands. The monastic estates, the economy of monasteries, food and drink, and hospitality for guests are subjects discussed in Chapter 6.

Monasteries in towns, from pre-Conquest foundations to the arrival of the friars, as well as the impact of monastic precincts on the topography of urban centres, are described in Chapter 7. The Dissolution occurred rapidly in England and Wales, and more slowly in Ireland and Scotland. The contribution of archaeology to knowledge of the process of closure and adaptation or demolition are examined in Chapter 8.

The reawakening of interest in monastic remains, the preservation movement, and the presentation of monastic sites to visitors today, are all topics of Chapter 9, which also provides some guidance on outstanding monastic sites to visit. In the Postscript, suggestions for future directions in monastic archaeology are put forward.

J. Patrick Greene

Acknowledgements

The writer of a book of this kind is heavily dependent upon the research and writings of others. I would like to thank the following people and organisations for their help, encouragement, and provision of information and illustrations: Dave Beard and Simon Mason (Museum of London), Julian Cross (Wessex Archaeology), Gail Durbin and Ken Glen (English Heritage Education Service), Glyn Coppack, Stephen Johnson, David Sherlock (English Heritage, Properties in Care), Derek Edwards (Norfolk Museums Service), Margaret Faull (Yorkshire Mining Museum), Mary Gryspeerdt (Somerset Rural Life Museum), Barbara Harbottle (City of Newcastle upon Tyne), Elizabeth Hartley and Brian Hayton (The Yorkshire Museum), Fred Hartley (Jewry Wall Museum, Leicester), Stephen Heywood (Norfolk County Council), Peter Hill (The Whithorn Trust), Mike Hodder (Sandwell Metropolitan Borough Council), Haidee Jackson (Newstead Abbey), Donnie Mackay (Royal Commission on the Historical Monuments of England, Newcastle Office), Phil Mayes and Robina McNeil (Greater Manchester Archaeology Service), David Miles (Oxford Archaeology Unit), Denis Mynard (Buckinghamshire County Council), Anne Partington-Omar (St Edmundsbury Borough Council), David Robinson and Christine Kenyon (Cadw), Peter Saunders (Salisbury and South Wiltshire Museum), Aighleann O'Shaughnessy and Ann Lynch (Office of Public Works, Ireland), Alistair Smith (Whitworth Art Gallery, Manchester), John Barnatt and Ken Smith (Peak National Park), Sian Spink (Royal Commission on Ancient and Historical Monuments in Wales), Judith Stones (Aberdeen Arts and Museums), Chris Tabraham (Historic Scotland), Blaise Vyner (University of York), Simon Ward (Grosvenor Museum, Chester), Margaret Warhurst (Norton Priory Museum Trust), Jason Wood (Lancaster University Archaeological Unit), Stuart Wrathmell (West Yorkshire Archaeology Service), Susan Wright (Bordesley Abbey Project) and my colleagues at the Museum of Science and Industry in Manchester. I particularly appreciate the advice and guidance provided by Helen Clarke, as Series Editor, in the production of this volume.

List of figures

1 *What are monastic houses?*

Monastic origins

An aspect of religious practice that appeared early in the Christian era was the desire of individuals to separate themselves from the distractions of society so that they might live a life entirely devoted to contemplation, prayer and the worship of God. It is hardly surprising that this should have occurred, as Christ Himself had established a compelling precedent by spending forty days and nights in the wilderness in spiritual self-examination. From this, and from the Apostle Paul's advocacy of the state of celibacy, as well as the conviction that riches were an undesirable encumbrance to those who wished to enter the kingdom of God, grew the motivations of those who chose the monastic life.

The original monks were hermits living in isolation – the word monk was derived from the Greek for 'one who dwelt alone'. However, some hermits began to live in communities. By the early fourth century the monastic movement had developed in the Egyptian desert, and from this source it spread throughout the Christian world. It was also in Egypt that the idea took root that a brotherhood of monks required a set of guiding principles to govern their lives. The leading figure of influence was St Anthony, whose teachings and ideals were given wider circulation through the *Life of Anthony*, written by Athanasius, bishop of Alexandria (Brooke 1982, 14).

It was also to North Africa that another strand of medieval monasticism could trace its origins. St Augustine (354–430), as bishop of Hippo, provided guidance to groups of men and women, each living in fervent but unregulated communities, on ways in which they could better organise their affairs. His conception of the monastic ideal, incorporating the life of contemplation and prayer with the virtue of hard work and an openness to the outside world, was developed to become the Rule of St Augustine. This was widely adopted in the medieval period by canons – men who lived in communities like monks, but who were also ordained priests. Canonesses also embraced the Augustinian rule, but as women were debarred from the priesthood.

The influence and asceticism of the North African desert monks was transmitted to parts of the Roman Empire in which communal hermitages had already become established. John Cassian was particularly influential. He left Egypt to settle in Provence in about 400. His teachings and writings examined the framework and objectives of the life of the monk. His *Collations* promoted the benefits of contemplation; in the medieval period a chapter of the *Collations* was read every day in most monastic houses.

The Rule of St Benedict

In about 530, in a monastery at Monte Cassino in Italy, St Benedict of Nursia wrote his Rule. It was to govern the administration of thousands of monasteries, and would regulate the lives of tens of thousands of monks (and eventually nuns as well) in the centuries that followed. The Benedictine Rule made great demands on those who followed it. Monks were expected to follow its instructions with total obedience. Poverty and chastity were required of every individual. Each day was to be spent in a rigorously organised routine of worship by the community, private prayer, eating and sleeping. Every hour, every minute, of an individual's life was determined by the Rule, for every day of the year. For anyone who is not a member of a religious order, it is difficult to imagine the extent to which a monk was expected to submit to the authority of the Rule, and the degree to which personal considerations were sacrificed to a totally inflexible regime. The strength of Benedict's Rule was in its recognition of human frailty. The ascetic life, wholly devoted to God, brought great psychological pressures upon those who entered it. The rigidity, the predictability, and the lack of personal choice were all essential supports to the person who had chosen such a strenuous and stressful life – particularly as individualism was regarded as a manifestation of pride and therefore something that the monk should struggle against.

The Benedictine Rule was the foundation upon which the entire structure of medieval monasticism in Western Europe was eventually built. Many reformers in later centuries put their own interpretation on Benedict's teachings, but all acknowledged his primacy. The canons of the Augustinian order, although not strictly speaking monks, were nonetheless profoundly influenced by Benedictine practice. The Augustinians came to adopt a similar pattern for regulating communities of canons and canonesses.

The manner in which monastic influences and practices spread from place to place in the sixth and following centuries is beyond the remit of this book to describe. A striking feature that must be emphasised, however, is the capacity of monastic movements to transcend political boundaries. In the case of the British Isles, ideas and influences flowed both to and from continental Europe. The Benedictine Rule was introduced to England in the seventh century. It had a great influence on two leading figures in the monastic movement in Northumbria – St Wilfred, who founded monasteries at Ripon, York and Hexham, and St Benedict Biscop, the founder of Monkwearmouth and Jarrow. But as Benedict's ideas permeated Britain, so Celtic monasticism was taken to the Continent by Irish monks. Monasteries on the Irish pattern were established as far afield as France, Switzerland and Italy; eventually they too came under the influence of the Rule of St Benedict. Missionaries also set out from English monasteries, the most famous of whom was St Boniface. He laid the foundations of the church in Germany, where he was martyred in 754. Women took part in missionary activity, establishing abbeys for nuns, or sometimes communities for both monks and nuns, particularly in Germany. One of the models for this kind of double monastery was Whitby, founded by St Hilda. As was usually the case, Hilda was of royal birth so consequently had access to the resources necessary to enter upon such an enterprise. The frequent choice of monasteries as burial places by kings and their relatives is an indication of the high regard in which they were held. They often became the resting places of the relics of saints.

Religious houses were susceptible to two principal dangers: decay from within, and attack from without. In the eighth century, Bede deplored the tendency of monasteries to drift away from the ideals upon which they had been founded. His strictures were echoed by reformers in subsequent centuries who, like Bede, saw the need to return to the basics of belief and observance. Bede described monasteries that had fallen under the control of laymen, where the members had wives and children, where a lavish life-style had been adopted, and where the brethren simply went through the motions of the religious life. Even the most assiduous pursuit of monastic ideals, however, provided no protection from assailants from the world beyond the precinct. Whilst individual members of a monastic community had renounced personal possessions, the monastery itself could present a tempting target for avaricious enemies. Inevitably, a monastery concentrated resources intended to sustain its inmates in their pursuit of the religious life. The church might also contain precious relics and furnishings. For Viking raiders in the ninth century they were enticing and vulnerable prey. Flight was often the only option open; the monks of Lindisfarne, for example, sought shelter at Norham on the Tweed before again fleeing to Carlisle carrying their treasured relics of St Cuthbert. After a further seven years' wandering they settled at Chester le Street.

The disruptions caused by Viking attacks and Scandinavian settlement damaged monasticism, but this was compounded by a decline in standards even in those communities unaffected by the Norsemen. By the middle of the tenth century, however, a movement for reform was under way, given impetus by developments on the Continent and by the support of English kings. Old communities were reformed to follow fullheartedly the Benedictine Rule, and new monasteries were established. Leading figures in the revival were Archbishop Dunstan of Canterbury and Archbishop Oswald of York, both of whom had experience of continental monasteries, and Bishop Ethelwold of Winchester. With their guidance, English monasteries adopted standards of observance of the Benedictine Rule and principles of administration that created a reassuring atmosphere of religious purpose and stability. This in turn gave rise to a remarkable flowering of religious art, music, architecture and learning.

Norman monasticism

The monasteries of Normandy also experienced the movement of renewal and reform in the tenth century. As a result, after William, Duke of Normandy's invasion of England in 1066, leading figures of the Norman church could be brought in to reorganise the English church on Norman lines. Lanfranc and Anselm, successive archbishops of Canterbury, were themselves Norman monks. In Norman England the climate of opinion was well disposed towards monasticism. King William himself set the tone, founding the great Abbaye aux Hommes in Caen in celebration of his victory, and Battle Abbey in Sussex as an act of penitence. His wife Mathilda founded the Abbaye aux Dames in Caen, also in 1066. Within a couple of generations of the Conquest, every cathedral and major abbey in England had been rebuilt in Romanesque style. The seats of bishops were established in nine important abbeys, the monastic churches becoming cathedrals of the reorganised Anglo-Norman church.

William's example in founding the abbeys at Caen and Battle was followed by members of his feudal aristocracy, who frequently used some of their newly-acquired English properties to endow a new monastery in England or Normandy. There were about fifty monasteries for men in England at the time of the Conquest. When Henry II ascended the throne less than a century later, the number had increased dramatically to about 500.

As spheres of Anglo-Norman power expanded, so too did monasticism. In Wales the Norman advance was marked by the building of castles and the establishment of towns. Benedictine monasteries were founded by the new landowners and endowed with lands which helped to consolidate Norman control (Soulsby 1983, 46). Abbeys were built at Chepstow, Monmouth, Abergavenny, Cardiff, Carmarthen, Brecon, Llandovery, Kidwelly and Cardigan. A Benedictine nunnery was established at Usk. In an apparent reaction to the identification of the Benedictines with Anglo-Norman power, nine Cistercian houses were founded by Welsh princes (Butler 1982). In Ireland as well, monasteries were used as an instrument of colonial control. The Abbey of St Thomas the Martyr, for example, was founded by William fitz Audelin in 1177 following the capture of Dublin by the English. It was kept under close royal supervision; the king had the right to appoint both the abbot and the prior. The founder's character was described by Gerald of Wales: 'There was no end to his craftiness – there was poison in the honey, and a snake in the grass. To outward appearance he was liberal and courteous, but within there was more aloes than honey' (Elliott 1990, 62). Fitz Audelin's soul clearly had particular need of the prayers of the monks.

A common feature of all monastic houses was the duty placed on the brethren to pray for the souls of the founders and their families, to provide a place of burial, to offer spiritual counsel, and often to admit the founder as a monk late in life. These obligations were not part of the Rule that governed the lives of monks, but they were usually specified in the abbey's foundation charter. The religious houses that will be examined in this book therefore had two major strands of responsibility – to the ideals of their order and to the preoccupations of their temporal supporters.

The layout of the monastery

Before looking at individual religious houses, it is worth examining the set of basic principles that underlie their planning. By the time of the Conquest these had become well established on the Continent and in Britain. They can be found in the houses of all the orders, although in the case of very small monasteries not all the standard features will be present. The investigation of deviations from the norm can reveal much about religious practice,

Figure 1. Thetford Priory, Norfolk, from the air. The cloister and surrounding ranges lie to the south of the church. To the south-east is the infirmary, arranged like a monastery-in-miniature around a tiny cloister. The gatehouse can be seen alongside the road to the north.

Photograph by Derek Edwards, Norfolk County Museums Air Photography Unit.

economic circumstances, constraints imposed by the location, the ambition of patrons or abbots, or any of a host of other factors.

The standard features of the monastic plan (figure 1) were a smooth blend of spiritual necessity and common sense. The dominant building was the church. This was the building that was first to be built in masonry. The reason was straightforward – the monastery was there for the Opus Dei, the Work of God. Construction of the church therefore had the highest priority, for within its walls the members of the community would spend the largest part of their waking hours in worship. It was also the building in which the founder might expect to be buried. Permanent domestic accommodation had to wait, often for decades, as the church building slowly progressed.

Precedence of construction was also reflected in scale. The church was the biggest, most impressive structure, not only because it had to contain the high altar, choir stalls and chapels, but because it symbolised the dedication of the entire establishment to the religious purpose.

The church was oriented so that the chancel containing the high altar was at the east end. This practice, which was of long standing but which has indistinct origins, meant that the complex of monastic buildings attached to the church was also aligned on an east–west axis. In reality churches were rarely laid out precisely to face true east, and sometimes, where the peculiar circumstances of the site demanded it, they could deviate markedly from the ideal. The extreme example is Rievaulx Abbey in Yorkshire where the fall of the ground towards the west meant that the Cistercian church had to be aligned north–south. Medieval references to the church simply treat the orientation as though it were normal.

A monastic church comprised three main units. The eastern part was the chancel in which the high altar was situated. Immediately to the west was the choir. This was lined, on the north and south, with sets of choir stalls. Here the brethren spent a major part of their day; both Benedictine and Augustinian traditions demanded a daily round of seven services. A screen, known as the pulpitum because it incorporated a pulpit, separated the choir from the third element of the church, the nave. Its use varied according to the order with which the monastery was associated, and also local factors. Thus the nave might have a purely ceremonial function, or it was used by lay brothers, or it could serve as a parish church.

The major monastic buildings were arranged to surround a courtyard, the cloister. Ideally this was square, but often the phased development of the buildings, or restrictions of the site, resulted in a rectangle or a parallelogram. Usually the cloister was built to the south of the church, to take advantage of sunlight which would otherwise be largely blocked out. Sometimes, however, overriding factors, such as the requirements of drainage or security, caused the cloister to be placed to the north of the church. Two groups of monasteries differed from this general rule. Friaries in Ireland commonly had the cloister on the north, for reasons that are far from clear. A higher proportion of nunneries than would be expected on purely functional grounds had a northern cloister, and it has been proposed (Gilchrist 1989, 253) that there may have been an association with the cult of the Virgin in this phenomenon.

Cloister buildings

In the description that follows, a monastery with its cloister in the conventional position on the south will be described; in essence the northern cloister involved a reversal in the positions of the church and refectory.

The cloister had two elements, the garth (garden) open to the sky, and the cloister walks – passages lining all four sides of the garth. They provided a means of covered access to the surrounding buildings. The north cloister walk also had desks for reading and study known as carrels; often a cupboard for the books was set into a nearby wall. As well as these practical functions, the cloister walks provided a setting for one of the most impressive rituals, the Sunday procession. Every Sunday morning, after the water had been blessed at the high altar, two monks toured the buildings sprinkling the holy water in all the rooms surrounding the cloister. At the same time, the remaining brethren processed through the eastern part of the church sprinkling holy water on each of the altars. They then left the church in procession, entering the east cloister walk. They were led by the bearers of holy water and the cross, flanked by acolytes holding lighted candles. The abbot was the last member of the procession, which progressed slowly round the cloister. The brethren returned to the church through a door at the northern end of the west cloister walk, opening into the nave. The nave altar was then sprinkled, and any other altars in side chapels. The brethren completed their procession by re-entering the choir through the pulpitum. On important feast days the procession was even more elaborate, with relics and shrines being carried.

The claustral buildings will be described in the order in which the Sunday procession passed them. Next to the church, to the south of the choir and adjoining the transept (in the case of a cruciform church) was a room which in some monasteries functioned as a sacristy where altar furnishings, vessels for the eucharist, candlesticks, etc. were stored. Sometimes, however, this space was occupied by a passage leading from the cloister to the monks' burial ground to the east of the church. To the south was the building which was next in importance to the church, the chapter house. A door, often flanked by a pair of windows, gave access from the cloister walk (sometimes through a vestibule). All the brethren gathered in the chapter house every morning to hear a chapter of the rule of the order read out to them, to discuss the day-to-day business of the monastery, and for confessions to be heard and punishments administered. Seating was arranged around the walls, with a special seat for the abbot in the centre of the east side.

Further south was the warming room. This room had a fireplace; in winter months the brethren might come here in the short gaps between services to restore some life to bodies chilled by long hours spent in the unheated church. The ascetic ideal restricted fires to the warming room, the kitchens, the guesthouse, the infirmary and, where present, the abbot's quarters.

On the upper floor above the sacristy, chapter house and warming room was the dormitory (sometimes called the dorter). A door led from the cloister walk to the day stairs which ascended to the dormitory. This was a long hall in which the monks' beds (straw-filled mattresses) were arranged side by side in two rows. Privacy was non-existent at an early date, but a characteristic of the development of dormitories is the introduction of partitions between beds (figure 2). At the northern end of the dormitory a door opened on to the night stairs. These occupied part of the south transept of the church. They are so called because in the middle of the night a bell was sounded to rouse the brethren from their sleep. They formed up in procession, walked down the night stairs into the church and proceeded to the choir stalls where they celebrated Mattins and Lauds. They returned to the dormitory for their second sleep, which ended at dawn with, again, the ringing of a bell and a procession to the church, this time for Prime.

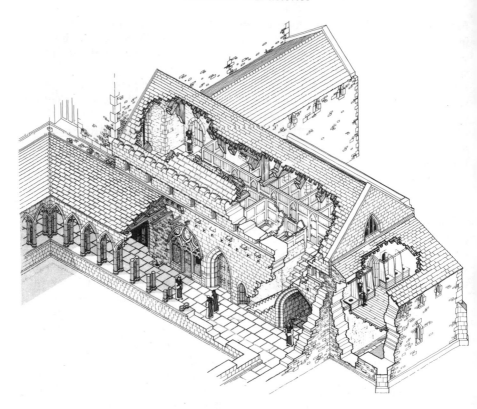

Figure 2. Reconstruction drawing of the east range of Valle Crucis Abbey, Clwyd. On the ground floor is the elaborate entrance to the chapter house. Above, the dormitory has been divided into compartments by wooden screens. The latrines are situated at the end of the dormitory.

Illustration by Chris Jones-Jenkins, reproduced by permission of Cadw: Welsh Historic Monuments.

At the southern end of the dormitory, or sometimes projecting from its eastern side, were the latrines. They consisted of a long row of wooden toilet seats over shoots or over a gap between two walls dropping down to a drain on the ground floor. Water flowed down the drain to provide, by medieval standards, a high level of sanitation (see figure 2). The importance placed upon a good drainage system is a striking feature of monastic planning (see Chapter 5). The availability of a source of water for the drain was often the decisive factor in determining the location of the monastery. Where a monastery was particularly inconveniently sited for a water supply, or in some very poor houses, the latrines emptied into a cess-pit.

On the south side of the cloister was the refectory, the hall in which the monks ate their meals. The first substantial meal was dinner, eaten after Mass in late morning. Before entering the refectory the brethren were expected to wash their hands at the lavatorium. This was a long basin supplied with running water, with towels stored nearby for all the monks. Usually the lavatorium was set into the wall of the refectory within the south cloister walk, but at some monasteries a free-standing structure was built into the cloister garth. The refectory itself was arranged to accommodate the brethren at long tables in the body of the hall. The abbot sat at a table on a dais at one end, sometimes with important visitors. Silence was observed during meals, during which passages from holy writings were read out by one of the monks. The side wall of the refectory therefore often incorporated a pulpit. Supper was eaten in the early evening after Vespers.

Adjoining the refectory on its western side were the kitchens where meals were prepared and passed through a hatch in the wall to the monks. On the west side of the cloister was another two-storey building, the cellarer's range (sometimes called the cellarium). This building provided secure storage for foodstuffs, drink, and other materials for which one of the monks, the cellarer, was responsible. A passage (often referred to as a slype) usually separated the northern end of the cellarer's range from the church. It provided a link between the cloister and the outer courtyard; through it important lay people, especially benefactors, might occasionally be invited, for example to take part in a ceremony in the chapter house. In most orders the upper floor of the west range served as the abbot's quarters. As a person of rank the abbot had a suite of rooms that would befit a substantial landowner, comprising a hall, chamber, and oratory (private chapel). The Cistercians had lay brothers in addition to monks, so in their abbeys the upper floor of the west range housed a dormitory for them. In those cases, the abbot had his accommodation in a separate building, once the early fervour which demanded that the abbot should sleep in the common monks' dormitory had subsided.

The buildings arranged around the cloister were the setting for almost all of the activities of a monk's life. The monastic complex was likely to have several more buildings, however. The infirmary was the most important. Its usual location was to the south-east of the claustral buildings (beyond the dormitory and the latrines). It was often placed to permit the infirmary latrine to empty into the main drain. The infirmary usually consisted of an open hall in which the beds of sick and aged monks were housed (figures 1 and 3). There was sometimes a chapel or an altar at the east end of the infirmary hall so that the inmates could still participate in the religious life. A kitchen served the infirmary, which had more relaxed regulations about diet, especially consumption of meat, than the monks could expect in the refectory. This doubtless helped the recuperation of the sick and of monks who had undergone bleeding – the deliberate opening of veins – that featured in most monastic houses.

Another important building was the guests' quarters, normally on the outer courtyard to the west of the cellarer's range. Hospitality to travellers featured as an obligation in the rule of most orders. Sometimes it was exploited mercilessly; members of the gentry travelling with large retinues of servants could be an enormous drain on the resources of an abbey, which might suffer particularly if it was on a popular route. The facilities consisted of a large hall, sometimes with chambers attached, and latrines. There might be a kitchen as well, unless the hall was supplied from the main kitchens.

Service buildings were located on the outer courtyard. These provided for the daily needs of the community. A brewhouse with malting lofts and kiln

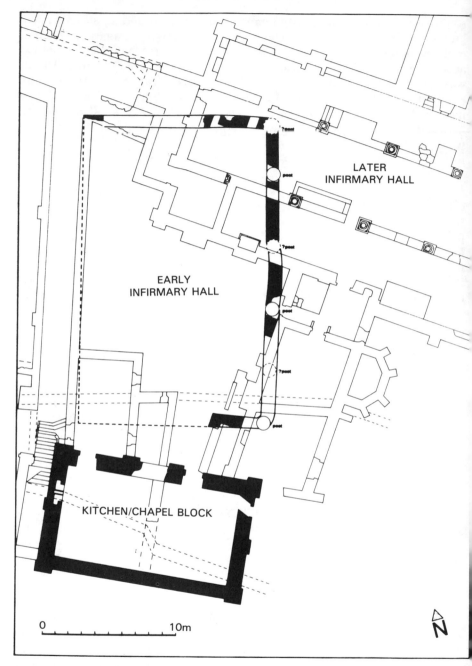

LATER
INFIRMARY HALL

EARLY
INFIRMARY HALL

KITCHEN/CHAPEL BLOCK

0   10m

N

Figure 3. Plan of the early infirmary hall of Kirkstall Abbey, West Yorkshire, with the larger infirmary complex that replaced it shown in outline.
West Yorkshire Archaeology Service.

produced the ale which was a major ingredient of the monastic diet (as much as eight pints of – admittedly weak – beer per person might be provided). A bakehouse produced bread which was served with all meals. There was often a granary, a stable, a smithy, and other attributes of a 'home farm' such as a dairy, a hen house, a slaughter house, and animal sheds. The outer court was made secure with a gatehouse, which often had two doors: a large one for horse-drawn wagons and riders, and a smaller one for pedestrians. The gatehouse was set in a perimeter wall, bank or moat system to protect the privacy of the monastery. In areas subject to military incursions, such as northern England and the Scottish Borders, perimeter walls and gatehouses were usually insufficient to prevent damage and looting.

The landscape surrounding a rural monastery often had a number of further features. One of these was a system of fishponds in which fish were reared for serving at the refectory tables. A watermill or a windmill (or both) ground cereals to supply the bakehouse. A herb garden was situated conveniently for the kitchens and infirmary. There was probably a vegetable garden and an orchard. The fields of the home farm were usually farmed directly by the employees of the abbey. Other land in the ownership of religious houses was farmed on a manorial system by tenants, or as granges staffed by farm workers or lay brothers.

Medieval monasteries had many features in common that allow a generalised description of the kind that has been given here. Like all generalisations however, it conceals the wide differences that existed between the houses of different orders, and the great variety of interpretations of the standard monastic plan that occurred within an individual order. There are usually good reasons why particular features were adopted, or why certain changes to the original design were introduced at a later date. These are issues that can be explored through archaeological enquiry, to provide a fully rounded view of monasteries and the lives of their inhabitants.

The remainder of this chapter consists of a number of brief sketches of monastic houses that have been the subject of at least some recent archaeological investigation. The selection is designed to provide a picture of the very wide range of monasteries that were established in Britain, and to introduce some of the monastic orders that were most numerous in the British Isles.

A Benedictine royal foundation: Battle Abbey

In 1066 the religious houses in both England and Normandy were organised on lines that followed the prescriptions of the Rule of St Benedict. For William the Conqueror therefore, it was not a matter of choosing a suitable order for the monastery he wished to create on the site of the battle that won for him the throne of England: it had to be Benedictine. The monks were sent from the abbey of Marmoutier in the Loire Valley to establish a new monastery in Sussex. They were faced with a situation quite different from that which pioneer monks usually expected. Normally the site of a monastery was determined by practical considerations. The Marmoutier monks, however, were faced with an inflexible constraint which removed

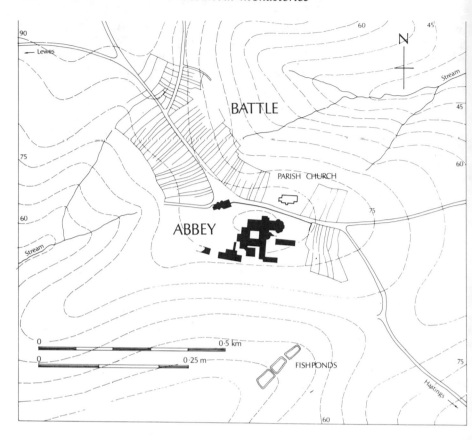

Figure 4. Plan showing the location of Battle Abbey, Sussex, in relation to the topography. The contours show the hilltop site that proved so troublesome to the builders.

Drawing supplied by John Hare, English Heritage.

from them any element of choice in the location of their new abbey. The Conqueror determined that the abbey church should be built with its high altar on the spot where Harold fell, as an act of penance (Brown 1981, 3). It was a singularly inconvenient spot, on a hill that required artificial levelling and which was without a water supply. The monks decided that it was impractical to build the abbey on the precise site of the battle, and therefore chose a better location to the north-west. When the king heard of the change of site he 'ordered them to lay the foundations of the church speedily and on the very spot where his enemy had fallen and the victory had been won', according to the chronicle of Battle Abbey. The monks, in consequence, were forced to come to terms with their unsuitable site and had to adapt both the hillside and the building designs to create a monastery on the standard plan. Despite the drawbacks of the location, Battle Abbey was to become one of the wealthiest monasteries of medieval England, and the focus for the development of a town (figure 4).

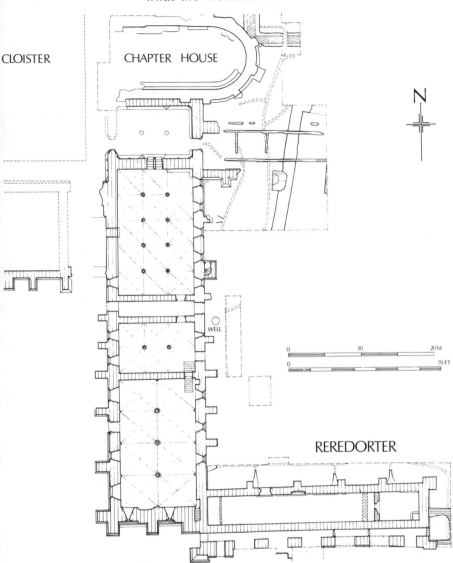

CLOISTER

CHAPTER HOUSE

N

WELL

0   10   20 M

0   70 FT

REREDORTER

Figure 5. Plan of the east range of Battle Abbey, showing the dormitory undercroft and the latrine block.

Drawing supplied by John Hare, English Heritage.

Limited excavations were carried out on the site between 1929 and 1934; more recently a three-year programme of excavation and investigation of the standing structures was organised (Hare 1985). Little survives of the Norman buildings because, like many wealthy monasteries, the monks were able to replace their original structures with a much grander assemblage in later years. Further drastic changes to the buildings followed the dissolution of the abbey which occurred in 1538. Nonetheless, it is possible to reconstruct a plan of the abbey showing those buildings that were standing at the Dissolution. The layout is much as might be expected of a wealthy Benedictine house. On the north was the church. Its plan is partly conjectural; it seems to have had a broad aisled nave, a pair of transepts with apsed chapels (i.e. with semi-circular eastern walls), and an aisled chancel that terminated in an ambulatory within an apse from which radiated three chapels. This Norman design was discarded when the eastern arm of the church was rebuilt on a larger scale. The new east end terminated in a chevet – a ring of radiating chapels around an ambulatory, which was a semi-circular route for pilgrims or processions around the eastern side of the high altar. The church was therefore clearly an impressive structure, both in its Norman and its expanded forms, which did full justice to the Conqueror's wish to create a suitable memorial on the spot where he had won the crown of England.

The Battle Abbey cloister was placed to the south of the church with the Norman chapter house built alongside the south transept. The remains of the chapter house were uncovered during the excavations in the 1970s (figure 5). It was a large building which, like the original church, had an apsed east wall. Further south the Norman and the later builders had to overcome the problems posed by the sloping site. A new abbot's hall was built in the thirteenth century on the west side of the cloister and a new dormitory on the east as part of the same operation. The latter occupied the usual position on the first floor, and was set on a series of four vaulted undercrofts which were used as a parlour, a warming room and a novices' room; the function of the fourth has not been identified. In order to provide a level floor for the dormitory, the undercrofts are of increasing height, with the southernmost, the novices' room, a particularly lofty structure.

A latrine block was built next to the eastern side of the dormitory at its southern end. Excavation has revealed details of its form. Because of the necessity for the latrines to be easily accessible from the dormitory, it too was a tall building. The latrines were arranged in a long line at first floor level; they emptied into the main drain on the south side of the building (figure 5). The drain had a stone flagged base and it sloped to the east. The wall on its southern side consisted of an arcade; each of the arches appears to have held timber shuttering. There was no stream to divert to flush the latrines, so the shuttering may have permitted liquids to seep through, soaking into the open ground to the south and east. Periodically the solid excrement could be dug out for disposal elsewhere.

On the south side of the cloister was the refectory, which was rebuilt in the late thirteenth century. Further south was a kitchen which comprised a central cooking area with hearths, surrounded by four other lower ranges. On the lower, southern side a cellar was needed to create a level platform for the square kitchen building.

Beyond the main monastic complex other buildings stood, only some of which have been investigated; they may include a sacristy and an infirmary. Because of the restricted nature of the hilltop, the outer courtyard was situated to the south of the main buildings rather than in the usual position to the west of the cloister. The monastic precinct was surrounded by a wall into which, in the mid fourteenth century, a great gatehouse was inserted.

It survives in remarkably complete form, dominating the town that grew up outside the abbey. It continued in use after the Dissolution as the highly impressive entrance to the residence of the new owner, Sir Anthony Browne, who converted the abbot's house and the outer courtyard.

A house of Augustinian canons: Norton Priory

King William's foundation of Battle Abbey is one of many examples of royal patronage of monastic houses in the eleventh century – a practice which was continued by successive rulers in the twelfth century. At first it was houses following the Benedictine Rule, and after 1077 its reformed variant from Cluny, that benefited from the Crown's support. From about 1104, however, a third order was available to potential monastic patrons. The Augustinian canons made rapid progress, with a large number of foundations in the first half of the twelfth century. Royal patronage was an important factor in ensuring the Augustinians' widespread success in England. Over 75 per cent of Augustinian foundations in the early period were established by Henry I, officials of his court, or members of the royal entourage (Dickinson 1950, 129). However, it was not only those who counted themselves members of the royal circle who founded religious houses. Increasingly, major landowners sought to ensure the protection of their souls and those of their families through the prayers of monks and canons in religious houses that they themselves had founded.

Norton Priory in Cheshire is an example of one such foundation. Its founder, William fitz Nigel, baron of Halton, was second in command to the earl of Chester and had the responsibility of, amongst other things, assembling a fighting force for action in Wales whenever the need arose. He possessed extensive land holdings, granted by the earl, spread widely throughout England. These formed the basis of the endowment he provided for the canons. One of his gifts was the church at Runcorn – a Saxon foundation which appears to have become the priory. This was by no means an unusual situation. Many founders took advantage of an existing religious community when setting up their monastery. The earl of Chester had done this twenty-one years earlier when he refounded a college of secular canons as the Benedictine abbey of St Werburgh (Burne 1962). The use of a parish church was not unique either – many Augustinian houses originated in this way (Robinson 1980, 35–6). The formula was acceptable to the local bishop, for the canons, as ordained priests, were subject to episcopal supervision. Indeed, the bishop occupied the position of abbot in the case of all but the most important Augustinian houses – hence the fact that the effective head of the household was the prior, who acted as the abbot's deputy in an abbey. This involvement of the bishop, however theoretical it may have been in practice, is one of the reasons for the popularity of the Augustinian order. Bishops were keen to promote it: a notable example was Bishop Malachy who introduced the order to Ireland as a reform measure, aimed at bringing clerks and married priests into line with established practice elsewhere in the church.

The canons moved to Norton in 1134, nineteen years after the foundation

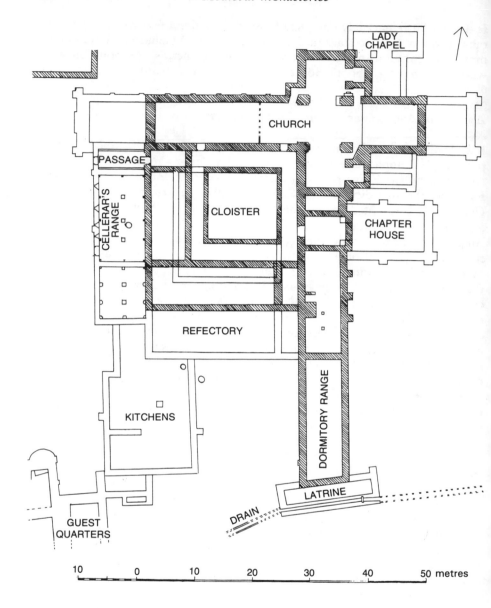

Figure 6. Plan showing the expansion of the buildings of Norton Priory, Cheshire, in the thirteenth century. The twelfth-century buildings are shown hatched, the thirteenth-century structures are in outline. The church was extended, a new chapter house and latrine blocks were built, and the south and west ranges demolished and reconstructed on a larger scale.

Drawn by Patrick Greene.

at Runcorn. It was by no means unusual for a change of site to occur relatively soon after the foundation of a religious house. At least twenty other English Augustinian houses moved site, usually only a modest distance – the average was 6 kilometres (Robinson 1980, 78). Cistercian houses tended to move over greater distances, and indeed showed a greater propensity to do so. Twenty-nine, a third of the English total, changed site, the average distance being 29 kilometres (Donkin 1978, 31–6; Donkin 1959, 251).

The site at Norton where the canons established themselves has been the subject of excavation on a large scale, directed by the writer between 1971 and 1982 (Greene 1989). As a consequence of the intensive nature of the archaeological and historic investigation, and the application of a range of scientific techniques, a great deal is known about this particular site. The aspects that are worth highlighting here are first, the form of the original buildings, and secondly, the way in which the canons were prepared to engage in an ambitious campaign of expansion when their endowment was supplemented by further gifts (figure 6).

The church, which was the first masonry building to be erected at Norton, was of a very simple plan – aisleless, cruciform, with tiny chapels opening from the eastern side of each transept. This basic design fulfilled the needs of a priory of modest size and pretensions (there would probably have been thirteen brethren). Although a number of Augustinian houses adopted this plan, it was not peculiar to the order; Cistercian, Premonstratensian and Benedictine examples can also be found as it suited a small community. The cloister was built in the usual position on the south. The east range joined the south transept, with a sacristy, the chapter house, and a warming room on the ground floor and the dormitory on the upper floor. The range terminated in latrines at its southern end. The refectory formed the southern side of the cloister, with the kitchens to the south-west. On the western side of the cloister was the cellarer's range; above this store was the prior's accommodation.

It was not long before the canons and their patrons developed greater ambitions for the house. By the end of the twelfth century a massive expansion was well advanced. A stream of additional gifts from successive barons of Halton and their principal retainers included land, property, churches, tithes, mills and even a salt-works. The increased income provided the means to sustain a greater number of canons, probably two dozen. The increased number of inhabitants necessitated radical changes to the original buildings (figure 6). The church was lengthened at the east and the west; a new chapter house was erected, twice the size of its predecessor; new latrines were added to the end of the dormitory sufficient to cater for the larger numbers, and the west and south ranges of the cloister were demolished to make way for much larger buildings.

Expansions on a similar scale probably occurred at many other sites, but without large excavations by modern methods, they will remain undetected. Changes could be brought about by other factors (see Chapter 4). At Norton, a fire caused extensive damage in 1236. This necessitated, amongst other repairs, the construction of a complete new cloister arcade wall. However the canons, instead of merely replacing the wall, used the disaster

Figure 7. The thirteenth-century cloister arcade, Norton Priory. The sandstone has been embellished with finely carved human heads, animals and foliage; part of a figure holding a book can be seen in the spandrel.
   Photograph by Patrick Greene, Norton Priory Museum Trust.

as an opportunity to embellish the priory with an arcade of superb quality. Trefoil arches, sixteen on each side of the square cloister, were supported by triple shafts. The capitals and flat surfaces were enriched with a glorious display of foliage, human, animal and grotesque heads, and a series of semi-relief sculptures of religious subjects (figure 7).

   Continued benefactions allowed the canons further to enhance the priory. On the south side of the outer courtyard a guesthouse was erected. Large chapels were added to the north and south transepts. The availability of resources to support the construction projects was closely linked to the existence of the transept chapels. The priory had become the burial place of the Duttons, wealthy landowners of knightly rank who took on the role of supporters of the canons played hitherto by the increasingly remote baronial family. The Duttons used the transept chapels as their burial place, and in the early fourteenth century commissioned a magnificent mosaic-tile floor to be made for the church and the chapter house. In the northern transept chapel, at least one Dutton grave was covered with a tile panel in the form of a life-size knight with a shield bearing the Dutton arms, surrounded by an inscription requesting prayers for his soul.

   Whereas prosperity often allowed a religious house to engage in building schemes, financial difficulties could call a halt to such projects. At Norton the mismanagement of the resources of the house attracted episcopal criticism in the first half of the fourteenth century. During this time of financial difficulty there was no further construction after the completion of the mosaic-tile floor. Likewise, an effective head of a monastic house could reverse a decline; at Norton the election of Richard Wyche as abbot in about 1366 heralded a period of renewal. For the community, it culminated in the papal elevation from priory to abbey; for Richard himself, the personal distinction was to be made president of the Augustinian Chapter (the triennial conference of the heads of all the houses of the order in England) in 1395 (Greene 1979).

A new status might result in greater ambitions on the part of the prelate. In the fifteenth century at Norton the prior's accommodation above the cellarer's range was extended in the form of a tower house fit for an abbot. A new gatehouse followed, and in the closing years of the fifteenth century or at the beginning of the sixteenth, an elaborate vaulted cloister-walk with windows was built to replace the open arcaded cloister walk that had been erected after the 1236 fire. These developments can be mirrored in very many monastic houses at this time. There are marked trends towards greater comfort in houses of most orders, characterised by the construction of enhanced accommodation for the prelate, the division of dormitories to provide individual cubicles for the brethren, and the replacement of draughty open cloister walks by fenestrated structures. The provision of quarters for the abbot that were as well appointed as those of a wealthy lay landowner resulted in their widespread use for exactly this purpose following the Dissolution. At Norton it was the expanded west range and the buildings of the outer court that were converted into a Tudor mansion following the sale of the monastery and its lands by the Crown in 1545.

A Cistercian monastery and its precinct: Bordesley Abbey, Worcestershire

A Cistercian abbey was founded at Bordesley in the valley of the river Arrow in about 1138. An ambitious programme of excavation and fieldwork began in 1969 and is continuing to produce fascinating information about the abbey church and its surroundings (Rahtz and Hirst 1976; Hirst, Walsh and Wright 1983; Hirst and Wright 1989).

The Cistercian Order was developed at Citeaux in Burgundy in the first decades of the twelfth century, principally through the efforts of two men, Stephen Harding (who came from Sherborne in Dorset) and St Bernard, abbot of the daughter house at Clairvaux. The order was characterised by austerity – a stripping away of elaboration from the liturgy and of ornament from the buildings in an attempt to return to the essence of Benedictine practice. The monks engaged in personal pursuit of perfection in the context of a rejection of the distractions of the world. The choice of sites for new monasteries was therefore governed by requirements of seclusion and self-sufficiency. This in turn encouraged the order to adopt a system in which there were two kinds of monks. Choir monks devoted themselves to worship and prayer, and lay brothers, exempt from learning, spent a much smaller proportion of their time in church so that they might carry out a greater share of manual work at the abbey and on its estates.

A striking feature of the Cistercian Order is its organisation. To ensure that all houses adhered firmly to the precepts of the rule, a system was devised whereby each abbey was inspected once a year by the abbot of the mother house; he had full authority to correct any errors or slackness that he found. In addition every abbot was expected to visit Citeaux for the general chapter which took place once a year. This was completely different to conventional Benedictine and Augustinian practice; it welded the Cistercians into a unified, international movement. It had a profound effect on the design of Cistercian buildings (Fergusson 1984; Stalley 1987).

The first Cistercian foundation in Britain was at Waverley in Surrey in 1128. The Cistercians were particularly favoured by King Stephen (1135–54) and his magnates. Bordesley was founded by one of these, Waleran, earl of Worcester, but he renounced his status after Stephen's defeat by Mathilde, who provided a new charter of foundation in 1141. Henceforth Bordesley was regarded as one of the ten royal Cistercian houses. It was not in the same league as monasteries such as Rievaulx, Fountains and Furness, but it was comfortably endowed, supporting a community of sixty people in 1332 (thirty-four monks, one novice, eight lay brothers, and seventeen servants). It was suppressed on 17 July 1538 and, unlike Battle and Norton, it was not converted into a secular residence. By the end of the month it was said to have been 'plucked down'. In September there was a sale of materials from the demolished abbey, including the iron and glass from the windows of the north side of the cloister, and the pavement of the east side of the cloister. It is an illustration of how quickly the creation of four centuries of monastic endeavour could be reversed (see Chapter 8).

The excavation of the abbey church has revealed in minute detail the changes that took place over those four centuries. Bordesley might easily have joined the list of Cistercian houses that changed site, for it is clear from the excavation that the high level of the water table was a recurring problem for the monks. Their difficulties, however, provided great opportunities for the archaeologists, for the church was refloored again and again to combat the dampness. As a result of the careful dissection of each floor and the features within it, changes over the years in the layout, liturgical arrangements and burial practice have been distinguished (figure 8). From the thirteenth century the church was embellished with a series of decorated tile floors – part of the drift away from the rigid austerity of the Cistercian Rule that occurred widely. Another example of the relaxation of strictures against ornament is to be seen in the new cloister-arcade wall built in the late fourteenth or fifteenth century (figure 9), an elegant and elaborate structure, the design of which has been reconstructed on the evidence of fragmentary foundations and pieces of carved stonework (Walsh 1979).

An outstanding feature of Bordesley is the state of preservation of the monastic precinct. Very extensive earthworks survive, particularly relating to complex systems of water management, but also covering the remains of the buildings and traceable as the precinct boundary (Astill 1989). There are two principal reasons why so much still exists. The rapid demolition of the buildings and abandonment of the site in 1538 removed a significant agent of change – a new owner intent on stamping his proprietorial pride on buildings and landscape. Agricultural modification of the land was inhibited

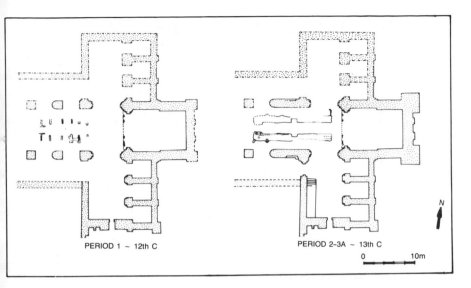

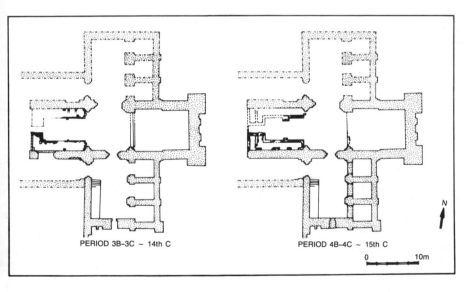

Figure 8. Plan of the choir of Bordesley Abbey, Hereford and Worcester, showing changes to the internal arrangements of the church from the twelfth to the fifteenth century.

Drawing supplied by the Bordesley Abbey Project.

by the irregularity of the surface, and by the wetness of the low-lying valley bottom. By the 1970s the importance of the earthwork remains was recognised and Redditch Development Corporation included them in an area designated for preservation as a public open space.

Many features of the precinct have been distinguished, largely by field survey but also by selective excavation. The site of the gatehouse lies to the

Figure 9. Reconstruction drawing of the cloister arcade at Bordesley Abbey, built in the late fourteenth or fifteenth century. This type of traceried, glazed arcade commonly replaced earlier open arcades.
Drawing by David Walsh, supplied by the Bordesley Abbey Project.

west of the church and from it the precinct bank can be traced towards the north. Next to the gatehouse stood the chapel at the gate (*capella ad portam*) which was available for worship by lay people, thereby preserving the solitude of the Cistercian monks. The site of the abbey buildings set round the cloister can be distinguished, although they are partly obscured by the spoil dumps of nineteenth-century excavations. The line of a conduit has been identified leading to the southern side of the monastic buildings. The dominating feature of the earthworks is an extensive range of fishponds with dams, leats, channels, flood protection banks and the sites of sluices. A large embanked triangular mill pond has been confirmed as such by the excavation of a watermill. A succession of timber structures with a wheel pit, a wood-lined mill race, fragments of wooden machinery and a metal-working forge have all illuminated the industrial side to the abbey's activities beginning in the twelfth century. To enable all these functions to be accommodated within the valley, the course of the river Arrow was diverted to follow a straight channel along the contour on the far side of the valley. Beyond the water management earthworks, the ridge and furrow of open fields has been found.

Oxford: a house of Franciscan friars in the city

In 1224 Franciscan friars (known as grey friars from the colour of their habits) acquired a block of land in the parish of St Ebbe in the western part of Oxford upon which they could build a friary. Their property extended across the city wall, so when, after twenty years, their success allowed the erection of a large church, they obtained permission to breach the wall. The church was built within the gap, and the wall was then joined up to the east and west ends of the building. Henceforth it became an integral part of the city's defences.

It was typical of the Franciscans that they should choose to establish themselves within a bustling city – even if it should require the expedient of straddling the boundary. The friars (Franciscans, Dominicans, Carmelites, Augustinians and the various other orders that were introduced to Britain in the thirteenth century) were a great contrast to the Cistercians and other contemplative monks. Instead of rejecting the world and its distractions, the friars were determined to be part of society. Wherever possible, therefore, they chose urban settings for their friaries, although in Ireland rural sites were also used.

St Francis, son of a wealthy merchant of Assisi, composed his rule in 1210. Like monks and canons, his followers took vows of chastity, poverty and obedience, and were obliged to live according to the rule in convents. However, friars were expected to model themselves on Christ's disciples, going out in pairs without money or possessions to teach the Christian way of life. They were mendicants – they obtained their necessities of life by begging. In practice, however, they attracted the support of benefactors, who were driven by motives of spiritual self-interest. The friars would have been unable to construct large churches without such assistance; the rapidity with which they spread across Europe testifies to the enthusiasm that they generated. The Franciscans arrived in England in 1224, three years after the Dominicans, under the leadership of Agnellus of Pisa. His party of nine people divided, one group going to London and the others heading for Oxford where they they obtained a house in the parish of St Ebbe as their base. The Dominicans and the Franciscans both appeared in Ireland in 1224, and in 1230 and 1231 the two orders established their first Scottish houses.

The Franciscans chose Oxford for one of their pioneer English houses because of the importance of the town. In the twelfth century it had become the ninth largest town in the kingdom. By the time the friars arrived the university had already been established, and they were to become heavily involved in its growth, encouraging the founders of colleges and taking part in administration. The most famous Oxford friar was Roger Bacon, the founder of modern scientific method. Despite its medieval eminence, however, practically nothing of the friary survived above ground when a massive redevelopment was planned for that part of Oxford in the 1960s. Rescue excavation between 1967 and 1969 revealed the remains of the friary church (Hassall 1972 and 1973; Hassall, Halpin and Mellor 1991). It had been comprehensively demolished following its surrender to the Crown in 1537, and above the footings of the walls 5 metres of material had accumulated as a result of the deposition of rubbish and the demolition of later buildings. Despite such difficulties, much was learnt about this important building and the way in which it developed.

The original friary included a chapel, infirmary and school. In 1248 Henry III issued a grant allowing the friars to breach the town wall for their new

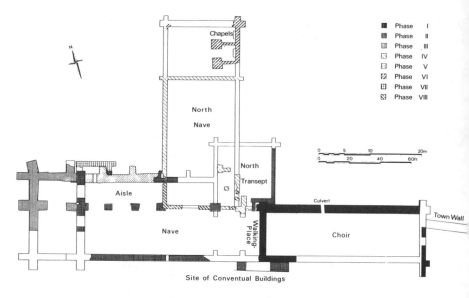

Figure 10. Plan of the church, Oxford Greyfriars, showing the growth of the building.
Oxfordshire Archaeology Unit.

church. The first phase of the church was typical of the Franciscans, although on a larger scale than most communities could aspire to. It had a long choir and a simple nave with a single aisle on the north (figure 10). The two units had their distinct functions which reflected the particular characteristics of the order. The choir was large enough for the friars to gather for worship, and the nave was designed to function as a preaching hall to which the people of the town would be attracted. Such was their popular success that it was soon necessary to create more room for the congregations by extending the nave and aisle westwards. This made the church about 75 metres long – the only larger friars' church in England was that of the London Franciscans.

The part played by the friars in teaching made increasing demands on space in the Oxford church. Another major expansion therefore took place, this time in the form of a long transept on the north side of the nave; it had seven chapels on its eastern side. This in turn was lengthened until it was 30 metres long with ten chapels. Despite the extent of destruction after the Dissolution, evidence of some of the internal arrangements survived when excavated. Much of the floor had been covered with tiles which had left their impressions in the mortar bedding. Fragments of window glass and pieces of carved masonry (found as demolition debris and in places still in position where they had been incorporated in later property boundaries) provided information on the appearance of the church. As friaries were predominantly urban establishments, their sites tend to have suffered destruction to a much greater extent than rural monasteries (see Chapter 7). Rescue excavations such as the Oxford Greyfriars site, and that on the nearby Dominican Priory

(Lambrick and Woods 1976; Lambrick 1985) are therefore particularly important for understanding this branch of monasticism.

Mount Grace Priory: a revival of asceticism in the fourteenth century

The Carthusian priory of Mount Grace in Yorkshire stands in marked contrast to Oxford's Franciscan friary. Whereas the friars chose to live in a bustling city and to mix with its inhabitants on a daily basis, the Carthusian monks became established in a remote location in which there was the minimum contact with each other, and a self-imposed isolation from the outside world. Unlike Oxford Greyfriars, Mount Grace still exists in a substantially complete state. Examination of the buildings reveals much about the life of the inmates (Coppack 1991). Excavations were carried out at the turn of the century (Brown and St John Hope 1905) and more recently (Coppack 1990, 78).

The monastery was founded in 1398 with the title House of the Assumption of the Most Blessed Virgin and St Nicholas of Mount Grace at Ingleby. The prior of La Grande Chartreuse in south-east France gave his assent to the appointment of the first prior of Mount Grace. Chartreuse was the headquarters of the order, which had its origins in the first half of the twelfth century, and drew its inspiration from the ideals of the eremitical life at the root of monasticism. The Carthusians reduced the liturgical element of their day to allow time for private prayer, contemplation, study and work. The labour that the monks specialised in was the copying of books. In consequence Carthusian priories became renowned for their libraries. The buildings reflected this change of emphasis. The church, chapter house and other claustral buildings were of modest size and there was no dormitory. Instead, a large cloister was surrounded with individual cells within which the monks spent the greater part of their lives in the solitude of the hermit.

The first Carthusian house in England was founded in 1179–80 at Witham in Somerset. Hinton Charterhouse was established in the same county in 1232. Ireland's only charterhouse, Kinalehin, was founded in 1252. However, it was in the fourteenth and fifteenth centuries that enthusiasm for the Carthusians flowered. At a time when support for the creation of new houses of other orders had dried to a trickle, the uncompromising commitment to the austere life attracted a number of patrons to support Carthusian foundations. Between 1343 and 1414, seven charterhouses were founded in England (Perth in Scotland followed in 1429). The London Charterhouse achieved the seemingly impossible by creating an oasis of quiet in the midst of the ferment of urban life.

Mount Grace was established in a totally different environment – the rural calm of north Yorkshire. The layout of the buildings differs greatly from the standard monastic plan, but it has an elegance of its own (figure 11). The lozenge-shaped cloister has five cells on each of the north, west and east sides. On the south are four cells, including one for the prior and one for the sacrist. Also on the south is the tiny refectory and chapter house. Alongside the southern buildings is the church. It started as a rectangle and

Figure 11. Mount Grace Priory, North Yorkshire – the south range of gardens and cells, one of which has been reconstructed.
Photograph by Patrick Greene.

was then developed into an aisleless cruciform building. Six more cells lay south and east of the church in a lesser cloister.

Excavation of some of the cells has recently been carried out. 'Cells' is a somewhat misleading term, for these were far from being prison-like. Each cell was of two storeys and was 8 metres square. The ground floor was divided into four compartments, two of which were lobbies, one with a door that gave access to the cloister walk and the other to the garden; the latter also enclosed the stairs to the upper floor. A third compartment served as the monk's living room. It had a fireplace and a two-light window. The remaining compartment was a bedroom and oratory. The upper floor was probably a workshop. A covered walkway led from the cell to an individual latrine projecting from the back wall of the precinct; on the north and south sides the latrines were placed directly above a drain. An enclosed garden was provided for each cell (figure 12). The entire arrangement was admirably suited to the life of personal devotion and work that were the hallmarks of the order. The avoidance of distraction is exemplified by the hatches in the cloister wall of each cell through which food was passed to the monks. They are built to a dogleg plan so that the servant delivering the food and the monk would not catch sight of each other and be tempted into conversation.

To provide for the bodily needs of the monks there was a kitchen adjoining the refectory and the cloister. Next to the gatehouse on the outer court was the brewhouse and bakehouse, with stables and granaries as well. The

Figure 12. The excavated garden of the reconstructed cell, Mount Grace Priory. Photograph supplied by Glyn Coppack, English Heritage.

provision of a supply of water to all the cells was achieved by tapping springs and carrying the water through conduits to a cistern in the cloister. From there a system of lead pipes took water to each cell, which had a tap housed within an arched recess. Spring water also flushed the latrine drains except those on the eastern side where the slope of the hill prevented it; they had cess-pits.

The Carthusians remained true to their principles to the end. This resulted in widespread popular admiration, although to the Crown it appeared as obstinacy. Two of the Mount Grace monks refused to subscribe to the Act of Succession in 1534, although eventually the house was surrendered quietly in 1539. The prior later became a monk at Sheen Charterhouse (Surrey) when it was refounded after the Dissolution under Queen Mary, in what was to prove to be a false dawn for a monastic revival.

Denny Abbey, Cambridgeshire: a house, successively, of Benedictine monks, Knights Templar, and Franciscan nuns

Battle, Norton, Bordesley, Oxford Greyfriars, Mount Grace – the one thing that all have in common is a continuity of purpose and ownership that endured until the Dissolution. One reason for that is that their endowments were substantial. It would be wrong to think that such stability was invariably the case. There were considerable numbers of small houses where it was a struggle to survive. Denny began life as one of these. Later, it fell victim to political actions that were totally beyond its own capacity to influence. Its vicissitudes resulted in possession by three different orders successively. The site was the subject of excavation from 1968 to 1975 (Christie and Coad 1980).

Denny began in 1159 as a dependent cell of the Benedictine cathedral priory of Ely. The monks commissioned a small masonry church, but probably remained in temporary timber living quarters during the short history of the cell. An examination of the standing masonry of the church and excavation of below-ground features showed that the Norman church consisted of a two-bay chancel, north and south transepts, and a two-bay nave only 8.23 metres long. After eleven years, possibly because of indebtedness, the site was transferred to the Knights Templar. This order had been established after the First Crusade to protect the holy places and the pilgrims they attracted. In 1128 the Templars adopted a rule based on that of the Cistercians. In Europe they lived in small communities called preceptories. The London Temple (founded in 1128 and moved to a larger riverside location in 1185) became the rich headquarters of the order in England. Denny was on an altogether smaller scale. It may have been used to house aged and infirm members of the order.

It appears that the short nave of the church was a result of the curtailment of building activities by the Templars when they took over the site. They proceeded to erect a series of buildings to the north of the church which may have been a hospital, refectory and dormitory. They were not arranged around a cloister on the standard monastic plan, although they were apparently built round a quadrangle. The Templar occupation of Denny came to an abrupt halt in 1308. The order had attracted enmity through its disputes with other orders of knights, and was regarded as being avaricious as a result of its great wealth. King Philip IV of France persuaded the pope to take action against the Templars for crimes and heresy. On 10 January 1308 the sheriff of Cambridgeshire took possession of the site and arrested the preceptor and ten brothers. The property, like many of the Templars' possessions, was granted by the Crown to the Knights Hospitallers. They failed to make any use of it so eventually it was granted in 1327 to Mary de Valence, widow of the earl of Pembroke. Denny began the third phase of its monastic metamorphosis, this time as a house of Franciscan nuns transferred here from Waterbeach, a less well drained location nearby.

The buildings, empty for nearly two decades, required extensive alterations and extensions to make them suitable for their new use. The chancel of the twelfth-century church was demolished and in its place was built a much larger church for the nuns. A cloister with surrounding ranges was erected to the north of the church, beyond an open court. The refectory, to the north of the cloister, still stands as a result of being converted into a barn after the Dissolution. Nunneries were, in general, provided with poorer endowments than male houses (Gilchrist 1989, 251). Denny was comparatively wealthy, with thirty-five nuns in residence at the Dissolution. In the sixteenth century most of the buildings were demolished, with the exception of those that could be converted for farm use. Surrounding the site are twelve hectares of impressive earthworks.

A double monastery of monks and nuns: Shouldham Priory, Norfolk

During the 1130s and 1140s an Englishman, St Gilbert of Sempringham, formed an order of canons and nuns (Graham 1901). His rule was influenced by that of the Cistercians, and he met St Bernard on a visit to Cîteaux in 1147. Despite the fact that the presence of nuns at Sempringham resulted in a rejection by the Cistercians of Gilbert's plan for affiliation, he adopted the Cistercian Rule as a basis of his rule for nuns. Gilbertine canons followed a rule based on that of St Augustine. In about 1190, the last Gilbertine double monastery of canons and nuns was established at Shouldham (Norfolk). All later Gilbertine houses were for canons alone.

During the extreme drought conditions of June 1989, remarkable traces of the buildings and the precinct of Shouldham Priory were recorded by the Norfolk Archaeology Unit (Edwards 1989). Despite the fact that the masonry foundations of the buildings had been robbed, the lines of the walls showed up as crop marks in aerial photographs (figures 13 and 14). The east end of the church had three chapels, each with an altar. Like the Gilbertine priory at Watton in Yorkshire (Hope 1901), the church was divided by an axial wall which separated the canons from the nuns. The nuns' cloister at Shouldham could be seen lying north of the church; that of the canons must have been to the south.

The northern side of the precinct appeared as a major, linear crop mark which must represent a large filled ditch. A complex of fishponds occupied a large area in the eastern part of the precinct. Another linear mark would

Figure 13. Aerial photograph of Shouldham Abbey, Norfolk, taken 26 June 1989. The east end of the church can be seen as crop-marks. In the foreground are boundary ditches and fishponds. The precinct ditch appears as a long arc running through the field to the right.
  Photograph by Derek Edwards, Norfolk County Museums Air Photography Unit.

seem to show the line of the drain which served the nuns' latrine block, and which flowed into the fishponds. Earthworks still exist in the south-western part of the precinct. Shouldham Priory is an excellent demonstration of the fact that even where no buildings of a monastery have survived above ground, aerial photography and other survey methods can produce considerable quantities of valuable information.

Summary

This chapter has described the characteristics of a variety of monastic orders through the case studies of sites where archaeology has made a contribution to their understanding. Sites occupied by Benedictines, Augustinians, Cistercians, Franciscan friars, Carthusians, Knights, Franciscan nuns, and Gilbertine nuns and canons have been described. This is not an exhaustive account of the orders whose houses were established in the British Isles (for that see Knowles 1948–59; for English houses, Knowles and Hadcock 1971; for Scotland, Cowan and Easson 1976; and for Ireland, Gwynn and Knowles 1970). Some of the other orders will be briefly introduced where appropriate elsewhere in the book. What will be apparent from the case studies is the rich diversity that exists beneath the

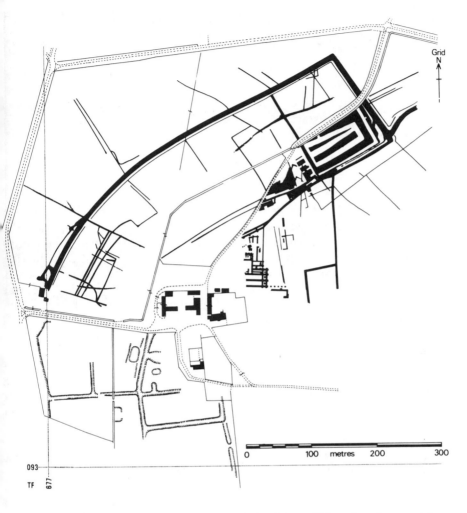

Grid
N

0   100   metres   200   300

093

TF   677

Figure 14. Plan of buildings and precinct of Shouldham Abbey, based on aerial survey. The east end of the church and parts of other buildings can be seen in the centre. An expanse of ditches and fishponds lie to the north and west. Earthworks survive to the south-west of the modern Abbey Farm.

Plan supplied by Derek Edwards, Norfolk County Museums Air Photography Unit.

blanket term 'medieval monasteries', and also the potential of using archaeological techniques in efforts to gain further insights into monasticism in the Middle Ages.

2 Archaeology and monasteries

In this chapter the growth of interest in monastic sites by antiquaries and historians will be traced, and the development of techniques of archaeological investigation will be described.

The beginning of interest

A surprising feature of the end of monasticism in England (though not in Scotland or Ireland where it was more a matter of lingering decline) was the speed with which those who had previously been sympathetic to the monks accepted their dispersal and manoeuvred to take advantage of the situation to augment their own possessions. Despite the disenchantment with aspects of monasticism shown, for example, by Chaucer in his portrayal of the friar in the prologue of the *Canterbury Tales*, religious houses were still being well supported right up to the Dissolution. Evidence of this is people's continued desire, expressed in wills, to be buried within monastic churches and to benefit from the prayers of the brethren as a means of achieving salvation. Often, the tradition of using a monastery as a family mausoleum had lasted for generations. Yet when it came to the acquisition of a monastic house from the Augmentations Office (the Crown's agency that dealt with the sale of such properties), there were few who seem to have been troubled by any scruples.

The evidence from excavation bears this out. When adapting a complex of monastic buildings as a gentleman's residence, the presence of burials of fellow landowners, albeit usually from a different family, did not prevent the digging of foundations, laying of drains or creation of gardens. It also appears to have been rare for a family to exhume its dead to be transferred to the local parish church. The impression given is of a widespread indifference to the fate of the dead in the scramble to benefit from what was available to the living.

Despite these attitudes, there were those who regretted the destruction of monasteries. Robert Aske, leader of the Pilgrimage of Grace, was executed for this act of rebellion; he wrote that 'the abbies were one of the beauties of the realm to all men and strangers passing through . . . they were great maintainers of sea walls and dykes, maintainers and builders of bridges and highways, and other such things for the commonwealth' (Knowles 1956, 3, 328). Three decades after the Suppression there were those who could write of the destruction with a sense of regret. Michael Sherbrook's account of the end of Roche Abbey in Yorkshire (quoted in Platt 1984, 231–4) was based upon the eye-witness accounts of his relatives:

> the church was the first thing to be put to the spoil, and then the abbot's lodging, the dormitory and the refectory, with the cloister and all the buildings there-about within the abbey walls: for nothing was spared but the ox-houses and the swine-

cotes . . . It would have pitied any heart to see what tearing up of the lead there was, and plucking up of boards, and throwing down of spars; and when the lead was torn off and cast down into the church, and the tombs in the church all broken.

Sherbrooke describes how the choir stalls were broken up to be burnt as fuel by those melting down the lead in furnaces. When he asked his father his opinion of the monks, he replied that he thought well of them, but this did not stop him profiting from the despoliation of the abbey for 'I did as others did'.

In following centuries the derelict remains of abbeys were to become the subject of sentimental regard from those who would have had little sympathy for the religion once practised within their walls. Shakespeare wrote of 'bare ruin'd choirs, where late the sweet birds sang'. Leland commented in his *Itinerary* on some of the former religious houses that he visited on his travels, which were partly concerned with the collection of volumes from monastic libraries for the royal collection. John Speed published a 'Catalogue of Religious Houses in England and Wales' in 1614 as part of his larger work. Monastic remains might even have moral value:

> We desire likewise to behold the mournful ruins of other religious houses, although their goodly fair structures be altogether destroyed, their tombs battered down, and the bodies of their dead cast out of their coffins; for that, that very earth did sometimes cover the corpse of the defunct, puts us in mind of our mortality, and consequently brings us to unfained repentance. (Weever 1631)

In the early seventeenth century Sir John Oglander carried out what was probably the first attempted excavation of a monastery, Quarr Abbey in the Isle of Wight, which he had inherited (Aston 1973, 249). 'I hired some to dig to see whether I might find the foundations but I could not.'

In 1655 Sir William Dugdale published the first volume of the *Monasticon*, which brought together a mass of documentation concerning the foundation of religious houses. Volumes two and three appeared in 1661 and 1673; they were to provide a bedrock of knowledge for monastic studies. In the seventeenth century these rarely concerned the architecture of monastic remains. It was memorials and heraldic representations that attracted attention. Books on the history of individual monasteries did, however, begin to appear, such as *Monasticon Favershamiense* (Southouse 1671). The author's intention was 'to rescue from the teeth of all devouring time and oblivion some memorials concerning the primitive state and condition' of Faversham Abbey (Kent).

In the eighteenth century there was a growth in topographical representation – notably by the Buck brothers who counted the occupiers of mansions built upon the remains of monastic houses amongst their potential clients (S. and N. Buck 1774) (figure 15). Another developing area was the writing of county histories, which usually included accounts of abbeys and priories based on documentary records. One of the earliest pleas for the preservation of the remains of a religious house, at least implicitly, was William Stukeley's description of Crowland Abbey in Lincolnshire which appeared in his *Itinerarium Curiosum* in 1725.

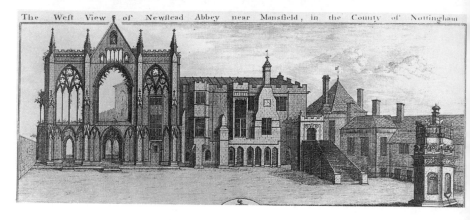

The West View of Newstead Abbey near Mansfield , in the County of Nottingham

Figure 15. Engraving of west front of Newstead Abbey, Nottinghamshire, by S. and N. Buck. On the left is the front of the medieval church, alongside which is the monastic west range adapted as a house. The structure on the right is a medieval cistern, probably moved to this position from the centre of the cloister. Illustration provided by Nottingham Museum Service.

The roof, which was of Irish oak finely carved and gilt, fell down twenty years ago: you see pieces of it in every house. The pavement is covered with shrubs for brass inscriptions, and people now at pleasure dig up the monumental stones, and divide the holy shipwreck for their private uses; so that, instead of one, most of the houses in the town are become religious. The painted glass was broke by the soldiers in the rebellion, for they made a garrison of the place. All the eastern part of the church is entirely razed to the foundation; and the ashes as well as the tombs of an infinite number of illustrious personages, kings, abbots, lords, knights, etc. there hoping for repose are dispersed, to the irreparable damage of English history. (Stukeley 1725, 1, 33)

A quarter of a century later Stukeley was commenting, in a paper delivered to the Antiquaries on 12 April 1753, on a similar case of casual digging on a monastic site: 'Yesterday I made a most agreeable journey, though it may be called a pilgrimage, to visit the venerable remains of Lesnes Abbey, at Erith in Kent . . . They told us they had dug up, from time to time, the foundations of the buildings, with many coffins of stone, corpses and monuments' (Stukeley 1770).

As the eighteenth century proceeded, monastic buildings became not only material for topographical illustration but also a proper subject for the land-scape artist. The value placed on monastic remains for their picturesque qualities began to foster an awareness of the need to preserve them, as is described in Chapter 9.

Interest in the Gothic was growing, however, fostered by people such as Horace Walpole who began to rebuild Strawberry Hill in Gothic style in 1750. Lacock Abbey, the Augustinian nunnery in Wiltshire that had become a secular mansion after the Dissolution, provided a ready-made basis for a 'Gothick' house. Ivory Talbot commissioned Sanderson Miller in 1754 to add a hall in the revived style to the surviving medieval buildings which included a beautiful fifteenth-century cloister, thus ensuring its preservation. Such enthusiasm, however, did not yet reflect itself in any general move to secure the preservation of the remains of monasteries. Richard Gough, who produced a new edition of Camden's *Britannia* in 1789, became aware on his travels of the state of neglect of many medieval buildings. 'One cannot enough regret the little regard hitherto paid to Gothic architecture of which so many beautiful models are daily crumbling to pieces before our eyes' (Gough 1768). However, scholarly study of medieval ecclesiastical buildings was developing, and resulted in publications such as a detailed examination of Ely cathedral priory and its conventual buildings (Bentham 1771).

The Society of Antiquaries of London developed a particular interest in tombs in the 1770s (Evans 1956, 154). This resulted in one of the first archaeological investigations of a monastic site to be carried out with care and then published – the opening of the tomb of Edward I in Westminster Abbey in 1774 (Ayloffe 1786). The Society's director went on to publish his great work on tombs (Gough 1786–96). He also described the remarkable line-impressed mosaic-tile floor in Prior Crauden's chapel at Ely (Gough 1792). He eventually resigned his office in 1797 in the controversy that split the Antiquaries over James Wyatt's destructive 'restoration' of Salisbury and Durham cathedrals. Irish monasteries also received attention. Motives could be mixed, as the preface to *The Antiquities of Ireland* shows: 'When the late Captain Grose had finished *The Antiquities of England, Scotland and Wales*, he turned his eyes to Ireland, who seemed to invite him to her hospitable shore, to save from impending oblivion her mouldering monuments, and to unite her, as she ever should be, in closest association with the British Isles' (Grose 1794). In the 1790s Irish Republicanism emerged as a defined political aim, but it is difficult to see quite how Grose's posthumous editor envisaged accounts of antiquities might support the Unionist cause. In fact the volumes contain accounts of many monastic sites that might be identified as much with control from Rome as rule by London. The engraved plates are a valuable record of the condition of monasteries in Ireland two centuries ago. Holy Cross Abbey (County Tipperary) provides the subject matter for the frontispiece, and Dunbrody Abbey (County Wexford) warranted two plates and a plan of the buildings (*ibid*. 44–6).

In the period that followed the Napoleonic War, the study of monasteries received a fillip from the renewal of visits to France. John Sell Cotman was one of the artists who painted monastic remains on the Continent. The most significant influence, though, was the demand by ecclesiologists and architects for models with which to inform their Gothic Revival creations. The vocabulary of the subject was substantially established by Thomas Rickman and Augustus Welby Pugin (Rickman 1819; Pugin 1821–31). By the 1820s some excavation was being undertaken to investigate monastic sites. The construction of the Yorkshire Museum on the site of St Mary's Abbey in York resulted in a large-scale operation to uncover the remains of the church, although the museum was built over the east range. The results of the excavation, illustrated with engraved plates (figure 16), were published in commendably full detail for the period (Wellbeloved 1829).

Another early publication described work at Wymondham Priory, Norfolk (Woodward 1836). Following the accidental discovery of two lead coffins on

Figure 16. The excavation of the south transept of St Mary's Abbey, York – an engraving published in 1829. Beyond the excavation is the King's Manor, originally built as the Abbot's House. York Minster can be seen in the distance.
    Illustration provided by the Yorkshire Museum.

Christmas Eve 1833, digging on a large scale commenced: 'I now have pleasure in stating that the ruins have been cleared to the level of their respective floors; and that a very excellent plan has been completed by an inhabitant of the town.' Woodward's brief report included a plate showing the location of the abbey with a plan of the church and a drawing of the seal. Nevertheless, it was ecclesiology that was the objective of most studies. For example, *The Monastic Ruins of Yorkshire* (Richardson and Churton 1843) was described in the notices of new publications in Volume 3 of *Archaeological Journal* (1846) as 'one of the most elaborate of the numerous publications occasioned by the present taste for and general study of Ecclesiology'. The reviewer continued 'wisely avoiding minute antiquarian detail . . . the author has furnished a pleasing and instructive narrative of each building illustrated'. The volumes are indeed handsome, particularly in respect of Richardson's lithographs, plans and drawings of architectural details such as sedilia, grave-slabs, mouldings and floor tiles.

In the late nineteenth century many monastic buildings were under threat. Sometimes this was the result of neglect; the owner of Glastonbury Abbey in Somerset, when urged by the Society of Antiquaries to arrest the decay, replied, 'Well, they are ruins now, and if they fall they will be ruins still won't they?' (Evans 1956, 333). More often the danger lay in a reckless approach to restoration. St Alban's Abbey suffered particularly badly, but Lincoln, Westminster, Rochester and Norwich cathedrals all required the

Figure 17. A visitor to the excavation of Chertsey Abbey, Surrey. Parts of walls have been exposed, and on the left a tile floor can just be made out.
   Photograph from the collections of the Surrey Archaeological Society.

Antiquaries' efforts to resist the restorers. Norwich at least was spared the dismemberment of its precinct by the construction of a railway through it in 1882. The foundation of the Society for the Preservation of Ancient Buildings by William Morris in 1877 was another response to the wave of destruction.

In 1885 William St John Hope became assistant secretary of the Society of Antiquaries. His name, and that of the man who was frequently his partner, Harold Brakspear, were prominent in monastic archaeology for the following three decades. Hope travelled widely to report on the state of buildings, often monastic. He excavated and published the results of his investigations extensively; his reports are still of immense importance to the understanding of many of the sites he examined. In 1910 Sir Charles Peers became Inspector (later Chief Inspector) of Ancient Monuments, and three years later the Ancient Monuments Act enabled monastic sites to be brought into guardianship. Peers established the methodology of preservation, which placed emphasis on the importance of standing remains as evidence that should be carefully treated, with 'restoration' always avoided. However, his clearance of sites such as Rievaulx and Byland in Yorkshire was of a particularly drastic nature.

Although reports of excavations of monastic sites continued to be published, there was no sense of breaking new ground. Indeed, the methodology of investigation remained stuck in a rut until the late 1960s. The manner in which an excavation of a monastic site was being tackled in, say, 1965 would have been entirely recognisable to an excavator working in 1865 (see figure 17). The questions being asked and the techniques of excavation remained basically unaltered; almost all other areas of archaeology had made great strides in theoretical and practical research.

The way in which the investigation of a monastic site was usually tackled can be illustrated by Harold Brakspear's account of Waverley Abbey in Surrey (Brakspear 1905). Waverley was the first Cistercian house to be established in Britain, in 1128. The introduction to the volume gives the background to the exercise. The Surrey Archaeological Society held a meeting at Waverley in July 1898 and

> as a result of the interesting account then given by Mr W.H. St John Hope, of what might be found below the turf, steps were taken to begin a systematic examination of the site at the expense of that Society . . . Excavations were started the following summer under the direction of Mr Hooper, and with the advice and occasional help of Mr Hope. The chapter house was first cleared out, followed by the monks' infirmary on the south side of the cloister. In the autumn of 1899, when the work had proceeded thus far, the writer was invited to undertake the agreeable task of examining and measuring in detail the portions exposed.

From that point Brakspear was in charge. In 1900 the church was explored, as well as the west side of the cloister. 1901 saw the lay brothers' infirmary and other buildings on the west side of the cloister exposed. In 1902, attention switched to the guesthouse and the brewhouse, followed in the next year by a block of buildings to the north-west of the church. 'After continual attempts to discover the gate-house, the further excavation of the site was abandoned, owing to the great expense that had been incurred and the profitless nature of the result in the northern part of the site.' Brakspear was commendably quick to get the results published in a volume issued to members of the Surrey Archaeological Society in respect of their annual subscription for 1904.

The publication will have impressed its recipients. Within hard covers embossed with the badge of the Society were 100 pages of text covering a general history of the abbey, its precinct, and sections dealing with twenty-five elements of the monastic complex. These were rounded off with discussions of building materials, the water supply, the fishponds, seals and daughter houses. The text was illustrated with three plans and sixteen photographic plates. The glory of the volume, however, was to be found in a pouch which formed part of the back cover. Here was a folded plan measuring 580 mm. by 745 mm., showing a vast assemblage of buildings, with eight colours used to indicate work of different dates. A further refinement was the application of a ground tint to show those parts assumed to have been roofed at the Suppression. Buildings covering an area of some 30,000 square metres had been revealed in just five years' work. How could this have been possible?

It is when one looks in more detail at the volume that the answers to this question emerge. There are no section drawings nor any other indication that stratigraphy was of concern to the excavators. When the photographs are examined this becomes horribly clear. Some of the digging seems to anticipate trench warfare; in other cases it looks like open-cast mining. Masonry remains stick up awkwardly amidst the delving, the subtleties of their relationships to floors, construction and destruction levels, and other stratigraphical features regarded as of no consequence. Indeed, the use of the term 'cleared out' to describe the examination of the chapter house in the introduction quoted above betrays the approach of the excavators. The object of the exercise was to recover the plan of the monastic buildings, and to assign dates to the stages of development. No other considerations applied. For the excavators, therefore, the strategy of finding and then following walls by digging along them was perfectly justified.

With such limited objectives the unravelling of a stratigraphic sequence was irrelevant. So too was the recovery and recording of objects – unless they happened to be visually appealing. Thus, architectural and other stone fragments appear stacked on walls near their point of discovery. Floor tiles fare rather better, with three plates of drawings. An ornamental enamelled bronze boss from a book cover even rates a colour plate. Pottery is disposed of as follows:

> A quantity of broken pottery of both brown and green glazed ware was found, but in no case was a perfect piece or sufficient fragments to make one discovered. One fragment, of a handle of twelfth-century green ware, should be mentioned. It consists of the head, shoulders, and arms of a soldier wearing a pointed helmet with a nose guard. The right hand is broken, but the left holds what looks like a snake which issues from the mouth.

Curiosity is the criterion – not the information that such material might be able to provide on, say, dating of structural changes, or trade patterns, or the life-style of the monks.

The evidence upon which the dating of the various buildings was fixed by Brakspear is of varying reliability. In the case of the church and chapter house, documentary evidence is available for some of the constructional events, and the assigned dates are probably broadly correct. Elsewhere, masonry mouldings are given as the source, though on a site such as Waverley where surviving remains were fairly slight, by no means all buildings could yield such evidence. Guesswork supplied the deficiency. There can be no doubt that a re-excavation of Waverley would find a site badly damaged by the excavators at the turn of the century, but nonetheless capable of yielding a considerable amount of new information. In particular, the development sequence implied by the big multi-coloured plan would be found to be a gross oversimplification. There will still be a great deal of stratigraphical and environmental information surviving. There should also be vitally important evidence of early, temporary timber buildings that provided the monks with their accommodation while the masonry buildings were being erected – of particular interest on a pioneer site such as this. Brakspear thought he had detected evidence of an earlier wooden building on the site of the infirmary.

The excavations undertaken by the Office of Works under Peers after 1913 differed from those of Hope and Brakspear in an important respect. The objective was not to recover the plan simply for publication, but to clear

Figure 18. Basingwerk Abbey, Clwyd, in course of excavation in the 1920s. Despite the difference in date from figure 17, the technique is essentially the same. The impression of 'mining' is emphasised by the rails for wagons to remove soil and rubble.
Taken from James 1925.

the site for preservation and display. The scale was therefore vastly greater. Photographs of work in progress show rail tracks along which labourers wheeled wagonloads of soil and rubble (figure 18). Peers' policy was to remove all material down to the latest phase of monastic occupation. In practice, it is clear that on many sites the removal of 'over-burden' went far beyond this. In consequence, not only were all the archaeological layers that resulted from the post-Dissolution history of the site removed without recording, but often the latest medieval floor surfaces were lost as well.

Excavation today

Although the work of archaeologists in the nineteenth century and first half of the twentieth century revealed the plans of many monastic houses, there was little attempt to produce other information that might elucidate subjects such as the life of the inhabitants. In retrospect this is perfectly understandable. Monasteries were proficient and assiduous at record-keeping. Despite losses at the Dissolution, vast quantities of documents survived. As a class, there was better documentation for monasteries than any other category of site, with the possible exception of the principal royal buildings. Monastic archives might contain cartularies (volumes of charters and deeds), the accounts of officials such as the cellarer (who was responsible for many categories of purchases), records of building campaigns, and estate accounts. With such riches, what possible information could archaeology add, beyond revealing the layout of the buildings? It would be wrong to be too critical of those in the nineteenth and early twentieth centuries who proceeded on the basis that the answer to that question was 'nothing'.

What is surprising is that such an attitude persisted after the Second World War. It can be seen in the way in which the Ministry of Public Building and Works tackled guardianship sites. Too often, right up to the 1970s, the policy was one of 'clearance' along the lines advocated by Sir Charles Peers. The supervision often consisted of no more than the occasional visit by someone from the Inspectorate of Ancient Monuments. The loss of information that might have been obtained by a careful, archaeological dissection of the layers was considerable.

From the late 1960s, excavations began to be organised on modern lines to a standard which established that there is still much that archaeology can add to existing knowledge of monastic houses. During the same period, exercises in field survey were carried out which demonstrated that there was a wealth of information about the environs of many abbeys, and their estates, remaining to be discovered. The rest of this chapter will describe the potential of monastic archaeology today.

Field survey

The conventional approach to the investigation of monastic sites, until the 1970s, concentrated attention almost exclusively on the cloister and the buildings that surrounded it. Today, whilst the church and claustral buildings are still important subjects for study, there is a range of other topics to pursue. One of these is the operation of the monastic house as an economic unit. As a result, the focus of attention has widened to take in the entire support system that provided the monastery with a surplus that might be invested in building activities, income to meet financial obligations, and its requirements to sustain the brethren on a day-to-day basis.

To achieve the broad objective of a comprehensive investigation of a monastic site requires the application of a range of techniques, of which field survey is one. Examples of the potential have already been described in Chapter 1, including the earthworks resulting from water management enterprises undertaken for the Cistercian monks at Bordesley, and the landscape features at Denny Abbey. A pair of surveys of particular interest are those of Marton and Moxby priories in North Yorkshire (Mackay and Swan 1989) (figures 19 and 20). The Augustinian Priory of St Mary was founded at Marton in the mid twelfth century as a double house of canons and canonesses. This arrangement was short-lived, and by 1167 the canonesses had been moved to Moxby. Both sites have extensive earthworks.

The earthworks on the site of a monastery are unlikely to be solely the

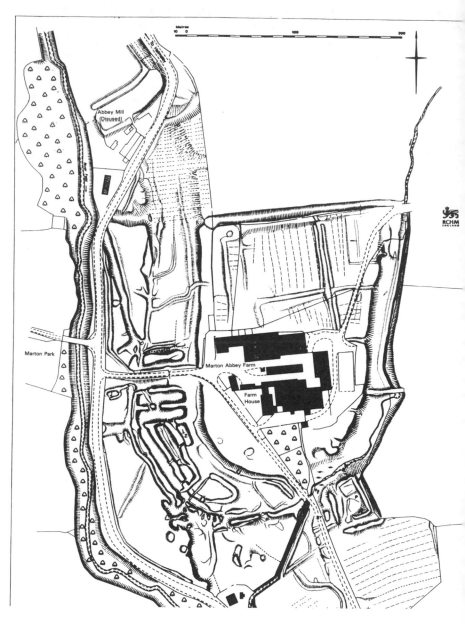

Figure 19. Plan of Marton Priory, North Yorkshire. The valley on the west is heavily modified by earthworks resulting from activities such as the construction of a millpond and fishponds of at least two phases. The river was removed from the valley bottom to flow in an artificial cutting to the west. The spur on which the priory was located (beneath the modern farm) was defended on the north by a large moat, which also enclosed an area of ridge-and-furrow fields.

Plan supplied by Royal Commission on Historical Monuments (England) after Mackay and Swan 1989. Crown Copyright.

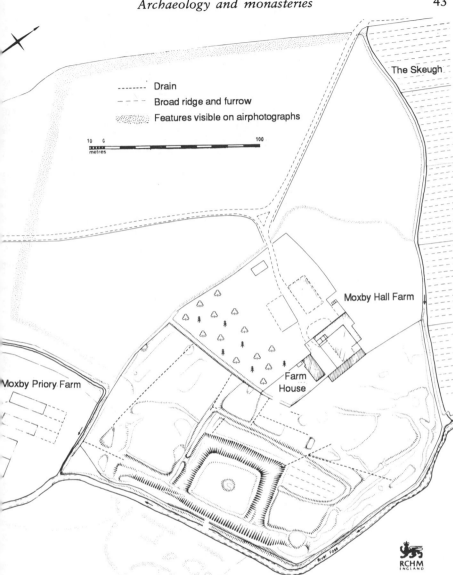

Figure 20. An earthwork survey of Moxby Priory, North Yorkshire. Most of the earthworks are medieval but the moated enclosure (possibly a garden) is part of the post-Dissolution occupation of the site of the nunnery (which lies beneath the farm). The embankment alongside the river was part of a millpond on the site of the medieval mill; it had a complex system of by-pass channels.

Plan supplied by Royal Commission on Historical Monuments (England) after Mackay and Swan 1989. Crown Copyright.

result of water management. The Royal Commission on Historical Monuments for England has carried out an extensive earthwork project in north Lincolnshire which has revealed complex patterns of earthworks at monastic sites such as Stainfield, Heynings and Orford (Everson 1989). Because RCHME studies are topographically based, all the earthworks on a site are recorded whether they belong to a monastery or an adjoining secular site, and irrespective of their date. Particular care is required for interpreting earthwork surveys of this kind. It is important that there should be a thorough knowledge of existing documentation which may throw light on individual features. An awareness of post-medieval developments is especially important in order to disentangle monastic features from the results of subsequent occupation. Such surveys have illustrated the enormous extent of the monastic precinct compared to its core of claustral buildings which often takes up no more than 10 or 15 per cent of the whole. Techniques of fieldwork in medieval archaeology, including recording, interpretation, the use of documents and publication have been set out by an expert practitioner, Christopher Taylor (Taylor 1974).

Aerial photography

The use of aerial photographs as a source of information about monastic sites is often undertaken in conjunction with field survey and documentary research. The potential was demonstrated in *Monastic Sites from the Air* (Knowles and St Joseph 1952). Religious houses also feature in two other books that deal with air photography and medieval remains (Beresford and St Joseph 1979; Platt 1984). In the case of monasteries with surviving masonry above ground, the view from the air allows the remains to be seen in their setting, whether that happens to be a rural landscape with earthworks, an urban location, or perhaps the parkland of a country house incorporating parts of the medieval buildings. In all cases, there is the potential to extract information that may not be apparent from other sources or from vantage points at ground level (for example figure 1, Thetford Priory). Aerial photography really comes into its own, however, on sites where apparently little remains. Vegetation marks, soil marks, slight earthworks brought to light by the sun low in the sky – all may be detectable provided there is systematic air survey. The ability to respond quickly to opportunities such as the 1989 drought is also essential, as in the case of Shouldham Abbey in Norfolk (figures 13 and 14). There is sometimes an opportunity to extract astonishing amounts of information from aerial photographs. Two outstanding examples are Wymondham Abbey (figure 21) and West Dereham Abbey (figure 22), both in Norfolk. In the case of other aspects of the monastic economy, such as the sites of granges, the evidence obtained from air photographs may go some way to making up for the deficiency of documents (e.g. Newlass Grange, Yorkshire – Beresford and St Joseph 1979, figure 67; Platt 1969, 222–3). An outstanding example is Monknash Grange (figure 64).

Figure 21. Wymondham Abbey, Norfolk, from the air, 27 July 1979. The nave of the monastery was kept as the parish church at the Dissolution. This photograph, taken at the height of the 1979 drought, shows the considerable extent of the monastic buildings, the foundations of which appear as parch-marks in the grass. The cloister and particularly the east range buildings can be seen to the south of the church, the choir, transepts and chancel of which underlie the modern graveyard.
Photograph by Eileen A. Horne, Aerial Archaeology Publications.

Geophysical prospecting

Methods of identifying buried remains using a variety of physical phenomena have been developed, mainly since the 1950s. The two main families of instruments are resistivity meters and magnetometers. The former measure variations in resistance to the passage of an electric current through the soil. The latter detect anomalies in the magnetic field. Electronic recording and processing of the results has made the handling of data much easier, facilitating what can be extremely time-consuming survey methods. Their application to monastic sites can be effective due to the standardisation of the monastic plan (see Chapter 1). One example of their use might be to determine whether, on a site where the location of the church is known, the cloister lies to the north or the south. If the site is threatened with destruction, the information gained can indicate where rescue excavation should be concentrated, or could even assist in decision-making over emergency preservation measures. At Bury St Edmunds geophysical survey was recently used in municipal parkland as a means of informing decisions on the management

Figure 22. Aerial photograph of parch-marks of the buildings of West Dereham Abbey, Norfolk. Only fragments of the abbey survive above ground, but as this photograph taken on 8 July 1976 shows, below the surface it is a different matter. To the west, at the top of the photograph, is the gatehouse from which a road approaches the main claustral complex (near the clump of trees). The buildings to the right may be the infirmary. There are several large outlying buildings which may be barns.

Photograph by Derek Edwards, Norfolk County Museums Air Photography Unit.

of the grounds. Results were found to confirm and amplify observations of parch-marks in turf produced by buried walls.

Geophysical methods are not without their problems, however. There are often factors which upset the results. Twentieth-century cables and pipe runs, nineteenth-century land drains, post-Dissolution tree planting and industrial activities, and variations in the sub-soil are all capable of distorting the readings. However, there are examples where geophysical prospecting has been of great benefit on monastic sites. At Norton Priory (Greene 1989), the presence of a moat system was suggested by an eighteenth-century estate map. A magnetometer survey pinpointed its position, and excavation was hastily arranged before earth-moving machines arrived to lay out playing fields (figure 58). In addition, a medieval iron-working site was discovered, due to the high magnetic anomaly resulting from the presence of quantities of slag. The complexity of interpretation of the results of a geophysical survey is well illustrated in the case of Vale Royal Abbey, Cheshire (S.J. Hyatt, in McNeil and Turner 1990, 74–7). A dot-density map was produced by a computer into which the results of a resistivity study were fed. Anomalies of high resistance are accounted for by features as varied as the drive leading to the post-Dissolution mansion, garden paths, the eastern walls of the church, modern trees, and the chapter house, possibly accentuated by the presence of a tile floor.

Structural recording and analysis

Where masonry exists above ground, the techniques of structural recording and analysis can provide considerable information about the history of the monastery buildings. This in turn can reveal something of the changing fortunes of the house. Structural analysis should always precede excavation, for it is not possible to frame a correct strategy of investigation without a thorough knowledge of the visible remains. It should also be a preliminary to consolidation or restoration so that these too are carried out with as great an understanding of the structures as is possible.

Furness Abbey in Cumbria has been the subject of a particularly intensive structural study, carried out on behalf of English Heritage by the Lancaster University Archaeological Unit. It provides a good example of what can be achieved in understanding a complex site without recourse to excavation.

Furness Abbey was founded in 1127 by Stephen, count of Boulogne and Mortain (later king of England). The monks, who followed the reformed Benedictine practice of the Order of Savigny, had settled at Tulketh, near Preston in Lancashire, four years earlier, but abandoned it in favour of Furness. It was a much more promising site and they appear to have made rapid progress in adapting it for their use and erecting buildings. After twenty years the Savignac order was absorbed by the Cistercians – a decision by the mother house that was vigorously opposed by the abbot of Furness who took his protestations as far as Rome, to no avail. Furness was highly successful as a Cistercian house. A rich endowment allowed a new set of buildings appropriate to Cistercian organization and practice to be built. Even depredations by Scottish invasions, which badly affected the estates in the fourteenth century, were only a temporary setback. Income from properties producing both wool and iron made Furness second only to Fountains Abbey in wealth amongst the Cistercian houses of the British Isles.

In consequence of such a substantial income, the monks were well able to invest in major building operations. Considerable portions of the structures still survive. The basis of the programme of structural recording embarked upon by the archaeological unit is photogrammetry, provided mainly by the Photogrammetric Unit at York University. For such large expanses of masonry, rising to considerable heights in parts of the site, photogrammetry

Figure 23. Drawing based on the photogrammetric and hand survey of the south face of the north wall of the north transept of the church, Furness Abbey, Cumbria. One of over 200 stone-by-stone base elevation drawings of Furness prepared on behalf of English Heritage.

Drawing supplied by Lancaster University Archaeological Unit.

the only practical means of obtaining measured drawings of wall faces. The only alternative – direct measurement of stonework – would require the erection of complete scaffolding to give access to all but the lower parts of the walls. This would not only be prohibitively expensive, it would also be much more time-consuming.

The basis of photogrammetry is the production of stereo pairs of photographs. From these, detailed stone-by-stone drawings can be prepared. The first step is to place markers at a series of points on the wall face, each one being accurately surveyed in. Photographs of the wall face are then taken from at least two different viewpoints using a special camera. The key to the method is the use of a computerised stereo-plotting machine capable of correcting the photographic distortions. These will result from diminishing perspective, variations in the plane of face of the wall (for example, openings such as doors and windows, and projections such as buttresses and pilasters), and distortions produced by the camera lens. A scaled drawing showing the entire face of the wall is then prepared (figure 23).

The drawing is the first stage in the recording process. There will always be gaps due to the fact that some areas of the wall are obscured – for example, by the branch of an overhanging tree, or the deep shadow cast by some projecting masonry. These must be measured in by hand, using, if necessary, a scaffold tower or a vehicle with an extending arm. Having completed the base drawing, a series of overlays can be prepared. These might include one showing different types of stone (a pair of binoculars will allow examination of the higher courses of masonry). Another could record differences in types of mortar. A third could be specifically designed to aid the process of consolidation, highlighting areas of decayed stonework, or where repointing is required. A fourth could be interpretive, showing the archaeologist's judgement of the structural phases of the building. This will probably be the final item following the production of the sequence of record drawings, for the raw material upon which judgements can be made is contained within the methodically compiled records.

The Furness Abbey survey has demonstrated the value of detailed study of this kind. Many people, beginning with St John Hope, had interpreted the remains, but it is with the discipline of an exhaustive structural survey and analysis that a full understanding of this complex site has become possible. The layout and detail of the Savignac church and the effect it had on its Cistercian successor has been one area where the survey has provided new information. The additional benefit of such a campaign is the fact that, of necessity, it takes many months to complete. The opportunity to get to know a site intimately, and to see it in a wide range of light conditions as the seasons progress, allow the subtle clues that can illuminate the building's history to be detected.

On a practical basis the results are of enormous value in informing the process of consolidation. The specific identification of areas of stonework and pointing that require urgent attention is part of the product, but of even greater value is the basic understanding of the structures that can pinpoint problem areas. One is the hitherto unnoticed crack which can indicate settlement and the longer-term danger of collapse. Knowledge of the structure's history can provide clues to the reasons for the problem. Examples include

walls built across drains that were part of an earlier phase, or recent changes to the water table that have precipitated the settlement of the foundations. Early detection of the problem, and the opportunity to devise a solution based on the best possible information, could avoid a serious situation of major structural failure, and could save considerable sums of money by permitting localised treatment.

Excavation

The preceding sections of this chapter emphasise the fact that excavation is but one of a range of techniques available to the archaeologist investigating a monastic site. Indeed, it will often be possible to gather sufficient information from a combination of documentary research and a range of surveys to make excavation unnecessary. Excavation is, by its very nature, a course of action of last resort because it is destructive. However skilled the excavator is in recording what is revealed by digging, the process itself removes the raw material upon which understanding is based. The opportunity to replicate the experiment to confirm observations and conclusions, which is the essence of scientific enquiry, is denied the excavator. Another trench, another site – the results are material for comparison and analogy, but do not constitute replication.

The unique and fragile nature of the evidence places a heavy responsibility on the excavator. This is true of any class of archaeological site. In the case of monasteries, however, there is also the practical question of their size and the complexity of the archaeological deposits. Excavation can only be justified if it can be carried out on a scale sufficient to reveal worthwhile information about the site. Sometimes small, strategic investigations may be required to provide a basis for informed decisions on conservation or restoration. However, it is a sad fact that of almost 300 monastic sites that have been subject to excavation, reported in the annual surveys in *Medieval Archaeology* for the years 1974 to 1990, a great number have not produced information of any substantial nature. Monastic sites, whether or not they are threatened with destruction, should be subject to a rigorous examination of the likely return on resources consumed by excavation and post-excavation work. Unless it is possible to mount a rescue excavation on a large enough scale to produce meaningful results, the exercise is unlikely to be justifiable. Urban sites subject to piecemeal development are a particular problem, as is discussed in Chapter 7.

It is the preliminary work described in preceding paragraphs that will pay dividends when hard decisions have to be made. It may, for example, be an intelligent course of action to abandon the remains of the claustral buildings to the mechanical excavators, with a watching brief in which information is salvaged on the basis of a procedure agreed with the contractor in advance. This 'sacrifice' may then enable the team to concentrate on some promising area of the outer courtyard or other parts of the monastic precinct.

In terms of the variety of stratigraphical, artefactual and environmental evidence, a monastery is likely to confront the excavator with as wide a selection of demands as any class of site. Masonry structures may exist as tanding buildings, or at least as large areas of walling projecting above the surface of the ground. On the other hand, all that may be left are the trenches dug to remove the stones of abandoned buildings and a scatter of debris, such as broken facing blocks, carved stones, fractured roof and floor tiles and shattered glass. Many sites will exhibit both extremes of the range, with many intermediate states of damage. The essence of excavation is therefore to disentangle the sequence of stages of construction and destruction, working backwards from the most recent events that have left their mark. The techniques have been well described elsewhere (for example Greene, K. 1990; Barker 1982; Harris 1979). There are particular characteristics of monastic sites, however, that make special demands on the excavator. One is the wealth that many enjoyed in the Middle Ages permitting a series of modifications, rebuildings, expansions and embellishments that few other classes of buildings experienced. Another is the long period of occupation experienced by many sites. Often, four centuries as a monastery were followed by a further four centuries of post-Dissolution life. Excavation may therefore be concerned with a sequence of events that takes up the greater part of the present millennium (as for example, Merton Priory in Surrey, figure 24).

Excavation of a monastic site is a process in which an extensive and complex web of threads have to be unravelled. The components are of a variety of types. There are layers of soil, such as construction surfaces with spreads of mortar and chippings of stone left by the masons; earth floors; tiles set on beds of mortar (or simply the impressions of tiles left in the mortar matrix); the pattern of wear on floor surfaces capable of indicating, for example, liturgical practices; the debris of destruction; scatters of rubbish, and many other traces of human activity. There are the elements of the walls themselves, including construction trenches and foundations. The masonry may show the impressions of tools used for dressing facing blocks and mouldings, as well as masons' marks which can be examined and recorded. There may be post holes showing the position of scaffolding; possibly plastered and painted surfaces to the walls; window and door openings, sometimes blocked as a result of changes of plan; trenches dug to remove stones for reuse, often at more than one date. Above all, the extensive nature of masonry remains places great demands upon the excavator, for the impact of particular events such as a destructive fire may be observed at widely separated locations within the monastic complex. To discern such phenomena requires qualities of excavation, observation, recording, correlation and interpretation of a high order.

A common feature of monasteries is their system of water supply and drainage. This too presents opportunities and challenges to the excavator. As such systems were often planned on an integrated basis to bring pure water to a site, and to remove waste, one research objective must be to understand how these twin demands were organised. Once again, this is unlikely to be achieved unless excavation is on an extensive scale. The main monastic drain serving the infirmary, dormitory latrines and the kitchens may well have undergone a series of modifications as the buildings were themselves changed. Improvements may have been introduced to enable the drain to function more efficiently. There will undoubtedly be many subsidiary drains

Figure 24. Excavation in advance of development, Merton Priory, Surrey. Work taking place to excavate and record the flint and mortar foundations and other features of the Augustinian priory as construction work for a hypermarket encroaches on the site. Looking east along the north aisle of the church with the lady chapel in the distance. The piling rig is standing on the area of the lay cemetery.

Photograph supplied by Department of Greater London Archaeology, Museum of London.

aking water from roofs and certain rooms such as the kitchen. If water was supplied through stone channels, these may survive. Lead pipes are found surprisingly often. Where it has been stripped out, however, it may be possible to locate the trench dug to remove the pipe. Often a chase cut in stonework will be the sole evidence for the former presence of a pipe. Abandoned drains can be a rich source of environmental materials, particularly human faeces which may contain food remains, and traces of bacteria and parasites which can provide evidence of standards of health. It is essential that the excavator has a full appreciation of the circumstances of the disuse of the drain if meaningful results of environmental analyses are to be obtained. It can in fact be difficult to assign a date to abandonment, which is essential if the results are to be related to the occupants of the monastery at a particular period of its history.

One particularly important aspect of the presence of an extensive network of drains is the opportunity it presents to tie together stratigraphical relationships over widely separated parts of the site. This is valuable in compiling a comprehensive picture of the developmental history of the site as a whole.

In addition to all the challenges of what could broadly be described as the archaeology of masonry buildings, a monastic site is likely to present the excavator with other types of evidence. There may be traces of early timber buildings such as post holes, beam trenches and scatters of burnt daub from wattle walls. There may also be later buildings that are timber framed, with either earth-fast posts, or cill-beams either set in the soil or (more likely) supported by a dwarf wall of masonry. Often these will be the subsidiary buildings of the outer courtyard. There are also likely to be ditches, stone-lined drains and possibly moats. All require of the excavator the identification of dates of construction, recuttings, abandonment, and relationships with other features.

Even when the earliest monastic activities have been identified and examined, the excavator's tasks are not complete. There is much to be learnt about the kinds of sites colonised by monastic communities. A rural monastery may have been established on marginal, uncultivated land or may have entailed the abandonment of fields or even a village. An urban monastery may have been placed in an uninhabited part of the town, or may have necessitated the removal of occupied tenements. A further possibility is that the monastery was established at an earlier religious site, for example a pre-Conquest abbey or cell, or a parish church. Excavation, and environmental research, can provide valuable evidence where charters may be frustratingly vague in their references to the circumstances of foundation. Beneath the monastic remains may be completely unrelated Saxon, Roman or prehistoric remains. At the other end of the chronological scale, the post-Dissolution history of the monastic site and its estates is an important subject for study. The way in which monastic buildings were adapted by their new owners, or were used as sources of building materials, can be investigated by excavation.

It will be clear from the foregoing that not only is excavation on a large scale essential if worthwhile results are to be obtained, but also that the volume of data produced by the process will be enormous. The use of portable personal computers and lap-tops on site can assist in the recording

and collection of stratigraphical information which can then be transferred
to a comprehensive data base. This will also hold data on finds and samples.
Techniques of stratigraphical analysis such as those derived from the work
by Ed Harris to cope with the complexities of urban archaeology in
Winchester are essential tools to the understanding of sites on the scale of
monasteries (Harris 1979).

Finds and environmental evidence

Even the most poverty-stricken religious house had standards of material
culture far exceeding the generality of medieval Britain. The monastic rule
may have forbidden individual possessions, but as institutions monasteries
formed part of the affluent crust on the top of medieval society. In consequence, excavation will usually produce large quantities of artefacts. These
are likely to fall into a number of categories.

Building materials may include carved masonry, ceramic roof and floor
tiles, painted window glass and lead cames, door furniture such as locks,
keys and hinges, iron nails, pipes and spigots (taps). Kitchen waste is likely
to include discarded animal bones from mammals, birds, fish and shellfish,
and also broken pottery vessels, vegetable remains such as pips and stones
of fruit, grain and seeds, and perhaps items of kitchen equipment such as
stone hand-mills and mortars or metal cauldrons and flesh hooks. Objects
associated with monastic life include writing instruments (for example,
dividers and parchment prickers, figure 25), book bindings and clasps, seals
from documents including lead bulla from papal documents, seal matrices,
pilgrim badges and reliquaries, liturgical objects such as candle sticks and
crosses, and leisure items such as dice and gaming pieces, coins and jettons.
The buildings of the outer courtyard may produce objects associated with
their specialist functions – brewhouse, smithy, stables, mill, barn, foundry,
dovecot, etc.

The study of artefacts from specific locations within the monastic precinct
can provide information about the uses to which buildings and other areas
were put. Thus a cloister, as a result of its use for a number of functions,
can produce a wide range of material. In the cloister of St Frideswide's
Augustinian priory in Oxford were found Nuremburg jettons (tokens used
in gaming), a lead bulla of Innocent IV (1243–54), copper alloy book clasps,
lace ends, iron knives, an antler side plate from a comb, a hinged manicure
set, and even two arrow heads of the type used for target practice (Blair
1990, 38–45). At Bordesley Abbey (Hereford and Worcestershire), the
excavation of the room situated between the south transept and the chapter
house produced finds that helped clarify its functions. It had been divided
into a book store and vestry. Amongst the objects discovered in the book
store were studs and clasps from book bindings and a lead stylus. Only the
choir stalls produced a similar concentration of book fittings (Hirst, Walsh
and Wright 1983, 103–22).

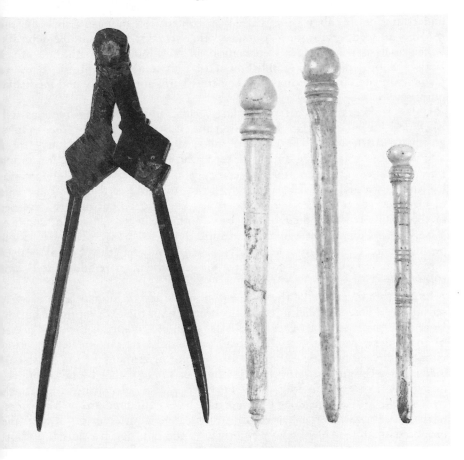

Figure 25. Pair of bronze dividers and bone parchment prickers found in Dissolution demolition rubble in the latrine of Bermondsey Abbey; they were used in the production of manuscripts. The dividers measure 94 mm. by 19 mm.; the largest parchment pricker is 88 mm. in length.

Photograph supplied by Department of Greater London Archaeology, Museum of London.

Environmental evidence and human remains

Environmental evidence obtained from many excavated contexts will greatly extend the information available from written sources (Shackley 1981). Large-scale sampling of the kind developed by the York Environmental Archaeology Unit is capable of providing, for example, truly representative collections of animal bones. In samples collected by conventional methods of excavation, relying as they do on visual recognition by excavators, the tiny bones of small mammals, birds and especially fish will be underrepresented. Modern sampling and identification techniques are essential for realising the full potential of investigating monastic diet (Jones 1989). Flotation usually forms part of mass sampling techniques. The opportunity therefore exists to understand more about the vegetable content of monastic diet by the recovery of seed, grain, pip, stone and other remains from suitable deposits. Pollen analysis can produce information on such topics as the nature of the landscape preceding the establishment of the monastery, or the types of plants cultivated in the monastic precinct as herbs for culinary and medicinal purposes.

Unless soil conditions are particularly acidic, human skeletal remains will be found inside the church and outside it, particularly in the monks' graveyard to the east. The cloister walks, chapter house and chapels may also produce burials. Anatomical research can give considerable information on such matters as stature, life expectancy, standards of health, blood grouping and dental hygiene. The results will not, however, reflect the full range of medieval society. The two main groups likely to be encountered are the monks themselves and their benefactors, both privileged classes in medieval society. Associated material may include items of dress such as buckles, pewter chalices, fabric from vestments (possibly only lengths of gold or silver thread may survive), wooden coffins, stone coffins, grave slabs, nails and shroud pins.

Excavators must handle the excavation and study of human remains with sensitivity. There need be no ethical concern about the excavation of burials from a monastic site, however. The excavation of remains of the dead is one of the oldest traditions of the Christian church. In the medieval period monks were enthusiastic exhumers of the mortal remains of the holiest of individuals. Few monasteries lacked bones of saints to be displayed in reliquaries or exposed on holy days. Provided graves and their contents are treated with respect, problems should not be encountered from the Roman Catholic Church or the successor orders. It is courteous to discuss the proposed treatment of human remains with the appropriate church authorities before excavation starts. Under civil law it will also be necessary to notify the coroner's officer in the local police force who will arrange for an inquest to be held. This will be no more than a formality.

3 Building a monastery

The decision to found a new monastic house set in train a series of events that were necessary to bring pious ambition to practical reality. Once an existing monastery had agreed to provide a nucleus of brethren, a site for the new foundation was required and there was an urgent need for temporary buildings to be erected. A construction team had to be assembled, led by a master mason, and the long job of building the monastery began.

In the case of most monastic houses, there is little detail recorded in charters and annals of the precise circumstances that surrounded the erection of the buildings. Careful selection of a site must always have been the crucial first step. A benefactor rarely disposed of his (or occasionally her) best land to found an abbey. Not infrequently, however, the founder required the monastery to be located in immediate proximity to his castle or manor house (Thompson 1986). This was true not only for Anglo-Norman lords, but also in the choice of site of many of the Cistercian houses founded by Welsh princes. Another factor in the case of some Welsh houses was the choice of a site with earlier sacred associations. Thus Valle Crucis (Clwyd) was established in the field of the early Christian memorial, the Cross of Eliseg, in view of the founder's princely stronghold that dominated the eastern skyline (Butler 1982b).

Despite such pressures, there was usually some choice of location within the founder's estates. The critical influences were prosaic – the need for water supply and drainage. Wherever possible the site incorporated a spring, stream or river that could be channelled to flow down the latrines. In consequence, most medieval monasteries were established in stream or river valleys; if necessary the cloister was built in the less favoured, colder position to the north of the church if that was the only way of ensuring a flow of water through the latrine drain. Nunneries, however, were built more frequently with the cloister to the north, perhaps because of an association of the north side of the church with the cult of the Virgin (Gilchrist 1989, 253). Irish friaries usually had the cloister to the north.

There were constraints in the siting of many monasteries. Sometimes churches were given to be converted into religious houses, as at Linlithgow (Lothian) where a chapel formed the basis of a Carmelite friary founded in the early fifteenth century (Stones 1989, 71). In these circumstances a monastery might find great difficulties in providing efficient systems of water supply and drainage. St Werburgh's Abbey at Chester was the successor of a pre-Conquest establishment. The monks had to arrange for a conduit to be built to carry water into the city to supply their precinct (Hewitt 1967, 72). Their drain also pierced the city walls to deposit the abbey's waste in the defensive ditch outside. The Chester cloister therefore had to be placed to the north of the church. On a smaller scale, the canons of Portchester (Hampshire) had a similar problem, for their priory was set within the massive walls of the Roman fort. Their solution can still be seen today, in the form of a row of nine masonry shoots which penetrate the mortar and flint wall, each originally serving a cubicle in the latrine building which lay at the southern end of the dormitory. As described in Chapter 1, the monks of Battle (Sussex) had a still more difficult problem as a result of their hilltop position (figure 4).

Site selection was therefore by no means an easy matter. About fifty Augustinian and Cistercian houses in England failed to get it right at the first attempt and were forced, for a variety of reasons, to move to a new location. Eventually the Cistercian Order became concerned about the selection of inappropriate sites. In 1194 the General Chapter decided to send two abbots to all sites being offered to the order. Such an inspection might have prevented the problems that arose at Stanlow Abbey, established in the 1170s in a remote spot on the southern bank of the Mersey estuary in Cheshire. At first sight it must have appeared a good location for a Cistercian house, far from habitation and close to a river. The Mersey, however, was the source of repeated problems with flooding. There were two particularly bad inundations in 1279 and 1287 (Hewitt 1967, 91). Pope Nicholas IV responded to the pleas of the monks and their patron, Henry de Lacy, earl of Lincoln, granting a licence in 1289 'to transfer themselves to the place where is the church of Whalley, their present place being near the sea, which sometimes floods the offices to the height of three feet, and prevents all access, so that the place is not fit to live in' (*Calendar of Papal Registers*, 1, 1893, 499). The Pope's mandate to the bishop of Coventry and Lichfield granting the church of Whalley described the monks' predicament even more forcibly. They 'fear that their house may be overturned by the sea' (*ibid.* 501). Eventually, in 1296, they settled at their new and agreeable site at Whalley in Lancashire, adjacent to the river Ribble but at an elevation clear of the highest waters. There is a graphic account of the flooding of Boyle Abbey (Co. Roscommon) by the River Boyle in 1471. After a hail storm with lightning and thunder 'a boat could have floated over the floor of the great church of the monks' (Stalley 1987, 32).

Once the site had been selected, the construction of temporary buildings began. Occasionally it was not the monks that arranged this, but the patron. At Pipewell in Northamptonshire this led to confusion. Having granted the land and erected the temporary buildings, William Batevileyn opened negotiations with two Cistercian monasteries, Garendon (Leicestershire) and Newminster (Northumberland). Two parties, each consisting of an abbot, twelve monks and some lay brothers converged on Pipewell, each convinced that they had an agreement with the founder. After arguments, the Garendon monks had to return home (Fergusson 1983, 78).

There are few contemporary accounts of the way in which the preliminary site-works were organised. Archaeological excavation has produced only a handful of examples of the earliest phases of a monastery's life. Fountains Abbey, the great Cistercian monastery in Yorkshire, has, however, a vivid description of its modest beginnings which excavation has amplified (Gilyard-Beer and Coppack 1986). It was the heroic circumstances of Fountain's origins that led to the writing in 1207 of the *Narratio de fundatione Fontanis monasterii*, based on the memories of Serlo, one of the first monks. In 1132 a dispute at the Benedictine St Mary's Abbey in York resulted in the prior and thirteen monks leaving. They had been urging the abbot and their brethren to adopt a simpler, more austere way of life. This they decided to try to achieve themselves. After some wanderings they ended up in the valley of the River Skell, described by Serlo as a place of horror and solitude, thick-set with thorns.

In the depth of winter the monks built a hut of rough timber, roofed with turf, beneath an elm tree. This provided shelter while they cleared some land for a garden and built a chapel, probably of wattles. By the spring of 1133 the brethren had decided to seek admission to the Cistercian Order, and sent messengers to St Bernard at Clairvaux. He dispatched Geoffrey d'Ainai who instructed the monks in Cistercian practice and supervised the construction of buildings; the employment of carpenters is mentioned. Problems were not at an end, however. Famine and poverty nearly made the community give up the struggle, but by October 1135 Fountains had achieved sufficient resources and stability to be admitted to the Cistercian Order. With increasing benefactions the erection of permanent buildings could start. The construction of a stone church probably began in 1136. In 1146, however, the products of a decade of endeavour were destroyed when Fountains was attacked and burnt by the supporters of the recently deposed archbishop of York. The abbot of Fountains had been a leading figure in the campaign for his deposition. Serlo describes how the monks watched as the buildings 'erected by the sweat of their brows enveloped in flames, and that only the oratory and offices adjoining it reserved for prayer remained half-consumed, like a brand plucked from the burning'. The monastery then began the task of construction again, eventually in the 1170s erecting 'sumptuous buildings'. In the first part of the thirteenth century another major building campaign took place to erect an aisled presbytery ending in the Chapel of the Nine Altars. This was needed because 'the church flourished like a vine and the congregation of monks was much greater than usual, so that there were not enough altars on which to celebrate, and the choir was too mean and dark for so great a multitude'. The precarious encampment beneath the elm tree had become one of the most powerful monasteries in England.

Serlo's narrative is very important in throwing light on the beginnings of Fountains. However, his account was not intended as a description of the development of buildings, but of the community they housed. There has been speculation and debate about the early building history of the abbey, which archaeology has now substantially resolved. Excavation took place in the south transept in 1979 and 1980 (Gilyard-Beer and Coppack 1986). The need to provide a sump for drainage led to the excavation, which was eventually extended to the whole area of the transept and the south crossing-aisle. The results were dramatic. At the lowest level, cut into the clays of the valley bottom, were twenty-one post pits and stake holes which were sealed by all later deposits and were thus primary to the site (figure 26). Despite later disturbances it was possible to identify two distinct buildings. The first building, defined by post-pits, was 4.9 m. wide and at least 7.6 m. long. In a number of the pits the posts had been sawn off at ground level, leaving 'ghosts' of the timbers in the pit filling; they had been carefully squared and were of 0.4 m. section. It was clearly a large building of carpentered construction, aligned below the later stone churches. The excavator concluded that it was the chapel or oratory of the abbey as reorganised by

Figure 26. Post holes of early buildings, and foundations of the original church, Fountains Abbey, North Yorkshire.
Photograph by Glyn Coppack, English Heritage.

Geoffrey d'Ainai in 1133, and that its sophisticated construction would accord with the mention of carpenters by Serlo. The second timber building lay to the south on a north–south alignment, with only three post-pits of its east wall in the area excavated, so it is not possible to identify its function.

Built directly above the levelled remains of the timber buildings was the first stone church, the south transept and part of the choir and presbytery of which had stood within the area excavated. The method of construction was deduced by the excavator. The second timber building was in the way, so its north end was taken down before the foundation trenches for the walls of the new building were dug. These were laid out around the first timber building, the oratory. Presumably it continued in use for some time until construction of the stone church had reached an advanced stage. The wall posts of the oratory were cut off at ground level and the stumps were left to rot.

The foundations of the new church consisted of rubble and mortar. There was evidence that the superstructure was built of ashlar masonry, and that there was an eastern cloister range of timber with a floor of pink mortar. The east range was eventually replaced in masonry.

The excavation revealed the effects of a major fire that had badly damaged the transept, its chapels, and the part of the east range which was uncovered. There was fallen wall plaster and mortar, ash, charcoal, and fragments of window glass. The masonry walls had been discoloured by the heat. There can be little doubt that the remains bore witness to the fire of 1146 that Serlo recalled. The church was repaired, but the decision to erect a much larger church a few years later necessitated the demolition of at least the chancel and south transept before its foundations could be dug. The nave, however, was left standing, and this may have served as a temporary chapel until the new chancel was sufficiently far advanced to be used for services. The east end of the new church was completed before work started on the nave. Timber scaffolding was used, set in post holes, and a group of larger posts may have supported a wheel used to raise blocks of stone to the masons working on the building. Much of this church survives to the level of the wall tops, and there was abundant evidence of the later building campaigns and modifications.

The excavation showed that Serlo's account was reliable, thereby illuminating the early struggles of this religious house. The monks, thrown on to their own resources, were hard put to build their hut of branches and turf. When Geoffrey of Ainai arrived, the task of providing temporary timber buildings was placed in the hands of professionals – the carpenters mentioned by Serlo, whose impressive structures were found in the excavation. The buildings are consistent with the limited documentary evidence which shows that at the Cistercian houses of Clairvaux and Meaux (Yorkshire) there were similar early timber buildings serving a variety of purposes. At Meaux, for example, there were two timber buildings erected in advance of the arrival of a group of monks from Fountains (Fergusson 1983, 78). This is consistent with Cistercian regulations for the founding of new houses which demanded as essential requirements a place to pray, a place to sleep, a place to eat, a place for guests and a place for a porter who could ensure seclusion. For a new Cistercian abbey, founded without the drama and crisis that accompanied the beginnings of Fountains, these minimum temporary facilities were to be provided in readiness for the first contingent of monks from the mother house. Thus, in 1139 Fountains sent an advance party of lay brothers to Haverholme (Lincolnshire) to construct buildings and set up workshops. Eight years later a group of lay brothers set out 'to build humble buildings according to the form of the order' at another daughter house, Kirkstall in Yorkshire (Fergusson 1983, 76). In very few cases is there any indication that the monks took a hand in the construction work. In many instances not even the lay brothers were involved. One of the best documented cases is that of Meaux (*ibid.*). The patron, William le Gros, provided land and supervised the erection of two buildings for the monks. The next stage, however – the erection of permanent masonry buildings – was supervised by Abbot Adam of Meaux. He appears to have carried out this role at Fountains and a number of its daughter houses, having been trained by Geoffrey d'Ainai and being therefore conversant with continental as well as English architecture. At Meaux, Adam had to replace one of the founder's wooden buildings with a larger one to cope with the increased number of brethren (about forty). Like its predecessor though, it was of two storeys with the dormitory below and the oratory above, and was in essence an adaptation of a type of secular manor house.

In Ireland, continental Cistercian practice was introduced at the pioneering abbey of the order, Mellifont (Co. Louth) by the monk Robert, who was sent from Clairvaux by St Bernard to 'assist with the buildings and other things necessary for the well-being of the house' (Stalley 1987, 41). Robert, like Geoffrey, must have started with the erection of timber buildings, but these have yet to be found in the excavation of any Irish monastery.

The necessity for temporary buildings was common to monasteries of all orders. Excavation at Norton Priory in Cheshire (Greene 1989, 73–9) produced valuable information about early timber buildings that served the needs of the Augustinian canons during the erection of their church and claustral ranges in masonry (described in Chapter 1). Alongside the entrance track which led into the outer courtyard was a building measuring 6.8 m. wide by at least 7.8 m. long, with posts set in pits dug 0.5 m. deep into the boulder clay. It was probably the porter's lodge; a very large post pit alongside, 0.7 m. deep, contained a post-pipe that was the 'shadow' of a timber with sides 0.58 m. by 0.46 m. This massive post must have supported the gate that the porter supervised.

An extensive area with timber features was found to the south-west of the eventual site of the cloister ranges. Despite damage and disturbance by later structures, the plans of several buildings could be distinguished. There were two phases, corresponding to a life of fifteen to twenty years for each building. On the evidence of documentary records from other monastic sites, it would not be surprising if it took forty years for the church at Norton to be completed and the dormitory range made habitable. The building that left most evidence was also the largest. Built in the second phase, it was 11.0 m. wide by at least 14 m. long. It was an aisled structure, with two rows of aisle posts each measuring 0.40 m. by 0.30 m., set in pits 0.6 m. deep, and smaller wall posts each measuring 0.22 m. by 0.18 m. set in pits 0.4 m. deep. It had a thick clay floor and a central stone-built hearth. This was surrounded by many small stake holes, which may indicate the presence of a screen, a spit, or even a fire-hood. The building probably had walls of wattle and daub – its smaller predecessor certainly did, for large quantities of burnt daub were found bearing the clear imprint of the wattles. The large aisled hall probably performed similar functions to the big building at Meaux, combining a dormitory with daytime living and eating space. The central hearth, however, indicates that it was a single storey high. Nearby were other timber buildings that may have operated as temporary kitchens. The permanent kitchens were subsequently built on this part of the site.

The Norton excavation revealed many interesting details of the constructional techniques of the carpenters. The post pits were large in all cases, and although the timbers were precisely placed in relation to one another, they were rarely in the centre of the pit. In some cases the posts had been chocked up on short lengths of plank. This suggests that the basic structural framework of each building was prepared in advance and then assembled on site, with the large post pits allowing adjustments during the erection of the skeleton of aisle and wall posts, purlins and principal rafters. In many cases the stumps of posts had survived. Like those at Fountains they had been sawn off at ground level (which is where they would have rotted). The timbers were of oak, and they had been neatly cut to precise rectangular section. These buildings were no humble huts, but large and professionally built structures that would not have been out of place as the dwellings of secular twelfth-century lords. For example, timber halls of similar scale, and also dating from the twelfth century, have been excavated at secular fortified sites such as Goltho (Lincolnshire), Barnard Castle (Co. Durham) and Rumney (Glamorgan) (Kenyon 1989, 98–110).

One further building at Norton was part of the complex of temporary structures. Lying west of the intended site of the church, it was built in a totally different way to the timber buildings and the permanent masonry buildings. The foundations comprised a broad trench in which rough lumps of sandstone had been packed, also incorporating square-section horizontal timbers in the middle, on the axis of the wall. Although the timbers had rotted, their position was clear as strips of grey clayey soil. They may have been used as a device to prevent subsidence – a technique of strengthening foundations that was widely used in the medieval period (Wilcox 1982). The building, only a small part of which could be excavated due to the presence of trees, may have functioned as a temporary church. If so, Augustinian Norton Priory had temporary buildings that would also have satisfied the specifications of the Cistercian charter that 'no abbot shall be sent to a new place without at least twelve monks and . . . without the prior construction of such places as an oratory, a refectory, a dormitory, a guest house, and a gate keeper's cell, so the monks may immediately serve God and live in religious discipline' (Fergusson 1983, 75). In fact, these precepts would have made sense for any new house irrespective of order, and a set of similar temporary buildings could be expected on most monastic sites.

Despite the likelihood that temporary buildings once existed on most monastic sites, very few excavations have produced evidence for them. Amongst Cistercian abbeys it is scanty (Butler 1982), and even in the case of a Cistercian church as thoroughly investigated as Bordesley the three slots cut into the clay beneath the intended site of the crossing are ambiguous, although they have been suggested as belonging to a temporary church (Hirst, Walsh and Wright 1983, 30). However, timbers found in early graves there may have been reused from temporary structures. At Sandwell Priory (West Midlands) evidence was found for the first, timber phase of the east range (Hodder 1989). The total number of sites producing even tenuous suggestions of early timber phases has been estimated as fewer than two dozen over a period of three decades of archaeological activity (Baker and Baker 1989, 261).

Why have so few temporary buildings been found? One reason is that, despite the large number of sites investigated archaeologically, the scale of excavation has usually been small and the quality often poor. However, given the massive size of the post pits at Fountains and Norton, similar features at other sites would be hard to miss. The second and more important factor must be that there has been an expectation that temporary buildings would be most likely to be found beneath their masonry successors. However, it is a false assumption that a monastery was built of timber that was then progressively replaced in masonry on the same site. Although there are some examples of the claustral ranges being built first of timber (such as Sandwell, figure 39), and the replacement of the first infirmary hall at Kirkstall (figure 3), it would have been far more logical for the temporary buildings to be placed away from the building site, so that as

normal a pattern of monastic life as possible could be established free of the
disruption and disturbance that inevitably accompanied construction. The
situation at Norton, where the temporary buildings were grouped around
what was to become the outer courtyard, might well be typical. However,
so little excavation has taken place in these peripheral areas that general
conclusions cannot be drawn (Baker and Baker 1989). The situation at
Fountains, with the masons forced to dismantle the oratory (if that is what
it was) during the course of construction may have more to do with the
particular circumstances of that abbey's foundation than with usual practice,
although at the Augustinian site at Gisborough (Cleveland) a building
erected on shallow foundations of rubble has been suggested as a temporary
church (Heslop forthcoming).

For urban monasteries, especially friaries, there was often no need to build
temporary accommodation, as an existing building could be acquired for the
purpose. However, in some cases temporary buildings were needed, and the
discovery of a timber building with a plaster floor at the thirteenth-century
Franciscan friary at Hartlepool (Cleveland) may be one such example
(Daniels 1986, 265–7). For the archaeologist, it may be difficult to
distinguish between a temporary monastic structure, and an existing building
demolished as part of the clearance of the site.

The other circumstance where temporary quarters were unnecessary was
where a monastery was established in existing buildings. Grove Priory in
Bedfordshire is one such example (Baker and Baker 1989, 265). In 1164 the
priory was founded in a high-status manorial complex. The result was a
monastery that in many respects also acted as the grange, and which did not
lead to the construction of cloisters or surrounding ranges.

Constructing the masonry buildings

Once the community was provided with its temporary quarters, a start could
be made on the masonry church. The first tasks were to clear and prepare
the site, by removing vegetation, levelling uneven ground, installing drains
or digging ditches, and if necessary spreading stone chippings (as at Norton)
or ferns (Bordesley) to provide a firm working surface. The next step was
to set out the plan of the church so that the trenches for the foundations
could be dug. The means used to mark out the site are unknown, but it
seems likely that pegs and twine defined the outline of the church, with
markers also indicating the intended positions of the claustral ranges. Foundation trenches were often surprisingly shallow. At Norton they were only
0.15 m. deep; they were filled with sandstone rubble and rounded pebbles
from the boulder clay, and were about 0.25 m. broader than the walls they
were to carry (figure 27). The Bordesley foundations were about 0.30 m.
deep, and were packed with a raft of water-worn pebbles, although between
the western crossing piers and the next piers to the west a sleeper wall of
flat slabs of stone occupied the foundation trench. The sleeper acted as a
strengthening device to hold the piers fast. Similar techniques have been
observed at Quarr (Isle of Wight), Buckfast (Devon), and Merevale
(Warwickshire) (Hirst, Walsh and Wright 1983, 229).

Figure 27. Foundations and lowest course of walls, Norton Priory, Cheshire. The wall on the right (part of the dormitory range) has been built up against the earlier wall on the left (the south transept). Both walls are faced with ashlar blocks with a rubble and mortar core, and have shallow foundations.

Photograph by Patrick Greene, reproduced by permission of Norton Priory Museum Trust.

Measurement

Archaeological investigation of twelfth-century monastic churches has provided some fascinating insights into the design principles and units of measurement used by their builders. Three elements of modern archaeological technique have made this possible. One is the identification of the earliest plan form in churches that have undergone later expansion and modification. Another is the uncovering of the lowest masonry courses of walls that are closest to the masons' original plan. The third factor is the degree of precision of measurement achieved in an area excavation of monastic buildings that could never be attained by trenching.

The architectural study of the church at Bordesley Abbey by D.A. Walsh is particularly revealing (*ibid.*, 207–87). The church was being constructed in the years around 1150 (see Chapter 1). This was the period of greatest Cistercian expansion, with large numbers of churches being erected by the order throughout Europe. Many were planned on what has become known as the 'Bernardine' arrangement – a flat-ended, aisleless presbytery and deep transepts, each with eastern chapels ending in a continuous flat wall. It is

Medieval monasteries

Figure 28. Remains of the church, Bordesley Abbey, Hereford and Worcester. The south transept during the consolidation of the excavated masonry to ensure its survival. On the left are the entrances to the transept chapels, and on the right are the first seven steps of the night stairs which gave access to the first-floor dormitory.

Photograph by Patrick Greene.

believed that this plan type, with a scheme of proportions to guide it, originated at Citeaux and Clairvaux, and was associated with St Bernard. The centralised control of the order made transmission and regulation of design principles possible. The use of simple ratios, such as 3 : 4 (suggested by Hahn 1957) and 1 : 2 (Bucher 1957) determined many of the relationships of the plan and elevation. However, there still remained immense scope for variations on the general theme.

At Bordesley (figure 28), Hahn's formulae which should determine relationships between the various components of the plan were only found to work in a very approximate way. However, when Walsh studied the units of measurement used by the medieval builders, it became apparent how such units were applied in setting out the church, and therefore the particular lengths that were important in the scheme as built. The degree of precision achieved by the masons is impressive. At the Yorkshire Cistercian houses of Rievaulx, Fountains and Kirkstall, as well as at Bordesley, the equality of pier spacing varies by little more than 10 mm. Such exactitude in establishing the layout was a prerequisite for the construction of a building of high quality, for on it depended the entire superstructure, including the rhythm and uniformity of arcading and fenestration. Such precision provides the archaeologist with confidence in determining the units of measurement used. At Bordesley, the basic unit was 0.295 m. A number of major parts could be divided into an even number of 'medieval feet' of this size. The foot of 0.295 m., which corresponded to the Roman foot, was widely used in Burgundy, so it appears that there was a Burgundian influence not only on the form of Cistercian buildings, but on the unit of measurement used in their construction (Walsh 1980). At Bordesley, analysis using this unit has revealed the application of simple ratios – 1 : 1, 1 : 2, 1 : 3 and 3 : 4.

At Norton Priory the use of the 'medieval foot' was tested against a comparison with the modern statute foot (Greene 1989, 82). Not only was the former shown to be the measurement used in setting out the church in the 1130s, but it also made apparent the procedures the masons employed. The most impressive degree of precision applied to the measurements that governed the overall layout of the cruciform church (figure 6). The total internal length in 'medieval feet' from the west wall of the nave to the east wall of the chancel was 152' 11"; the total length across the transepts was 76' 6", a ratio of 2 : 1 achieved with a margin of error of only 1 in 1836. When these lengths are broken into their components, it transpires that the nave and the choir both had intended lengths of 60' 0" and the chancel 30' 0" – a ratio of 2 : 2 : 1 that was achieved with a maximum error of only 5". Furthermore, the length across the transepts resolved itself into three sections of 25' 6" (length of north transept, width of choir, length of south transept).

It seems likely that the Norton masons set out the church by using a base line along the south wall of the nave and chancel which was built to a near-perfect straight line. A Pythagorean set of 65, 60 and 25 provided a means of measuring out the length of the nave (60') and its width (25' – in fact the actual width was 24' 9") with a perfect right angle between them. This rectangle could then be extended to establish the basic layout of the choir and the chancel, with diagonals checked to confirm accuracy. The transepts were laid out using the 25' 6" module, probably employed in the form of two overlapping squares with sides of 51' 0" (the details of the procedure are given in Greene 1989, 82–3). Using the nave wall as a base line, the basic layout of the cloister could also be established at this stage. Again, the dimensions correspond closely to the postulated foot of 0.295 m. The cloister walks were 9' 0" broad, the length across the cloister garth 35' 11", the length across the entire cloister 61' 11", and the internal width of the west range 20' 0". Once these dimensions had been established, the building of the cloister and surrounding ranges could wait until construction of the church was nearing completion.

The use of the foot of 0.295 m. at Norton in the 1130s shows that it was not a peculiarly Cistercian unit of measurement. As more sites are investigated to elucidate methods of laying out, it will become easier to understand the procedures that were in general operation in the medieval building industry. They can be detected in the very largest ecclesiastical structures, as work at York Minster has shown (Philips 1985). A number of studies have recently demonstrated that it was common for medieval masons to use the 'root-two formula', which is based on the ratio of the side of a square to its diagonal, in designing buildings and their components such as column piers and arcades. The abbey built for Edward the Confessor at Westminster in the 1050s has produced evidence that it was laid out according to the root-two formula. The length of the nave and the length of the church are related by means of the side of the square cloister and its diagonal (Fernie 1987). At St Frideswide's Abbey, Oxford, the builders of the Augustinian church in the twelfth century used the root-two formula in both its plan and elevation (Blair 1990, 152).

There are two basic preconditions for success in determining the planning schemes of medieval architects. A thorough understanding of a building's constructional history is essential. So too is accuracy of measurement. A note of warning also needs to be struck. It is easy to be seduced into finding schemes and neat measurements simply by looking for them during the recording process. The use of metric units for the record provides a useful means of adopting an objective approach. There is also the danger of ascribing mystic significance to what were essentially practical matters, or of pursuing exotic schemes (such as the use of Norse units claimed at Torre Abbey, Devon) (Watkin 1914).

Sometimes there is documentary evidence of the specifications for the construction of a monastery or one of its elements. One example is the large lady chapel added to the church of the Augustinian nuns at Lacock (Wiltshire). It was built on the south side of the presbytery; its foundations were found in excavations at the turn of the century (Brakspear 1901). The agreement signed in 1315 by the abbess, Johanna de Montefort, and the benefactor who financed the new structure, Sir John Bluet, set out what was expected. It was to be 59 feet long and 25½ feet wide. There were to be four windows – one on each gable and two on the long side, all well glazed and barred with iron. Two arches were to be pierced through the wall to provide the link with the church, as large as could be safely constructed between the buttresses, but not taken down below the string course under the windows because the canoness's stalls occupied the space beneath in the church. The chapel roof was to have a good, painted ceiling. Work was to be completed within twelve years – two-thirds in the first eight years and one-third in the last four years. Sir John provided the cost of construction, which amounted to 200 marks (Talbot 1876). This amount of detail, doubtless agreed in advance with the master mason, would have been sufficient to give abbess and patron a clear idea of what to expect, and to form the basis of detailed design by the mason. The length of time envisaged by the contract is worth noting. A dozen years would not have been considered excessive for the erection of a masonry building, even one of relatively modest size such as this. Evidently the construction was carried out faithfully to the specifications, for Brakspear's excavations revealed foundations of the chapel with internal dimensions of 60 by 26 feet (measured off his plan).

The builders

The detailed design of a monastery was carried out by the master mason whose role was a blend of contractor and architect. He and his work-force were almost invariably laymen. Of a total of some 1,200 English architects in the period 1050 to 1550, only eighteen might possibly have been clerics (Harvey 1972, 81). The idea that monks built their monasteries themselves is a widespread misconception that owes its origin to three factors: the early Cistercian ordinances, which included an element of manual work; the attribution of buildings to individual abbots in documents (where 'built by' really means 'commissioned by'); and the heroic exploits of the monks of Buckfast Abbey in Devon who, in the thirty-one years from 1882, entirely reconstructed their monastery by their own hands. In reality, with seven services a day, the work of God left the medieval monk or canon with no time to become a builder. That activity was entrusted to the professionals.

Building materials

During the search for a suitable site for a new monastery, and while the preliminary work was being carried out, an assessment of sources of stone and other materials will have been made. A number of factors influenced the choice. Tradition of use was one. Another was availability, and here the assistance of the patron in granting lands with potential for quarrying was important. Where a choice of stones existed, ease of transport and quality of stone affected the selection. Thus the masons might prefer a lower quality stone that was available close to the site to a superior stone that was found at a distance. For some purposes, however, for example window mouldings, the quality of the superior stone might outweigh the disadvantages of its location. Thus many monasteries on the south coast of England used Caen stone from Normandy, not only because of its excellence, but also because large quantities could be more easily carried by ship down the River Orne and across the Channel than could be brought by road from inland quarries in England. In Ireland, the Cistercian monasteries of Dunbrody (Co. Wexford) and Graiguenamanagh (Co. Kilkenny) used large amounts of a fine yellow sandstone quarried at Dundry, near Bristol, and brought by ship across the Irish Sea. Both monasteries, and also the other five Cistercian sites where the presence of Dundry stone has been identified, were conveniently placed near rivers up which the cargoes could be brought (Stalley 1987, 32). It is probable that much building stone was transported as a commercially-valuable form of ballast.

Stone was usually obtained by quarrying, but if a redundant structure with suitable building materials existed nearby it could prove a good source. At Lanercost Priory (Augustinian, Cumbria), the south wall of the church incorporates hundreds of small, square ashlar blocks taken from Hadrian's Wall. St Alban's Abbey (Benedictine, Hertfordshire) is partly built of material from the Roman city of Verulamium, including ceramic bricks.

The skills and knowledge of a geologist can play a valuable part in a detailed archaeological study of a monastery, as work at Rievaulx Abbey in Yorkshire has shown (Senior 1989; Weatherill 1954). Rievaulx was the first Cistercian monastery in the north of England, founded by Walter l'Espec for monks from Clairvaux in Burgundy in 1131. When building work started, low-quality Lower Calcareous Grit from near the church was used for walls intended to be plastered and also as rubble in wall cores. Facing stones were

cut from brown Marine Sandstone from 0.8 km. up the valley of the river
Rye.

In the second phase of construction, further grants of land made stone
available that was easier to cut and shape. Deltaic sandstone was used at
Laskill to build the monastery's wool-house, and another source of the stone
at Weathercote Quarry over 20 km. from Rievaulx was exploited for the
monastic buildings. Huge quantities of sandstone were extracted in quarries
that were worked along the ridge that had once formed the channel of the
delta. The stone was faced at the quarry and brought down almost finished.
This was more efficient than carrying unworked stone, as the weight to be
transported was minimised. This was an important consideration, for over
100,000 tonnes were extracted of which half was left at the quarry as waste.
The large heaps are still there. One of the buildings for which this stone was
used was the chapter house, with other stone obtained closer to the site used
for infill.

It has been suggested that the River Rye was canalised to provide a means
of transporting stone to Rievaulx (Weatherill 1954). It is now thought that
the channels which exist as landscape features are the result of diversions of
the course of the river to define the boundary between Rievaulx and Byland
abbeys more precisely, and to provide more space in the vicinity of the
claustral buildings. The stone was in fact carried using wagons and sleds.

Transport of stone was an expensive element of the budget. At Vale Royal
Abbey (Cheshire) in the years 1278, 1279 and 1280, 35,000 cartloads of
stone were carried 9 km. from the quarries at Eddisbury. The wages paid
to the quarry workers, £104, was far exceeded by the carters' remuneration
which totalled £357 (Brownbill 1914). Vale Royal, as a personal project
funded by Edward I, benefited from great financial resources that enabled
building operations to proceed rapidly on a lavish scale (although in later
years when the money had dried up the monks were left living in their
temporary quarters for decades). With over thirty cartloads of stone being
taken along the Cheshire roads on an average day, Vale Royal may have
been exceptional. However, in the vicinity of any religious house during a
phase of construction, the sight of horses pulling wagons loaded with
building materials will have been a familiar one. Large quantities of sand and
lime were needed to make mortar. Timber was required for roof structures,
joists, floorboards, panelling and scaffolding. Lead was used for flashings,
roof coverings, pipes and window cames; and iron for nails, brackets and
hinges. Stone that split easily into slabs was used for paving and roof covering, such as Thackstone found at Kirkstall Abbey (Moorhouse 1990).

Building operations

The organisation of construction is mainly known from documentary sources
(Knoop and Jones 1949; Harvey 1972). It is a subject upon which
archaeology can provide valuable additional information. One example of
the potential for research is the excavation of a medieval quarry, that could
show in detail the techniques used to extract, sort, shape and move blocks
of stone. The working conditions of quarrymen could also be better

understood. Similarly, accommodation and working areas at the building site are of interest. The first entry in the Vale Royal building accounts for January 1277–8, under the heading 'wages of carpenters', is a payment of 45 shillings for making lodges and dwelling houses for the masons and other workmen. In June 1279, 1,400 boards were purchased for a new lodge, and in April 1280 a further 1,000 boards were obtained for yet another lodge. During this period the number of masons employed rose from forty-one to fifty-one (Brownbill 1914). These large timber buildings would undoubtedly leave archaeologically detectable traces if their undisturbed sites could be located. Indeed, care would be needed to distinguish them from the monks' temporary quarters. The lodges were used for cutting stone – at Vale Royal six barrow-men were employed for taking stone to be cut at the masons' lodge. They also probably served as canteens for rest-breaks and refreshments. The need for accommodation at an isolated spot such as Vale Royal explains the reference to dwelling houses, but on the majority of sites it is probable that the masons would have stayed in nearby villages or towns. A builders' compound probably existed on most sites during major phases of construction, containing not only a lodge in which the masons worked and some accommodation for labourers, but also stores for materials, stockpiles of stone, a grindstone for sharpening tools, and possibly even a smithy for preparing and repairing tools. Such certainly existed at Vale Royal, and at its quarry. The range of tools upon which the blacksmiths worked was wide – at Vale Royal masons' axes, hammers, wedges, picks, hoes, spades, trowels, buckets and sieves were all in use. So too were 'lines for the layers of the walls' (Brownbill 1914). Masons and carpenters were also provided with protective gloves (Knoop and Jones 1949).

It has been suggested that the buildings with wattle-and-daub wall panels found beneath the guesthouse at Kirkstall Abbey were used by the builders in the late twelfth century (Wrathmell 1987). A builders' yard was identified beneath the infirmary at Kelso. The rarity of builders' compounds may be explained by the desire of monks to distance themselves from the distractions of a gang of worldly, boisterous builders, whose accommodation was, therefore, probably placed on the fringes of the outer courtyard or on the side of the church away from the cloister. Until excavators look extensively at these areas it is unlikely that much more will be learnt about masons' lodges and yards.

In contrast, a great deal has been discovered about the methods of constructing monastic buildings in masonry. Walls usually consisted of stone facings and a core of rubble and mortar. Where suitable stone was available, the masonry of the outer face consisted of carefully-cut blocks, dressed using a chisel, axe or adze, and laid in courses of uniform height. These rectangular blocks, known as ashlar, were roughly tapered using a mason's hammer to ensure good adhesion between the wall core and its face, with mortar from the core extending into the voids between the facing stones. The wall was built one course at a time. The facing blocks were placed in position over a convenient length of wall, with the alignment facilitated by the use of a horizontal string, and verticality with a weighted line. Stone rubble was then tipped into the core space, and sand and lime mortar poured in (figure 29). The procedure would be followed around the entire circuit of the

Figure 29. The south transept and part of the east range, Sweetheart Abbey, Dumfries and Galloway. The fine sandstone ashlar facing blocks of the church walls contrast with rounded granite boulders used for the wall cores, and for the entire walls of the chapter house and the other parts of the east range. The opening in the transept wall is where the night stairs entered the dormitory above the vault of the sacristy (which was entered from the church through the door at ground level).

Photograph by Patrick Greene.

part of the building being erected before the next course was laid. This ensured that the mortar was able to harden sufficiently to be able to support the weight of the next course without bulging. The complex chemical processes involved in the hardening of mortar would continue over a lengthy period, the core eventually becoming at least as significant a component of the weight-bearing structure as the ashlar. When there was a danger of frost during construction, the exposed core was covered with straw or bracken to prevent the mortar from freezing.

Where no suitable stone for ashlar was available, so-called rubble facing was used. This consisted of pieces of stone with a flat outer face, placed in position and bedded in mortar, and raised in a series of rough courses corresponding to the equivalent ashlar courses. In Ireland, the limited demand for ashlar before the introduction of the monastic orders in the 1130s and 1140s meant that few quarries producing suitable stone existed, and there were few masons with the skills to use it. In consequence at an abbey such as Mellifont the early buildings are largely of rubble construction (Stalley 1987, 32). Once the walls had received a coat of plaster and a lime

Figure 30. Entrance to chapter house, Glenluce Abbey, Dumfries and Galloway. The walls are neatly built of slate rubble on a sandstone plinth. Openings, such as the early-sixteenth-century doorway to the chapter house, are framed with sandstone. The holes in the wall once held the timbers of the lean-to roof of the cloister walk.
Photograph by Patrick Greene.

wash, and had lines marked on the surface to represent the coursing of ashlar masonry, they would not have looked so very different to the real thing, for ashlar was often given the same treatment. Where rubble facing was necessary, the corners of the building and the frames of openings were often built of more easily shaped free-stone. Such frames were usually erected in advance of the rest of the wall and were held in position by scaffolding as the masonry was built up to them. Glenluce Abbey (Dumfries and Galloway) is typical of this form of construction (figure 30).

Archaeological investigation can reveal details of the masons' techniques. Stonework uncovered by excavation, especially that buried by, for example, floor materials soon after erection, often shows fresh marks of tooling that have become weathered on standing walls. The use of different tools for facing, or carving details, can help distinguish different phases of building history on a site. Marking-out lines inscribed on to the surface of stonework can show how the masons designed components such as complex mouldings (figures 31 and 32). Even where ashlar has been completely robbed out, the position of its face can sometimes be detected in the form of a line inscribed on the upper surface of the foundation stones. At Vale Royal Abbey, marking-out lines revealed how the entire architectural scheme for the chevet

Figure 31. Marks on paving at Gisborough Priory, Cleveland, where masons rebuilding the church used the flat surface to design the profile of the moulding of the nave arcade (the scale is one metre in length).
    Photograph by Cleveland County Council Archaeology Service.

addition to the east end of the church was set out in the 1350s (figure 84). The chevet comprised thirteen chapels, alternately polygonal and four-sided, around an ambulatory and semi-circular choir (Thompson 1962). A stone set on the axis of the chevet had inscribed upon it a set of lines that corresponded to the complex vaulting of the elaborate building. On a smaller scale, marking-out lines on an individual carved block show how a mason set about cutting it – for example, by scribing round a template for a piece

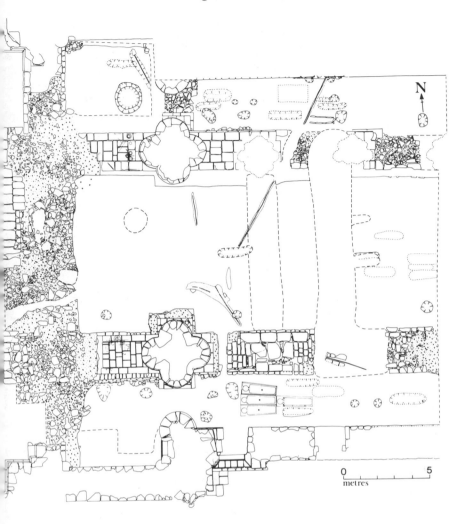

Figure 32. Plan of the nave, Gisborough Priory. The paving has been used for designing the vaulting of the nave arcade in two locations.
  Drawing supplied by Cleveland County Council Archaeology Service.

of moulding on the end of the block and then inscribing guide-lines to follow.

Masons' marks

Masons' marks are frequently found on medieval buildings, including monasteries. Their function seems to have been twofold – to establish responsibility for the execution of particular pieces of work, and to assist in verification for payment of wages. The latter purpose may also account for what seem to be tally marks – a series of lines scratched on to a stone. The archaeological examination of a monastery should include a methodical record of masons' marks, which on weathered standing masonry may only survive faintly. Oblique lighting – either from the sun, or arranged artificially for this purpose – can make otherwise invisible marks appear. On unweathered masonry, masons' marks may be clear, and other inscribed lines may be detected. In the late-twelfth-century passage through the west range at Norton Priory are tally marks, circles inscribed by a mason's dividers, and the outline of mouldings where a pointed implement has been used to scribe around a template. None of these would have been visible after the completion of building work, for the wall was given a coat of lime-wash. They have no profound or mystical significance, but are the result of casual activity by one or more masons engaged upon the construction of a particularly beautiful building (Greene 1989, figs. 45–50).

There is no uniformity over the use of individual marks by masons, so on some buildings none will be found and on others they may be present in profusion. Where there are numbers of marks they can provide information about the size of the labour force, as each mason will have had his own 'signature'. Twelve masons worked on the big building campaigns at Melli-font in the thirteenth century on the evidence of masons' marks, and at Holycross (Co. Tipperary) a team of about twenty masons left intricate floral and interlace marks in the fifteenth century (Stalley 1987, 42–3). There was great mobility in the medieval building industry, and it may be possible to detect the arrival and departure of individuals as a long construc-tion campaign progressed. The appearance of the same group of marks on separate parts of the same building can also establish that they were being erected contemporaneously, or in close succession. It is rarely possible to trace the movement of a particular mason from site to site, however, for masons' marks are frequently very simple. A mason joining an existing team could find the symbol he had been using already in use, and he would therefore need to adopt a new mark. There is potential, though, for recognising the presence of a group of masons with members in common at more than one site by a widespread collection of marks. Such an exercise in matching could be achieved using a computer database, and a program designed to recognise such groupings and to test the statistical significance of the coincidence of marks. Where a good fit was found, other diagnostic characteristics such as tooling and moulding details could be used as corroboration. In this way the movements of a construction team, albeit with a somewhat fluid membership, could be followed. It would also be necessary to take account of secular buildings, as masons would be unlikely to work only on monasteries and churches.

The transmission of styles

The influence of building styles and the transmission of architectural ideas has been studied with reference to a number of monastic sites. The use of particular types of mouldings in portals, windows, arcades and vaulting, for example, and details of sculpture – foliage, figures, or geometric – are the raw material for the architectural historian and archaeologist. The complex

Figure 33. The church of Jedburgh Priory, Borders, seen from the cloister. In the foreground is the south wall of the nave. Beyond are the tiers of arcading: the nave arcade, surmounted by the clerestory, with the triforium above that.
  Photograph by Patrick Greene.

web of influences at work on one building during a particular phase of its development is well illustrated by a study of Jedburgh Abbey (Borders (Garton 1987). The Augustinian house was founded by King David I in about 1138. Construction of the church was proceeding much later in the twelfth century, with sculpture in the Transitional style (figure 33). There are marked similarities with the Augustinian abbey of Hexham in Northumberland, with which Jedburgh may have shared the same architect. The strongest influences are, however, from Yorkshire, with the treatment of piers, mouldings and waterleaf capitals derived from the county's Cistercian tradition. Garton suggests that the Augustinian house of Bridlington in Yorkshire could be a significant connection, with further influences from southern England and northern France derived from Dunstable in Bedfordshire (another Augustinian house). The employment of masons from different traditions to work at the same time but on different sections of the building may account for the presence of features such as waterleaf capitals in both 'early' and 'late' stages of the building campaign. A study such as this emphasises the mobility of masons, which accounts for the rapid spread of architectural ideas and techniques of decoration. Masons did not restrict themselves to a particular order of monks or canons. Another mode of transmission, however, operated in the form of the clients – abbots and priors – attending meetings at other monasteries of their order and instructing master masons working on their own establishments to emulate features they had seen on their travels.

At Norton Priory, the canons employed a master mason, Hugh, from Catwick near Beverley in Yorkshire (Greene 1989, 89). In twelfth-century Cheshire there was little tradition of building in masonry, whereas to the east of the Pennines there was considerable activity and expertise. It is not surprising, therefore, that Yorkshire was the source of Norton's builder, who employed decorative motifs such as beak-head voussoirs (wedge-shaped blocks carved with fantastic beasts whose beaks gripped the mouldings of door frames). Norton's choice was also influenced by the fact that the original canons came from a Yorkshire house, Bridlington Priory, the founder of which was related to Norton's founder. In the middle of the thirteenth century, following a disastrous fire, Norton's cloister arcade was rebuilt. The master mason who built and embellished this beautiful structure may have come from the West Country, or had learnt his techniques of carving by working there (*ibid.*, 118). The building which had most influence on English ecclesiastical architecture in the thirteenth century, however, was Westminster Abbey. It may be the ultimate origin of the style of sculpture used on the Norton cloister.

There is great potential for extensive work tracing the activities of master masons using particularly individual styles, although the disappearance of many medieval buildings does place considerable difficulties in the way of detecting complete itineraries. The recovery of masonry from the excavation of monastic houses can be an important part of such studies as the archaeologist can provide valuable contextual information. The work of Dr R.K. Morris of Warwick University in compiling a database of moulding profiles has demonstrated the potential, applied, for example, to the study of the chapter house of St Albans Abbey. Carved architectural fragments ecovered from an excavation may be in a far better state of preservation han those that have been exposed to the eroding effects of the elements or he enthusiasm of Victorian church restorers. They may also bear traces of painted decoration. Sculpted and moulded stone frequently had its decorative effect enhanced with bright colours. Excavations at St Augustine's Abbey, Canterbury, produced sculpture that included an elegant foliage capital painted with a dark brown background to give the impression of depth and with leaves highlighted in sky blue and pink. Vault ribs were painted with black, red, pink and white decoration (Geddes 1983, 95). Stonework from St Mary's Abbey, York, with well-preserved painted plaster surviving on the surface, is displayed in the Yorkshire Museum. Even austere Cistercian buildings were permitted some splashes of colour. This included stencilled decoration, as is shown by the discovery of a lead stencil, for painting six-lobed rosettes, in excavations at Meaux Abbey in Yorkshire (Park 1986, 194).

Carpentry

In admiring the work of masons, it is easy to overlook the part played by equally important members of the construction team – the carpenters. This is because much of their work was temporary by nature, and where intended to be permanent has suffered a greater degree of damage or disintegration than masonry structures. In reality, though, it was impossible to embark upon the construction of a masonry building without the participation of carpenters.

The presence of carpenters as the first building workers at Fountains Abbey, erecting temporary timber quarters for the monks, has already been noted. So too has the provision of lodges made of boards for the masons. The next requirement would have been for scaffolding as the walls rose above the first metre or so in height. Post holes for scaffold poles have been found on a number of sites (e.g. Bordesley: Hirst, Walsh and Wright 1983, 33–4; Fountains: Gilyard-Beer and Coppack 1986, 158; Gisborough: Heslop forthcoming). Scaffolding is shown on many medieval manuscript illustrations of building work. It consisted of tall vertical poles and long horizontal poles lashed together with rope (figure 34). Planks provided walk-ways and working surfaces, and ladders joined the various levels. Blocks of stone and buckets of mortar were lifted using hoists or a windlass with a pulley over which the rope passed. The stone blocks could be raised by lashing them to the rope, or by using a cradle (medieval hoisting machinery is described in Hewett 1985, 188–99). Mortar was mixed on the ground and was either lifted to the building stage with a hoist or windlass, or carried up ladders by a labourer using a hod on his back. The considerable heights to which builders erected medieval monastery churches demonstrate the skill of the carpenters in providing a framework that enabled the masons to work at such elevations. Tall scaffolding structures were tied into the masonry building as it was built, to provide stability to what would otherwise have been a very insecure framework. When the building had been completed the scaffolding was dismantled from the top downwards. The timber ties into

Figure 34. Model of scaffolding, Norton Priory, based on the evidence of medieval manuscript illustrations. The scaffolding poles are lashed together and are set on horizontal planks. One labourer mixes sand and lime to make mortar; the other operates a winch to lift a block of stone to the level at which the masons are working.

Photograph by Patrick Greene, reproduced by permission of Norton Priory Museum Trust.

the masonry were either sawn off flush with the wall, or removed and the socket filled with a small stone block. These 'putlog' holes can be seen on the face of many buildings; they show the form of the scaffolding framework (figure 81). The absence of post holes for scaffolding does not mean that it was not used. Where there was a danger of the poles sinking into soft ground such as wet clay, they were set on short planks or slabs of stone, as is shown on some manuscript drawings.

As external walls rose in height, carpenters were needed to construct the centering for window and door heads. The mason would place in position the blocks of stone that formed the sides of the opening. At the point from which the arch was intended to spring, the carpenter built a wooden structure, the upper surface of which corresponded exactly to the intended soffit of the arch. The mason could then set the elements of the arch on the framework, and once the last, usually the central, block was in position, the structure was self-supporting and the centering could be removed. If the centering was for one of a series of identical windows, it would be reused. Large windows with complex tracery required centering of equivalent complexity.

In buildings with masonry vaulting, the carpenter was again required. Simple groined vaults, of the type found in the undercrofts of eleventh- and twelfth-century monastic claustral ranges, were built using centering in the form of semi-circular barrel vaults intersecting at right angles. The upper surface of the capitals of columns and wall-shafts helped support the centering. Each vault was constructed from the corners with large, long blocks of undressed stone or ashlar placed in successively higher rows, with mortar for greater adhesion. The strength of the vault derived from the wedge-like role of each block of stone, enhanced by the downward pressure of the whole mass. As soon as the vault was complete the centering was removed. In the case of ribbed vaults, the centering was designed to support the ribs which, when complete, formed part of the next stage in building each vault – and after completion assumed the major role of support. In Ireland, barrel vaults were frequently supported by wickerwork centering. Its use can often be detected in the form of impressions of the wattles in the mortar of the soffit of the vault (Stalley 1987, 130).

Structural timberwork

Carpenters were involved in many other aspects of the construction of a monastery. The claustral ranges had wooden floors and roofs. An impressive example covers the dormitory at Durham Cathedral Priory. Most cloister walks were built originally with a lean-to timber roof, although many were later replaced with stone-vaulted structures. The majority of churches had timber roofs, and even in those with masonry vaults a wooden structure supported the roof covering. The quality of the joinery was often outstanding, as has been shown in studies of, for example, St Frideswide's Priory in Oxford (Blair 1990, 195–204). The lady chapel still has its original roof of c. 1320–40, and the chapter house roof has been dated to the second quarter of the thirteenth century on the basis of dendrochronological sampling. Other monasteries with important timber roofs include Bath Abbey (Avon), Malmesbury Abbey (Wiltshire), Pershore Abbey (Worcestershire), Canterbury Cathedral Priory and the Lincoln Franciscan Friary (Hewett 1985). One of the greatest achievements of medieval carpentry was the creation, between 1328 and 1342, of the octagonal lantern over the crossing of Ely Cathedral Priory. Its construction, in a relatively light material, was a cautious but elegant response to the collapse of the masonry crossing tower in 1322.

Many fixtures within monastic buildings were made of timber, of which the finest were the screens and choir stalls. Surviving examples which show the outstanding quality of carving achieved by medieval carpenters include the late-fourteenth-century choir at Chester (St Werburgh's Abbey), the choir stalls of the late fifteenth century at Lancaster, the pulpitum at Hexham Abbey (Northumberland), and the central screen at Dunstable (Bedfordshire). Amongst the medieval doors to survive, all with highly decorative hinges, are those at Abbey Dore (Herefordshire), Whalley Abbey (Lancashire) and Beaulieu Abbey in Hampshire (Geddes 1986).

Considerable amounts of timber were needed for the construction of a monastery. It was either obtained from managed woodland which formed

part of the monastery's estates, or by gift from benefactors. Royal suppor
for monastic houses was frequently expressed in the form of grants of oak
from the king's hunting parks.

Glaziers and bell-makers

Specialist craftsmen were engaged to carry out tasks requiring a particula
expertise. Glaziers were commissioned to make and fit coloured glass in th
windows of important buildings. Bells were used to signal the principa
events in the monastic day, so were required at all monasteries. Unless it wa
in or near a town with an established bell foundry, a bell-maker would b
required to travel to the monastery to cast one or more bells to hang in th
tower of the church (or in some early Cistercian churches which had n
tower, in a belfry on the gable). Bell pits, in which bells had been cast, hav
been found in excavations at Norton Priory (Greene 1989, 118–22)
Pontefract Priory (Yorkshire), Taunton Priory (Somerset), Tintern Abbey
(Gwent: Courtney 1989, 117–21), Gisborough Priory (Cleveland: Heslop
forthcoming), Kirkstall Abbey (Yorkshire: Duncan and Wrathmell 1986) and
Ludlow Friary (Shropshire: Klein and Roe 1988).

The method of making a bell is well understood as a result of these
discoveries. A two-part mould was made in a pit about 1.5 m. deep using
a mixture of clay and horse dung. The inner part, the core, was shaped to
the desired profile of the bell using a rotating device known as a strickle. The
'false bell' of clay was then built up on the core. The outer mould, the cope,
was then formed over the false bell. After the entire assemblage had been
hardened by lighting a fire around it, the cope was lifted off, the false bell
was removed and the cope replaced. Bell metal (an alloy of copper and tin)
was melted in a furnace on the edge of the pit. The furnace was then tapped
and the metal flowed into the void between the two parts of the mould.
When the whole assemblage had cooled, the cope was broken away to
release the bell, which was then finished by hand, filed and polished. It was
carefully transported into the church where it was hoisted into position.

Bells crack easily, so a bell-maker had little alternative but to travel to the
monastery where the bell was required. Henry Michael of Lichfield was
commissioned by Croxden Abbey (Staffordshire) to recast a bell that had
cracked (Hibbert 1910, 95). He worked on the site for the whole summer
of 1303 and his first attempt was a failure, but on All Saints Day he was
at last successful. A bell-pit is a feature that is to be expected in the excavation of a monastery. The size of the pit and the presence of burnt material
can produce a strong anomaly on a geophysical survey. One likely location
for the foundry is within the church, in the centre of the crossing, from
where the bell could be hauled directly up into the tower. Alternatively it
might be placed outside the church in a position that was convenient for the
bell to be manoeuvred inside and lifted into the tower or belfry.

Two bell-pits were found at Norton Priory. One, about fifty metres to the
north of the church, had been used to cast a large tenor bell in the twelfth
century for the newly-completed church (the date was confirmed using radio-
carbon dating). The second was found to the west of the church beside the

ntrance track to the outer courtyard. It too had been used to cast a tenor
ell in the mid thirteenth century, almost certainly to replace the twelfth-
entury bell following a disastrous fire in 1236 (Greene 1989, 118–22). At
iisborough the bell-pit was found beneath the tower where it had been cut
nto the rubble foundation layers. It measured 1.60 m. in diameter and was
.92 m. deep (Heslop 1987, 178). At Tintern a bell-pit had been dug in the
outh-east corner of the guest hall, to the west of the church. The rim of the
ell mould was found in position; it had been used for casting a bell with
rim diameter of 0.34 m. (Courtney 1989, 117–21).

Most monastic bells were destroyed at the Dissolution. The Augmenta-
ions Office sale agreements usually reserved to the Crown all bell metal.
ells have survived in monasteries that became cathedrals or parish churches.

Floors

The floors of monastic churches in the eleventh and twelfth centuries were
imple, usually consisting of beaten clay or a spread of mortar. In some areas
where suitable stone was available, flagged floors were laid. There are good
urviving examples at the Cistercian abbeys at Shap and Furness in Cumbria.
The excavation of the church at Bordesley showed that reeds had been laid
on the earliest floor, which was essentially the surface of the sand and clay
nake-up which had been spread within the presbytery and choir (Hirst,
Walsh and Wright 1983, 35). Soon after 1200, however, a new floor was
aid in the choir as part of a programme of architectural changes. This floor
consisted of square ceramic tiles set diagonally to the axis of the church. The
iles themselves had not survived, but their impressions were present on
patches of the lime-based bedding material (*ibid.*, 157). The introduction of
floor tiles is a feature of a great many monastic churches in the thirteenth
century. They were harder wearing than clay floors and considerably more
attractive. The Bordesley floor was installed at a particularly early date. In
the period 1260–1280 a replacement floor was laid, also consisting of square
tiles set diagonally, some plain and others decorated, but surviving mainly
in the form of impressions in the bedding. In about 1330 yet another tile
floor was laid in the choir and presbytery, of which a very large area of
impressions survived. This showed that the floor consisted of diagonally-laid
tiles divided into zones by narrow bands of tiles running parallel to the axis
of the church. It has been estimated that this floor contained about 7,300
tiles of which 400 tiles or fragments were recovered in the excavation; only
a few were *in situ*. A combination of plain and decorated tiles made up this
floor. The decorated tiles consisted of continuous designs, in which the
pattern on each tile is a repeating motif, and also groups of four and sixteen
tiles in which the pattern is produced by assembling these numbers of tiles
together. In the fifteenth century, following flooding, a dirt floor covered the
choir and presbytery, but in the early sixteenth century a final tile floor was
laid in the choir. There was little remaining in position, but it was clear from
the fragments that the excavators found that it had been made up of tiles
reused from the previous floor. These must have been lifted and stored
during the period of the dirt floor; they were laid to a broadly similar

Figure 35. Part of the thirteenth-century tile floor uncovered by excavation in the north transept of Graiguenamanagh Abbey, Co. Kilkenny. Two-metre scales. Photograph by Con Brogan, Office of Public Works, Dublin.

attern. The excavators concluded that few, if any, new tiles were bought fter the early fifteenth century (*ibid.*, 167).

No other monastic church excavation has revealed such a full sequence of looring as that at Bordesley. The attachment to tiles, over a period of three-nd-a-half centuries, as the best floor material is striking. It is representative of monastic churches generally, however. During the thirteenth and four-eenth centuries most monasteries in the British Isles embellished their chur-hes with tiled floors, often of highly attractive design. The extent of the loor partly depended on the resources of the house. It might only be laid n the presbytery, choir and chapels. Sometimes tile floors were also provided for the transepts and nave, and the chapter house. At the 'remonstratensian abbey at Titchfield in Hampshire, the cloister walks were iled. Denny Abbey (Cambridgeshire) had a tiled floor in the fourteenth-entury refectory (Christie and Coad 1980). The abbot's house at Warden Abbey in Bedfordshire had a particularly fine mosaic-tile floor (Webster and Cherry 1975, 233). Malvern Priory (Hereford and Worcester) even has wall iles. In Ireland, the entire church at Graiguenamanagh (Co. Kilkenny) was paved with tiles (Bradley and Manning 1981) (figure 35). Their use was associated with the economic status and artistic affiliations of Anglo-Norman Ireland, for no tiles have been found west of the Shannon (Stalley 1987, 214).

The techniques used by medieval tile-makers to decorate their products were varied and ingenious (Eames 1980; Eames and Fanning 1989). Some floors, such as the mosaic floor laid at Norton Priory in the early fourteenth century, were produced by teams of itinerant craftsmen who set up a kiln at the monastery to manufacture tiles on the site. The remains of the Norton kiln were excavated. Together with waster tiles (which had developed faults during firing) and areas of the floor which were found in the church, the kiln provided a great deal of information about the techniques of the tile-makers (Greene 1989, 132–44). It was also the basis of an exercise in experimental archaeology in which a replica kiln was built and fired on several occasions, and a replica tile floor was created (Greene and Johnson 1978).

The Norton floor showed close similarities to a mosaic-tile floor in Prior Crauden's chapel at the cathedral priory at Ely in Cambridgeshire. That floor was laid in 1324 (Eames 1980, 91). The mosaic-tile floor found in 1974 at Warden Abbey belonged to the same group. The three floors share a range of characteristics, including a number of geometric patterns, the use of star-shaped tiles in borders, the embellishment of individual tiles with stamped decoration – particularly rosettes – and the presence of mosaic lions composed of several individual tiles with the hair of the mane represented by flame-like incisions in the clay. Particularly striking is the picture-mosaic placed in front of the altar at Ely. It illustrates the Temptation, with Adam and Eve, and the serpent coiled around the tree. Loose tiles at Warden were found to have come from an identical scene, with the same templates used to produce tiles at both sites. At Norton also, tiles from a picture-mosaic were found, and elements of a life-size figure of a knight which must have covered a grave. Tiles with letters inscribed on them came from a marginal inscription to the tomb, asking for prayers for the person buried beneath. Heraldic tiles linked the floor to a local benefactor family, the Duttons. At

Warden, elements of the figure of an abbot were found – these too may hav
covered a grave. Some had written 'labels' inscribed on the sides to help i
the assembly of complex designs. The fact that one of the tile-makers wa
literate is a surprising discovery in an age when literacy was rare outside th
ranks of the clergy. The picture that emerges from the study of the Norton
Ely and Warden floors is of a group of highly talented craftsmen travellin
through England and accepting commissions to create their beautiful floors
At Norton it seems that a member of a wealthy landowning family finance
the production of mosaic floors for the choir, transepts, presbytery, chapte
house and chapels, including the large lady chapel in which his family wer
buried, some time during the period 1315–24. From Norton they moved t
Ely where Prior Crauden was engaged in the construction of a lovely chape
to the south of the cathedral church, and made the floor in 1324. After El
they eventually went to Warden where the superb floor was made for th
abbot's lodgings. There may of course have been intermediate stops on thi
route. Archaeology may reveal more about the origins of these tile-makers
and may provide further evidence of their activities at other sites. Like s
many talented craftsmen in the medieval construction industry, it is clea
that they made no distinction between the orders to which the monasterie
in which they worked owed allegiance. Of the three at which their product
have been studied, one was Augustinian, one Benedictine and one Cistercian

Tile-making was not only the preserve of itinerant craftsmen. Where ther
was sufficient demand, a tile factory might be established to serve a numbe
of customers. At Danbury in Essex, a tile works comprising two kilns, &
workshop, a drying shed, and accommodation for the workmen all within
a ditched roadside enclosure was excavated (Drury and Pratt 1975). The
two-colour tiles were made in the late thirteenth and early fourteentl
centuries, and were supplied to secular and religious customers in the
locality, including Beeleigh Abbey, Leez Priory, and the Dominican Priory ir
Chelmsford. At Hailes Abbey (Benedictine, Gloucestershire) a tile works wa
established to produce tiles for the extended eastern end of the church, whicl
was being built to house a shrine containing a phial of the Holy Blood. I
led to the establishment of a commercial tile industry providing its product
to customers throughout Wessex (Eames 1980, 280).

The manufacture of tiles was not solely directed towards the supply of
products to monasteries, but they were the most important and demanding
consumers. Some of the commissions led to the production of decorative
floors, and even individual tiles, of very great quality. Indeed, two-colour
tiles made for Chertsey Abbey (Benedictine, Surrey: Eames 1980, 141–71)
are amongst the finest examples of medieval art in Britain.

4 Growth and rebuilding

Most medieval monasteries in Britain had a life-span of three or four centuries. During such a long period of time they inevitably underwent many changes. The nature of those changes, their scale, the date at which they occurred, and the reasons why they took place can all be illuminated by the techniques of archaeology. The story will be different for every monastery, and even houses of the same size belonging to the same order, founded at the same time, are likely to follow diverging paths. Nonetheless, there is a range of developments of general application that may be encountered in the study of a particular religious house; this chapter examines such phenomena.

Expansion of the monastery

The principal agent of change in the early years of a monastery's existence was organic growth. The opportunity to expand, and the pace at which it occurred, depended on the support of a monastery's patron and benefactors. Where this was forthcoming on a generous scale, a dramatic transformation of the buildings could result. A good example is Tintern Abbey in Gwent (Craster 1956; Robinson 1990). This, the second Cistercian abbey in Britain, was founded by Walter fitz Richard, lord of Chepstow, in 1131. Subsequent holders of the title bestowed lavish gifts on the monks, and Tintern became the wealthiest monastery in Wales. The church and domestic ranges seem to have been completed by about 1160 (figure 36). There are strong similarities with the plan of Waverley Abbey in Surrey, the first Cistercian house in Britain, founded three years before Tintern (Brakspear 1905). Both had simple cross-shaped churches without aisles; that at Tintern was just 48.5 metres long. Its cloister lay to the north, and the foundations of both the dormitory and refectory ranges were traced in excavations at the turn of the century (Brakspear 1934).

By 1200, Tintern's dormitory range had been extended, probably as a result of an increase in the number of monks. A large latrine block was added to the dormitory, and the chapter house was enlarged. A similar process of enlargement occurred at Norton Priory (figure 6). During the thirteenth century the Marshall family, earls of Pembroke, continued the flow of benefactions to the monks. The abbey was able to increase its complement further, but the domestic ranges were inadequate to cater for their numbers. A programme of enlargement began in about 1220. The original refectory was demolished and a new, larger replacement was constructed in the manner that had become characteristic of Cistercian planning. Its axis was north–south, and it occupied the central part of the site of its predecessor, extending well to the north. In the two spaces created to the east and west, a warming room and kitchens were built. The latter served the monks' refectory, and also that of the lay brothers, who were provided with an entirely rebuilt west range with dining accommodation on the ground floor and a

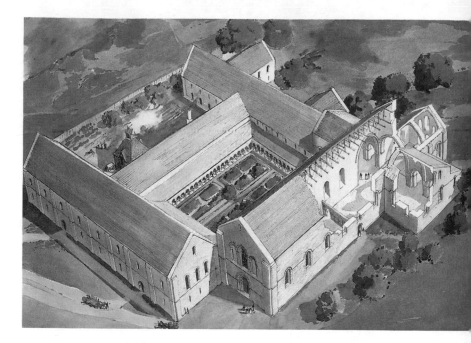

Figure 36. Drawing of the possible appearance of the buildings of Tintern Abbey, Gwent, in the late twelfth century. At this date Cistercian churches, following strictly the instructions of the order, were built without a tower over the crossing.

Drawing by Terry Ball, reproduced with permission of Cadw: Welsh Historic Monuments. Crown Copyright.

dormitory above. The remodelling of the eastern range began, including the refashioning of the chapter house with an impressive entrance from the cloister and a new vaulted roof. The ground floor of the range, to the north of the chapter house, housed the novice monks; it was substantially reshaped. A new building attached to the east range was constructed as the abbot's lodging. As the thirteenth century progressed, building work continued. The recruitment of further lay brothers necessitated an extension of the west range, increasing its capacity by a third. A large infirmary was erected in the late thirteenth century. Recent excavation has shown that an aisled guest-hall, similar to such halls at Kirkstall and Waverley abbeys, was also built in the thirteenth century (Courtney 1989).

The Tintern monks did not restrict their rebuilding programme to their living quarters. In 1269 the decision was taken to replace the twelfth-century church in its entirety. The resources to undertake such a radical and expensive operation were provided by Earl Roger Bigod, who was named as the builder in a chronicle which recorded its completion thirty-two years later (1301). The new church, which survives in a remarkably complete state (figure 37), was a much grander structure than the original church. It had an aisled nave and an aisled presbytery with stone vaults, and a central tower over the crossing. The west front was particularly magnificent, with

Figure 37. The interior of the thirteenth-century church at Tintern Abbey, looking eastwards from the aisled nave towards the crossing arches and the chancel
  Photograph by Patrick Greene.

a central doorway flanked by decorative arched wall panels, all set beneath a beautiful seven-light window.

To build a new church as part of an existing monastery was a more demanding exercise than the construction of a new religious house, for the simple reason that the daily round of worship had to continue uninterrupted. At Tintern the new church was placed a little to the south of the twelfth-century building. Although the entire plan of the new church was laid out, work concentrated on its eastern part. The strategy was to complete the building to a point at which it was possible to transfer the services from the old church. The new structure therefore rose to a point at which it encased the eastern arm and south transept of the old (figure 38). By 1288 it was possible for the monks to transfer services to the new building. Thereafter the process must have been one of completion of the church in stages, with a progressive dismantling of the original church. When this had taken place the north transept could be built, and the extended cloister provided with a new cloister walk. Even after the completion of the church in 1301, work continued on the claustral buildings.

It must have been extremely difficult to pursue a life of worship and prayer in the midst of the inevitable disruption of a construction site. The dust and dirt, the noise, and the presence of building workers whose style of life was so different to that of the monks, must have been unendurable at times. Some compensation will have been provided by the gradual

Figure 38. The thirteenth-century church of Tintern Abbey in course of construction. This imaginative drawing shows the structure rising alongside the twelfth-century church, with the chancel and south transept at an advanced stage and with a masons' yard operating in the area of the nave.

Drawing by Terry Ball, reproduced with permission of Cadw: Welsh Historic Monuments. Crown Copyright.

revelation of the qualities of the church as each part took shape, even if those who witnessed the laying of the foundations did not live long enough to see the completion of the entire building.

At Neath Abbey (Glamorgan), a strikingly similar church rebuilding took place in the years 1280–1330 (Butler 1976). The church was of almost identical ground-plan and size to that at Tintern. Excavations have failed to reveal the remains of an earlier church, although it is certain that there must have been one, erected soon after the monastery was founded in 1130 (a year before Tintern's foundation). There is a strong case for modern investigation of Neath Abbey to compare its development with that of Tintern. Of particular interest would be information on the earliest buildings. Neath was a member of the community of Savigny, which resembled so closely the Cistercian order that the two strands of monasticism joined in 1147. A comparison of Tintern and Neath could reveal whether early Cistercian and Savignac monastic buildings were designed on similar lines.

The comprehensive nature of the rebuilding that took place at Tintern, and which is implied by the dates of the standing remains at Neath, has implications for the study of any monastic site. If it appears that there is a large gap between the date of foundation and the dates of buildings known from their standing or excavated remains, then there is a strong likelihood that the original buildings were demolished to make way for new structures. Archaeological investigation should therefore be designed on the assumption that traces of the early buildings remain to be located by geophysical survey or excavation, or even to be recognised as incorporated in standing masonry. Another conclusion to be drawn is that there are dangers in using mouldings and other architectural features from a monastery of known date of foundation to date other ecclesiastical structures, unless it can be proved that they really do belong to the original buildings. The discovery of the original church at Fountains (Chapter 3) is a good example of this principle. It is the church built in about 1150 after the fire, designed in the style that originated in Burgundy which was widely adopted by the Cistercians, that architectural historians had wrongly assumed was the 1130s church.

Modest though they may have been in comparison with the structures that replaced them, the original churches at Tintern and Fountains were large compared to the first church at Haughmond Abbey in Shropshire (Webster and Cherry 1980, 240–1). Excavation in 1975 revealed the remains of a tiny cruciform church just 17 m. long. The nave had been extended in the second quarter of the twelfth century and a cloister was added at the same time. All this was swept away at the end of the twelfth century when the abbey was totally rebuilt on a very much larger scale (Blair, Lankester and West 1980).

Small monasteries

There was nothing inevitable about the expansion of a monastery. If financial resources were insufficient, even the original plans might fail to be achieved. Sandwell Priory (West Midlands) is an example of one such religious house; excavation has shown that the church was never completed as intended (Hodder 1989). The Benedictine priory was founded in the mid twelfth century. The church was found to have an elaborate east end, comprising a long central choir flanked by shorter chapels each side, and transepts with projecting chapels (figure 39). The grave of the founder, William fitz Guy de Opheni, lord of West Bromwich, was found next to the high altar. The stone coffin had been placed in position during the initial construction of the church. The foundations had been dug for a nave, but pottery from levelling material indicated that it had not been completed until the late thirteenth century. A rough foundation appears to have supported a temporary screen wall separating the east part from the unbuilt nave. The nave was eventually built as part of a general rebuilding necessitated by the collapse of the tower in the mid thirteenth century, which included the contraction of the east end through the demolition of the side chapels. The

Figure 39. Sandwell Priory, West Midlands: the crossing and south transept with, in the foreground, the apsed transept chapels.
Photograph supplied by Sandwell Metropolitan Borough Council.

modest claustral ranges were built to the north of the church, with masonry structures replacing timber temporary buildings.

Although Sandwell's original foundation endowment permitted the construction of the east end of the church on an ambitious scale, support to enable development to the same standard cannot have been forthcoming. It seems that Sandwell never supported more than four monks; in 1361 and 1380 there was only one monk and he was the prior. As a small monastery with slight resources, Sandwell was selected for closure by Cardinal Wolsey in 1525. There were two monks at this date.

Sandwell was by no means an exception. Many of the small Augustinian houses that were founded by members of the lesser gentry, particularly in East Anglia (Robinson 1980) failed to attract subsequent benefactions, resulting in a constant struggle for survival. Beeston Priory in Norfolk is one such example (figure 40); it never seems to have had more than six canons (Heywood 1989). Many nunneries were founded by the same social group, probably because they too were relatively inexpensive to establish, leading to similar financial difficulties. Although nunneries usually managed to arrange their buildings on a claustral plan, sometimes lack of resources prevented the replacement of timber buildings with masonry structures (Gilchrist 1989, 252). For small monastic houses, changes to the buildings were more likely to be occasioned by structural failure and lack of maintenance than the aggrandisement to which their wealthier counterparts could aspire.

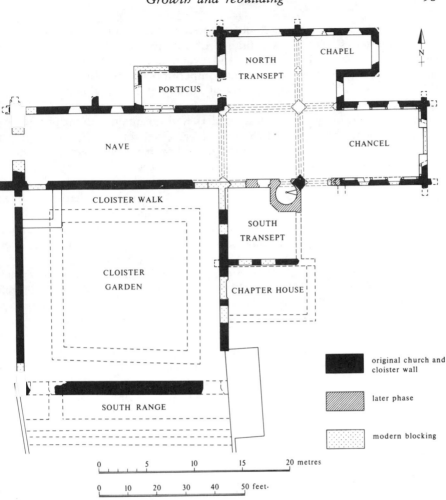

Figure 40. Plan of Beeston Priory, Norfolk. Although the scale of the priory was small, the church had all the elements of much larger monasteries.

Drawing by Steven Ashley, supplied by Norfolk County Council Planning and Property Department.

Changing religious practices

Physical alterations to the structures of a monastery could result from changes in liturgy, observances or religious devotions. Modifications to, or departures from, the rule of the order might also result in changes that have left their mark in the archaeological record.

An example of the influence of changes in monastic practice on the form of buildings is the ordination of Cistercian monks as priests, with the consequent need for chapels at which they could celebrate mass. The great eastern arm of the church at Fountains, built in the first part of the thirteenth century, terminated in the Chapel of the Nine Altars to satisfy the needs of the large number of monks. A quite different change in practice for Cistercian monasteries was the acceptance of burials of lay people within the church. The reason was prosaic and pragmatic. Cistercian houses found themselves at a disadvantage in the competition for benefactors' support if they could not offer the opportunity of burial within the abbey. It therefore quickly became acceptable for Cistercian houses to accommodate the burials of their wealthy supporters. Other orders had no qualms about providing a resting place for patrons and their families. Often one of the transepts, or the chapels opening off the transept, would become a family mausoleum. At Sandwell Priory it was the south transept that served this purpose (Hodder 1989, 188). The burials of men, women and children took place here throughout the history of the priory. Research on the skeletons at Birmingham University has revealed the presence of a metopic suture – an abnormal joint down the middle of the forehead – in nearly 50 per cent, compared to 9 per cent of the present-day population. This suggests that they were related, almost certainly belonging to the benefactor family.

A monastery might find itself required to create space for ever-increasing numbers of burials. This could necessitate changes to the church, particularly in the form of enlarged chapels opening off the transepts. At Norton Priory, excavation of the north transept showed how a tiny chapel only large enough to accommodate an altar, was replaced by a succession of chapels, expanding to make room for more burials (Greene 1989, 123–8). Members of Norton's principal benefactor family, the Duttons, were buried in the chapel, and in the early fourteenth century it was embellished with a beautiful mosaic-tile floor that incorporated their arms. The chapel continued in its role as mausoleum for the family into the sixteenth century.

Lady chapels

The Norton Priory chapel, the burial place of the Duttons, was dedicated to the Virgin Mary. The great majority of monasteries had St Mary as their patron saint. The cult of the Virgin became increasingly popular in Britain, and monasteries shared in the enthusiasm for shrines to Our Lady. In consequence, lady chapels were added to many monastic churches. Often they were built as an extension to the east end of the church, as at the great Benedictine foundations at Gloucester, St Albans, Canterbury, Tewkesbury (Gloucestershire) and Sherborne (Dorset). An alternative location was the one used at Norton, to the north-east. Examples of lady chapels in this position include the Cluniac monasteries of Thetford (figure 1) and Castle Acre in Norfolk, Augustinian Lilleshall Abbey (Shropshire), and Benedictine Ely Cathedral in Cambridgeshire where the lady chapel was built as a separate structure to the north east of the church to which it was connected by a passage.

Shrines

The construction of chapels dedicated to the Virgin, usually containing a

venerated image of her, was an extension of the practice of creating shrines
to house the relics of a saint. Relics credited with miraculous properties
conferred fame on the monastery that possessed them. The attraction of
pilgrims to worship at the shrine, and to seek relief from medical or social
ills, provided the opportunity for the monastery to benefit financially
through gifts, and the sale of indulgences and relics. Some shrines could
become so popular that a settlement might grow up at the gates of the
monastery to cater for the needs of pilgrims. Whithorn (Dumfries and
Galloway) is the outstanding example, with its power of attraction persisting
for more than a thousand years (see Chapter 7).

The murder in 1170 of archbishop Thomas Becket in the Cathedral Abbey
at Canterbury gave rise to the most popular cult in Britain. The destruction
of the choir of the church by fire in 1174 necessitated extensive rebuilding.
Income from pilgrims enabled it to be completed on a lavish scale by a
French architect, William of Sens. The body of the martyr was buried in the
crypt at first, but in 1220 it was placed in a magnificent shrine in the eastern
arm of the cathedral. The pilgrims who flocked to Canterbury learnt of the
miracles attributed to the intercession of St Thomas through the representations in the twelve windows of the Trinity chapel. About half of the original
late-twelfth and early-thirteenth-century glass survives. The shrine does not,
for the magnificent confection of gold studded with precious stones was
destroyed at the Dissolution in 1538.

The martyr's shrine may have been the principal attraction for pilgrims,
but Canterbury also possessed a multitude of relics besides (Platt 1984, 77).
There were the entire bodies of St Dunstan, St Odo, St Wilfred, St Anselm
and St Aelphege, as well as reliquaries containing bones and objects
associated with many other saints. Pilgrims bought souvenirs and protective
charms at Canterbury to mark the completion of pilgrimages. Many have
been found in London; Becket was born there and became Londoners'
favourite saint. The extensive collections of pilgrim souvenirs in the Museum
of London contain, for example, a mass-produced thirteenth-century lead
ampulla (holy water flask) inscribed in Latin, 'Thomas is the best healer of
the holy sick', which emphasises the curative properties associated with the
Canterbury shrine.

Few other monasteries in Britain could rival Canterbury's quantity and
range of relics, but many aspired to the possession of a popular shrine.
Relics might figure among a founder's endowment. Vale Royal Abbey
(Cheshire) received a piece of the cross upon which Christ was crucified. It
had been seized by Edward I during his campaign in the Holy Land in 1271–
2 (Brownbill 1914, 9). Fragments of the 'True Cross' were claimed by
numerous monasteries. The Augustinian canons of Waltham Abbey (Essex)
benefited from Henry II's penance following Becket's murder. He spent
heavily on the buildings, which contained a shrine with a fragment of the
True Cross. A stone mould for casting cross-shaped ampullae inscribed in
Latin, 'Sign of the Holy Cross of Waltham', was found at Coleman Street
in the City and is in the collection of the Museum of London. Vale Royal's
Cheshire neighbour, Norton Priory, claimed another Holy Cross. In 1287
the annals of Whalley Abbey recorded the miracles it had brought about:
'speech lost for five years by one person, and sight by another, have been

restored by virtue of the holy cross of Norton'. A large chapel added to the east end of the church was probably built to accommodate a shrine containing the holy cross (Greene 1989, 129–32). The most favoured location for an important shrine was in the eastern part of the church, beyond but in close proximity to the high altar. This necessitated special arrangements to enable the monks to continue to celebrate services in relative peace whilst admitting large numbers of pilgrims to the shrine. In consequence, the acquisition of an important relic was often followed, as at Norton, by major building works to provide an appropriate setting. At Hailes Abbey (Gloucestershire), a chevet chapel was added to the east end of the church following the gift of a phial of Christ's blood in 1270 by Edmund, the son of the founder, Richard Duke of Cornwall. The foundations of the chapel were found in excavations in 1900 (Brakspear 1901). The shrine was placed in the centre, with an ambulatory around it that enabled pilgrims to see it on three sides. Five semi-octagonal chapels radiated from the ambulatory. The arrangements at Vale Royal were similar (figure 84).

The ownership of an important relic could lead to the entire reconstruction of the church. The decision to remodel the church at Holycross (Co. Tipperary) during the period 1450–1500 was almost certainly connected with the monastery's possession of a piece of the True Cross. The design of the new church incorporated two shrines in which relics might be kept (Stalley 1987, 115). Possession of a relic could have political value. The most celebrated relic in Ireland was St Patrick's staff, which according to the *Life of St Malachy*, written by St Bernard of Clairvaux, was the staff used by Jesus himself and which Patrick was given on an island in the Mediterranean (Ronan 1990). The staff, in its gold and jewelled case, was seized by the Anglo-Normans and placed in one of their foundations, the Augustinian Holy Trinity Priory (now Christ Church Cathedral) in Dublin, which henceforth became one of the chief places of pilgrimage in Ireland.

There was no guarantee that relics and shrines would be as attractive to pilgrims as their promoters hoped. The monks of Glastonbury were disappointed by the lack of popular response to St Patrick and St Dunstan (Platt 1984, 77). It was only when in 1191 they staged a fraudulent excavation in which they claimed to have found the bodies of King Arthur and Guinevere, conveniently identified by a lead cross inscribed 'Here lies buried the renowned king Arthur on the Isle of Avalon', that they succeeded in capturing the public's imagination. Fashion played a large part in the response of pilgrims. There were few shrines where the popularity of the early Middle Ages endured until the Dissolution, and even in the cases of such well known pilgrim centres as Canterbury and Hailes, income from this source was greatly diminished. Amongst Augustinian houses, only Walsingham (Norfolk) retained its drawing power, with an income from offerings exceeding £260 recorded in the *Valor* in 1535 (Robinson 1980, 259).

Excavation was carried out at Walsingham Priory in 1961 (Green and Whittingham 1968). To the north of the large priory church were found the remains of the 'Holy House' that had been built on the site in the early twelfth century, some years before the foundation of the priory in 1153. It had been carefully preserved by the canons, eventually becoming the focus of pilgrimage associated with the cult of the Virgin. The excavators found

Figure 41. Pilgrim badges found in Salisbury. 1 and 2, St Thomas of Canterbury. 3, Rood of Grace, Boxley Abbey. 4, Our Lady of Walsingham Priory. 5, St Edith of Wilton Abbey. 6, St Etheldreda of Ely Cathedral Priory. 7, St Edmund of Bury St Edmunds. 8, St Werburgh's geese, Chester Abbey. 9, St Bridget of Syon Abbey. 10, St Alban (whose head hangs from the tree alongside which stands his executioner).

Reproduced with permission of the Salisbury and South Wiltshire Museum.

that the Holy House had been encased in a chapel, described as a 'novum opus' by William of Worcester when he visited Walsingham in 1479. The Holy House had become itself a venerated relic, enclosed in the new work which formed a kind of large reliquary.

Archaeology can play an important role in investigating the popularity of centres of pilgrimage through the study of souvenirs. The citizens of Salisbury (Wiltshire) were probably typical of the inhabitants of most medieval towns in their enthusiasm for pilgrimages. On their return from visiting a shrine, some of them threw their pewter ampullae and cap badges into the River Avon and the Millstream. Pilgrim souvenirs from these two riverine sources, found between 1975 and 1987, have recently been published (Spencer 1990). Most citizens undertook return journeys that could be completed within three weeks. The more adventurous visited shrines in churches and monasteries as far afield as Germany, the Low Countries, France, Spain and Italy. Amongst the shrines in England, hat badges and ampullae (figure 41) were brought back from monasteries at Canterbury, Boxley (Kent), Westminster, Hailes, St Albans, Bury St Edmunds, Ely, Walsingham and Chester, and nunneries at Wilton (Wiltshire) and Syon (Middlesex).

Damage by fire

Changes to the buildings of a monastery were not only the result of planned modifications by an abbot, his community, or due to the ambition (spiritual or secular) of a patron. Involuntary change might be brought about as a consequence of damage to the monastic buildings. Of all the threats, that of fire was the most devastating, because once it had taken hold there was little that the monks and their servants could do to halt its progress. A masonry building might appear fire-resistant, but in reality the timber components, especially of the roof, made it vulnerable. The account of the fire at Canterbury in 1174, written eleven years later by one of the monks who witnessed it, Gervase, shows how a conflagration might start and spread (Cotton 1938). It broke out in nearby houses from which sparks were blown into the air by strong winds. Some landed on the roof and found their way between the lead covering and the timbers supporting it. The wood was decayed in places and this made it more flammable. The lead began to melt, and suddenly the building was enveloped in flames. By the time that the fire had burnt itself out, only the nave was left, in which the brethren established a temporary altar. 'The grief and distress of the sons of the church were so great that they howled, rather than sang, mattins and vespers,' before contemplating the awesome task of rebuilding. It was five years, seven months and thirteen days before the monks could return to the choir. When Gervase was writing five years after that, construction work was still not complete.

Pershore Abbey, a Benedictine monastery in Worcestershire, was unfortunate enough to be affected by fire on more than one occasion. One outbreak is recorded in 1102. In 1223 the eastern arm of the church was entirely destroyed by fire, and the structure that still remains (now the parish church) is the result of the rebuilding. Thirty-six trees were donated from the royal forests, and in 1239 the new structure was consecrated. However, another disastrous fire broke out in 1288. It originated in the bakehouse and spread to neighbouring buildings, to the claustral ranges, and to the church. The tower collapsed, and the roofs of the nave, choir and transepts were destroyed. Forty houses in the town were burnt down (Andrews 1901).

Lightning was another threat. In about 1235 the chronicler of St Albans Abbey (Hertfordshire) recorded two lightning strikes within three years – despite the papal seal which had been placed on top of the tower in the belief that it had the power to drive away such storms (Platt 1984, 82).

Excavation has produced several examples of the devastating effects of fires. An account of the fire which destroyed the church at Fountains in 1147 has already been given (Chapter 3); fires were not only the result of accident but also of war and civil disturbance. At Norton Priory, a fire in 1236 was mentioned in the annals of Whalley Abbey (Greene 1989, 110). The fire may have started accidentally in the kitchens, for a thick layer of ash and charcoal, including burnt planks and a carbonised wooden bowl, were found there. The kitchens were timber-framed and would have burnt fiercely once alight. A south-westerly wind would have spread the fire to the refectory and then the dormitory range. With wooden floors, straw-filled beds and the roof timbers ablaze, the fire could reach the church. Here the excavation produced further evidence of its effects, including charcoal, ash, lead droplets, nails and sandstone roof-slab fragments in the choir and transepts. The east end of a church was at particular risk in a fire because the tower would act as a giant chimney. Burning timber choir stalls would turn the crossing into a furnace, the destructive power of which the brethren were helpless to combat. Bells would break free, shattering on impact with the ground. The Norton bell was recast a few years later. The cloister also required total reconstruction – the delicate open arcade of twin shafts was particularly vulnerable to falling roof timbers and blocks of masonry.

A disastrous fire swept through the buildings at Valle Crucis Abbey (Clwyd) in the mid thirteenth century (Evans 1987). Dressed stonework of the church is discoloured to a deep red in places where falling roof timbers burnt fiercely against it. Traces of the fire, in the form of a layer of burnt material, were found in excavations in the south range (Butler 1976). It is possible to distinguish the masonry erected before the fire from that built afterwards, and to identify repair work, for example to the west side of the crossing tower.

Gisborough Priory (Cleveland) is another site where recent archaeological examination has produced evidence of a fire (Heslop forthcoming). Excavation of the north aisle revealed scorching of the paving and the columns, probably the effects of a fire that is known to have occurred in 1289. It necessitated the rebuilding of most of the nave and all of the chancel (figure 32).

When a fire had burnt itself out, the masonry shells of the affected buildings might still be standing. Once they had overcome the shock of the disaster, monastic communities often displayed remarkable powers of recovery. From adversity, the resolution not only to repair the damage but to build on a grander scale than before seems often to have inspired the

Figure 42. South facade of the fifteenth-century south transept of Melrose Abbey, Borders. The niches above the door, in the buttresses and above the window once contained statuary arranged in an iconographic scheme.
    Photograph by Patrick Greene.

brethren. There is certainly nothing inferior in the work of repair carried out at Canterbury, Fountains, Norton, Valle Crucis or Gisborough. Fire-reddened stonework was incorporated in the new work, though doubtless covered with a lime wash to help erase the painful memories.

For monasteries on the English–Scottish border, warfare brought repeated destruction. In 1385, for example, the English forces of Richard II retaliated after an incursion by Scottish and French troops and, in the words of a contemporary Scot, 'saving nothing and burning down with fiery flames God's temples and holy places – to wit the monasteries of Melrose, Dryburgh and Newbattle' (Richardson, Wood and Tabraham 1989, 28). The reconstruction of Melrose Abbey was carried out with a confident spirit despite the trauma of its deliberate destruction. The church was built with a magnificent east window, with on the exterior a sculpture of the Corona-tion of the Virgin at the apex of the gable, and descending inhabited niches containing angels and a mitred abbot (Cruden 1986). The south transept has a similarly impressive facade (figure 42). Much of the church (although probably not the east window) was rebuilt under the direction of John Morow, who placed panels recording his achievement in the walls. From this we know that he came from Paris and 'had in keeping all mason work'. Melrose is therefore one of the very few medieval buildings to carry the name of its architect.

Structural problems

Changes to the structure of a monastic building, particularly the church, could cause the building to collapse. The most frequent cause of subsidence and structural failure was the overloading of foundations. This was particularly a risk in the case of crossing towers. Although not monastic, York Minster provides a vivid illustration of the problems that can occur in a large medieval church (Phillips 1985). Excavation took place as a result of the need to prevent collapse in the twentieth century; the roots of the problems, however, were medieval. The excavators discovered that the late-eleventh-century foundations had suffered severe deformations largely due to the enormous loads imposed by additions to the building. The first imposi-tion of excessive loading on the Anglo-Norman substructure below the cross-ing occurred during the mid thirteenth century when the construction of a magnificent new tower over the north transept led to serious distortion. Attempts at underpinning in 1407 failed to prevent a serious collapse. Other great churches that suffered collapses include Winchester, Gloucester, Lincoln, Ely and St Albans.

Smaller monastic churches were not immune either. Dramatic evidence of such a calamity was found in the excavation of Bordesley Abbey. The source of the problem seems to have been the unstable subsoil fill of an ancient stream or spring underlying the north-west crossing pier. Subsidence of the pier foundations of the twelfth-century church may have occurred, leading to the collapse of the northern and western crossing arches (Hirst, Walsh and Wright 1983, 255). Following rebuilding, the problem was repeated. The new north-west crossing pier collapsed again in the early fourteenth century.

Figure 43. Collapsed masonry of the crossing pier, Bordesley Abbey, Hereford and Worcester. The masonry can be seen embedded in the natural clay, which has been forced upwards in a surrounding ripple.
Photograph supplied by Bordesley Abbey Project.

One section of five courses of masonry came hurtling down to embed itself, through the floor, into the subsoil, which rippled upwards under the force of the impact (figure 43). The masonry was so firmly embedded that attempts to lever it out failed, and the medieval builders simply laid the replacement floor over the top. On this occasion the problems with the subsoil may have been exacerbated by the construction of a larger tower than that of the original church. The monks were determined not to repeat the mistake, and a new north-west pier was built on a massive foundation. Other alterations also suggest a determination to erect or heighten the crossing tower. The excavation of the church at Bordesley has revealed the complexity of change that one monastery might experience. Structural failure, problems with the water table, liturgical changes which resulted in the moving of the choir stalls (figure 8), and the desire to embellish the building all led to an almost bewildering series of modifications that required excavation of the highest quality to disentangle.

The temptation to build or heighten a tower was something that no abbot or prior with the means to fund the exercise seems to have resisted. There were several motives. The spiritual symbolism of a steeple soaring towards heaven was matched by the practical consideration of providing a lofty belfry from which the sounds of the abbey bells would carry over a wide area. Patrons and benefactors within earshot would be reminded of the unceasing

Figure 44. Crossing arch at Llanthony Priory, Gwent, distorted as a result of movement in the south-west pier supporting the tower.
Photograph by Patrick Greene.

round of prayers being offered on their behalf. There was also the personal
ambition of the prelate to leave a highly visible reminder of his achievements.
The huge tower at Fountains Abbey, 52 m. (170 ft.) high, has on its west
face the mitre, crozier and initials of its builder, Abbot Huby (1495–1526).
Whilst he was determined to record his responsibility for the erection of the
tower, its spiritual power is signified by a band of Latin inscription beneath
the embattled parapet and beneath the two upper tiers of windows. The
verse from the first epistle to Timothy reads: 'Now unto the king eternal,
immortal, invisible, the only God, be glory for ever and ever' (Gilyard-Beer
1970, 35).

By building a new tower on its own foundations at the northern end of
the north transept, Marmaduke Huby was ensuring that his tower was safe
from collapse. He had learnt from experience, for one of his other building
works was the reinforcement of the crossing and the transepts following an
earlier, damaging attempt to build a tower over the crossing. At two other
northern Cistercian abbeys, Shap and Furness in Cumbria, the construction
of crossing towers had disastrous consequences, and at both it was decided
to build a tower on its own foundations at the west end of the nave. Augustinian Bolton Priory in Yorkshire adopted the same solution. The construction
of buttresses to support the tower at Llanthony Abbey (Gwent) prevented
collapse, but the distortion of the crossing arches is pronounced (figure 44).

A further cause of collapse was the piercing of walls with arches,
particularly when aisles were added to a previously aisleless church. The
buttressing effect of the walls against the tower was lessened once arches had
been inserted in them. The frequent practice of enlarging window openings
could weaken walls. It is an unusual monastery that has not at some time
of its existence suffered serious problems with the stability of at least one of
its buildings.

The remodelling of cloisters

Apart from the tower, the parts of a monastery most likely to undergo
radical change were the cloister-walks. Only in the case of monasteries
established at a relatively late date was the structure of the cloister likely to
be the same in the sixteenth century as it had been in the plan that followed
the foundation. The cloister-walks of monasteries founded in the eleventh
and twelfth centuries consisted of a path covered by a lean-to roof which
was supported by an open arcade of masonry on all four sides of the cloister
garden. In northern Europe this arrangement, well suited to the warmer
south, seems to have proved too draughty and chilly. There are numerous
examples from the fourteenth century onwards of the replacement of open
arcades by enclosed passageways incorporating glazed windows. The open
arcades at Rievaulx (Yorkshire) and Newminster (Northumberland) are both
re-erected from fragments found on the sites during excavation. In Ireland
a number of cloister-arcades have been successfully re-erected, for example
at Mellifont (Co. Louth). In contrast to the paucity of early examples,
numerous later cloisters survive, particularly in those English monasteries
that became or continued as cathedrals at the time of the Dissolution, such

as Gloucester and Chester. In Ireland, fine cloisters have survived at Jerpoint, Co. Kilkenny, built in the fifteenth century to replace an earlier cloister. They are embellished with figure sculpture including St Christopher, a knight and a monk. The Jerpoint cloister, and many of the other late medieval cloisters in Ireland, continued to be built with open arcades. One of the finest glazed English cloisters, at Lacock in Wiltshire (Augustinian canonesses), has survived as a result of its incorporation into a post-Dissolution house.

On many sites, even where there are substantial remains of buildings, all trace of the cloister-walk has disappeared. The potential for rediscovery has been demonstrated at Bordesley Abbey (Walsh 1979) (figure 9). Fragments of the fifteenth-century structure, with its traceried windows, were found buried beneath the fallen stone of the south transept. The design of the Transitional cloister arcade at Haughmond is known as a result of the recovery of fragments from the foundations of the cloister that replaced it. A similar situation existed at Norton Priory where a sequence of four cloisters was discovered (Greene 1989) (figure 7). At Roche Abbey (South Yorkshire) the open, late-twelfth-century arcade survived until the Dissolution. The recovery of fragments from demolition rubble has enabled its original form to be reconstructed (Coppack 1990, 70). The lesson to be drawn from the examples of Bordesley, Haughmond, Norton and Roche is that excavation can produce evidence of the form of earlier cloister structures even if they have been replaced.

The principle that evidence of the form of the superstructure can survive even on sites that have been subject to extensive damage applies to all monastic buildings. The growth of a monastery inevitably involved demolition of obsolete structures. It made sense on economic and practical grounds to reuse material where possible. The archaeological investigation of a monastery should therefore take account of the potential for recovering information that can be used to reconstruct, on paper, structures long vanished. In particular, carved masonry is likely to be found as rubble in foundations, wall-cores, and levelling layers. Wood could also be reused, so the study of standing timber buildings, or roofs, floors and partitions of masonry buildings should be carried out with an awareness of the information on the form (and date, through dendrochronology) of earlier structures. It can also apply to grave-slabs and grave markers. The extension of the monastic church and chapels eastwards frequently encroached upon the brethren's graveyard. The living might think nothing of using their predecessors' graves as building materials, as the eastern wall of the lady chapel at Norton Priory showed (figure 45). Human remains were not always treated in quite such a cavalier manner. Charnel pits may be encountered in which the skulls and larger bones from graves disturbed during building work have been gathered up and interred as a group (figure 46). The repair of Canterbury necessitated just such an exercise (Cotton 1938, 12): 'In digging the foundations, Master William was obliged to take out the bones of several holy martyrs, which being carefully collected were re-interred in a large trench.'

Figure 45. East wall of the lady chapel, Norton Priory. The large blocks in the foreground, and in the buttress on the left, are grave-slabs, incorporated into the foundations when the chapel was extended. An earlier ditch can be seen (filled with water) on the right; the other water-filled feature is a nineteenth-century land-drain which cuts the medieval foundations.

   Photograph by Patrick Greene, reproduced by permission of Norton Priory Museum Trust.

Changing circumstances

Monastic houses were often profoundly affected by changes in external circumstances over which they had little control. The Cistercians, for example, were particularly badly affected by the Black Death in the middle of the fourteenth century, and the labour shortages that resulted from it. Numbers of lay brothers had been declining before the epidemic, but by the end of the fourteenth century they had disappeared entirely. The effect on the monastic buildings was mainly seen in the west range, the upper floor of which had been the lay brothers' dormitory, and the nave of the church. At Valle Crucis (Clwyd) for example, the monks' choir stalls were moved east, and a stone screen wall was constructed across the nave and north aisle in the early fifteenth century, thereby concentrating religious activity in the eastern part of the church (Evans 1987). Other changes at Valle Crucis moved it far from the original Cistercian pattern. The dormitory occupied the upper floor of

Figure 46. Sandstone coffin used as charnel pit, Norton Priory. The skeleton of the person originally buried in the coffin can be seen, with in the foreground a jumble of skulls and other bones found by the medieval builders and placed in the coffin.

Photograph by Patrick Greene, reproduced by permission of Norton Priory Museum Trust.

Figure 47. Reconstruction drawing of the abbot's hall in the east range of Valle Crucis Abbey, as it could have appeared in the early sixteenth century. The use of the building has changed radically (compare with figure 2); the cloister-walk is no longer roofed and an external stair leads to the abbot's hall, alongside which is his private chamber, and on the right are apartments for his guests.

Drawing by Chris Jones-Jenkins, Cadw: Welsh Historic Monuments.

the east range, in its usual position. At first it would have been an open hall with the straw-filled mattresses arranged in two rows. The first departure from this austere arrangement was probably the insertion of screens to divide up the space into individual cubicles (figure 2). In the later fifteenth century, however, it ceased to be the monks' dormitory entirely. The abbot, who had previously had a house to the east of the east range, converted the dormitory into a comfortable residence for himself (figure 47). It comprised a hall, a private chamber, and apartments for his important guests. The monks, whose numbers had declined anyway, probably lived in small lodgings created in other parts of the monastic complex. Even the cloister seems to have been abandoned at this stage, and an external timber staircase constructed to give access to the abbot's hall. Valle Crucis had become unrecognisable as a Cistercian abbey in comparison with its early-thirteenth-century beginnings.

5 Water management

For a medieval monastic house, the management of water was a matter of ensuring a reliable supply, and of getting rid of waste and excess water in an efficient manner. This technically complex balancing act was not always successful, as the evidence of rising damp at Bordesley (Chapter 4) and floods at Stanlow and Boyle (Chapter 3) testify. Nevertheless, the use of water is an outstanding feature of medieval monastic houses which few secular establishments came close to emulating (Bond 1988 and 1989).

The decisive nature of water supply in determining the location and the layout of a monastery has been described in Chapters 1 and 3, which also pointed out the differences that applied to Irish friaries and some nunneries in the placing of the cloister to the north of the church. In the vast majority of cases, however, functional considerations prevailed, with the cloister placed where the latrine drain could be supplied with a constant flow of running water. This might be difficult to achieve in the case of monasteries of pre-Conquest foundation that had not been established near running water, and new urban monasteries that had failed to find sites near a spring, stream or river. Even these were a small minority; most monasteries in towns succeeded in acquiring access to a reasonably plentiful supply, to make the conventional arrangement of buildings workable. Monastic water management went far beyond the confines of the latrines, however. This chapter examines the extensive nature of the control and organisation of water resources by monastic communities, including watermills, weirs, fishponds, moats, drainage ditches, land reclamation and sea defences.

The Canterbury water system

There can be no better starting point for an examination of the utilisation of water within a monastery than the remarkable twelfth-century 'birds-eye' drawing of Canterbury Cathedral Priory (figure 48). It was found, with a smaller drawing of part of the system, inside a psalter in the library of Trinity College, Cambridge (Willis 1868; Hayes 1977). The pair of drawings seem to have been executed in about 1160 and together form a comprehensive explanation of the intricacies of the monastery's system of supply and drainage. The drawings repay detailed study as the system incorporated many features that are to be found at other monastic sites.

The system at Canterbury was installed in the time of Prior Wibert (1151–67) who is known to have been responsible for building the latrines and the water tower in the cloister. The plan was given a colour key: green indicated the incoming supply, red the distribution system, and yellow showed rainwater collection and drainage. Stand-pipes, waste pipes and stopcocks were also identified.

The source was in the Scotland Hills about 1.5 km. to the north-east of Canterbury. Both drawings show the aqueduct following a course through

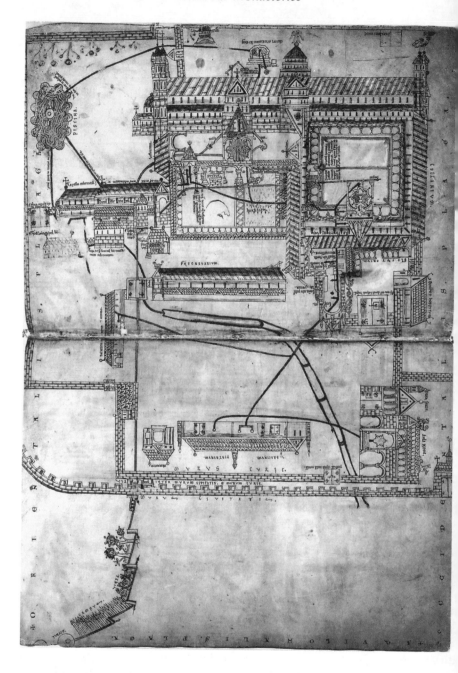

Figure 48. The water-supply system of Canterbury Cathedral Priory. The spring is shown in the bottom left corner, and the pipes can be followed around the precinct and the greater and lesser cloisters. The main drain flows out beneath the wall, bottom right.

Reproduced by permission of the Masters and Fellows of Trinity College, Cambridge (Ms R.17.1, f.284v/285r).

ornfields, a vineyard and an orchard. The monks had to come to an agreement with their neighbours, the Augustinian canons of St Gregory's Priory, o permit repairs to the aqueduct where it crossed their orchard. The canons vere allowed to use a branch of the aqueduct in exchange for a basket of heir best apples every September. Pipes that formed part of the canons' water-supply system have recently been found beneath the floors of the kitchen and refectory (Hicks and Tatton-Brown 1991, 104).

On its route to the monastery from the conduit house, which protected the spring, the water flowed through a succession of five settling tanks to remove silt and sand. After passing through the town wall, the aqueduct led to the water tower. From the water tower lead pipes distributed the supply to different parts of the monastic complex. Two important destinations were the lavatory in the great cloister, and the lavatory opposite the door to the infirmary. Here the monks washed their hands before meals. Other places on the main route were the cistern in the outer cemetery, the prior's cistern and water-tub, the lavatory under the north hall, the brewhouse and the bakehouse, the great kitchen, the bathhouse, the refectory, the infirmary kitchen, the infirmary hall, and finally the latrine building. Excess water flowed into a stone-lined fishpond and the prior's water-tub before joining waste from the bathhouse and rainwater from the roofs and gutters of the great cloister. The accumulated waste water flowed into the main drain which led to the latrine building. Then, carrying human waste products as well, the water flowed through a large sewer beneath Green Court and the town wall to empty into the town ditch. The drain was found during building work in 1946 – it measures about one metre high by one metre wide, with a paved base and a masonry barrel vault. The system continued in use in a modified form after the Dissolution and still operates to a limited extent (Tatton-Brown 1983).

The Canterbury drawings were probably produced to assist with maintenance of the system. Its main elements existed on most monastic sites of any size. They will be considered individually here.

Source of supply

Whilst a channel carrying water diverted from a river or stream was the ideal means of flushing the latrines, this was not the case as far as the piped water supply was concerned. By utilising one or more springs on a hillside above the monastery, a head of water could be established. Water brought by pipes (wood, ceramic or lead) could fill a tank in a water tower or conduit house in the monastery. From the tank, lead pipes could carry water under pressure to various locations in the monastery. The spring could be protected from pollution by a well-house. The source used by St Augustine's Abbey at Canterbury survives and has recently been excavated (Coppack 1990, 84). It consisted of a polygonal tank of flint and Caen stone fed by twenty-five separate springs through stone-lined channels. Well-houses can be seen at Haughmond Abbey (Shropshire), and at Mount Grace Priory in North Yorkshire three well-houses were excavated and reconstructed in the 1960s (figure 49). In Lincoln, water was brought into the town to supply the

Figure 49. Well-house at Mount Grace Priory, North Yorkshire, reconstructed after excavation in the 1960s. The stone channel in the foreground would have originally incorporated a lead pipe taking water to a central cistern in the cloister. The well-house itself contained a large lead tank.

Photograph by Patrick Greene.

Dominican priory through a lead conduit. This formed the basis of a supply to the town in the post-medieval period. The water supplies to many urban monasteries were utilised in this way after the Dissolution.

An urban monastery might find itself at odds with its town over the supply of water. A bitter dispute broke out in the thirteenth century between the Augustinian abbey of St Thomas the Martyr, and the mayor and citizens of Dublin (Jackson 1990). At an inquisition held in 1259 it was proved that the city had far exceeded the rate of abstraction of water from two rivers owned by the canons, the Dodder and the Poddle, that had been agreed in 1244 when a supply to Dublin was being organised. The piped system served Dublin Castle and conduits in the streets used by the inhabitants; it had also been extended to four religious houses within the city. A solution was arrived at to ensure a just division between the abbey and the city. A wedge-shaped masonry pier known as the Tongue was built in the Poddle to partition the water in such a way that the smaller portion flowed into the city watercourse.

In a flat area it might be impossible to obtain a supply from an elevated source, in which case water could be pumped to a water tower or raised manually in buckets. More information is required about the actual methods used. A small, poor monastery might never achieve an integrated supply, relying solely on water drawn by hand from a well or stream.

Settling tanks have rarely been found in excavations, which is not surprising as they are likely to be some distance from the parts of the complex that usually attract the attention of excavators. When field survey work is taking place in the vicinity of a monastery there should be an awareness of their possible presence; they might be detected in the form of earthworks or by geophysical survey. Parts of filters have been found at Westminster Abbey and Fountains Abbey.

The extensive nature and complexity of a water-supply system is well illustrated by the Carthusian priory in London (Hope 1903). The London Charterhouse was founded in 1371 and initially it seems to have drawn its water from wells. Provision of a regular supply did not begin until 1430. The prior and convent acquired a spring in Islington. The plan which was prepared to show the entire system still exists in a remarkably complete form. It is pictorial and is extensively annotated. Figure 50 is a tracing of the portion of the plan which shows the cloister and surrounding buildings. The canons had to obtain their supply about 1.5 km. distant from the priory because nearer sources had already been tapped by the Priory of St John of Jerusalem at Clerkenwell, and the nuns of Clerkenwell. Both their sources were shown on the plan, which also indicated roads and property boundaries. The plan was drawn as a working document to help with the maintenance of the system, to show changes to it, and to indicate agreements with other property-owners over whose land the water was carried.

The Charterhouse supply started at a series of springs and 'wells', these apparently being cisterns in which sediments were allowed to settle out. The water was carried by a stone conduit to the first 'receiving house'. This was shown on the plan as a rectangular building with a dividing wall. The northern half was coloured blue to indicate that it was the cistern. The water entered the cistern through a lead pipe with a perforated rose. A brick-built

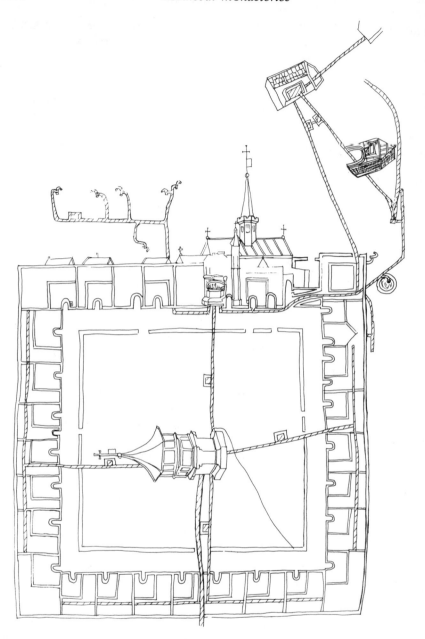

Figure 50. The system for distributing water within the cloister of London Charterhouse. This drawing is a tracing by the author of the original medieval plan. The church is shown at the top, and cells with gardens line the cloister. In the centre is the elaborate cistern from which water is distributed to the four ranges, and to the flesh kitchen and gatehouse (top right).

utter carried away overflow water. There was a fall of 20 m. in the 1.5 km. distance to the priory, so considerable water pressure would have resulted. To regulate it there was a gradual increase in the capacity of the pipe system as the water neared the second receiving house. The single lead pipe that left the first receiving house was doubled, and then trebled. Settling tanks, and features labelled 'Susparails' were shown at intervals along the system. Susparails seem to have been another device to prevent excess pressure developing in the system, with a vent to remove air as a precaution against bursts. They may have doubled as settling tanks. There was a considerable incentive to remove silts and sand and organic material. Quite apart from the desire for pure water, there was a need to avoid blockages that would be difficult to locate and remove. The second receiving house was entirely taken up with a reservoir. It had inlet and outlet pipes, and a large plug in the bottom to enable it to be drained for cleaning. The outlet pipe led to an elaborate octagonal cistern in the cloister, from which water was piped to each of the monk's cells.

Distribution

Lead pipes were the usual means of distributing water to the various parts of the precinct such as the cloister lavatory where the monks washed their hands before meals, and the kitchens. At the London Charterhouse, and at other Carthusian monasteries, the task was complicated by the fact that the brethren's individual cells each required a supply. The plan shows (and the notes on it describe) the arrangements in considerable detail. The octagonal cistern supported a square lead tank into which the main pipe discharged. The supply pipe descended with branches leading to the four cardinal points. The southern pipe ran to a lavatory built into the cloister wall. The drawing shows it as an ornamental cistern with a row of taps and a trough. As well as the cells, the system supplied the laundry, the buttery, the brewhouse and the kitchens. There were even supplies for four taverns outside the precinct wall – The Elms, The Hart's Horn, The Windmill and The White Hart.

Lengths of lead pipe have been found at numerous monastic sites, although it is rare to find long runs, as redundant lead was both valuable and easily reused. The technique of manufacture was quite different to that employed today, in which pipes of circular section are continuously extruded. Medieval plumbers would make a pipe from a rectangular sheet of lead about a metre long which was bent over a wooden rod. Molten lead was then poured along the join to seal it. Lengths were jointed using molten lead to seal the junction. Taps were of bronze, and operated in a similar way to the type of spigot still used on traditional beer barrels.

Even if little or no lead pipework has survived on a particular site, much can be learnt about the system from other clues. The ancient removal of a buried pipe will result in a linear feature that can be traced in the course of excavation. Frequently, as at the Carmelite friary in Aberdeen (Stones 1989, 38), lead piping was placed in small trenches filled with clay to provide secondary sealing; even where the pipe had been removed it was possible to follow its course marked by the strip of yellow clay. Other information can be gleaned from stonework. An example is the lavatory at Whalley Abbey (Cistercian, Lancashire). The lavatory consists of a long trough set into the wall on the south side of the cloister. Metal pipes and fittings were doubtless stripped at the time of the Dissolution, but it is still possible to see how the stonework was cut to accommodate a pipe. The chasing follows a course up the wall from the floor of the cloister-walk to the left of the trough. It then turns to run horizontally above the trough before stopping at its end. A number of chasings descend a short distance from the horizontal pipe recess; these must have terminated in taps. Another chasing descends from the base of the trough to floor level. This must have held the drainage pipe which took the waste water beneath the cloister walk floor to empty into the cloister drain.

Lavatory structures

The washing of hands before meals was a characteristic of the rules of all monastic orders. The Observances used at Augustinian Barnwell Abbey in Cambridgeshire (Clark 1897) stress the need for this instruction to be assiduously followed, and include prohibitions on the sharpening of knives at the basin, and blowing noses on the towels.

There were two main types of lavatory. The most common was the rectangular trough of the kind described above at Whalley. One of the most impressive examples, at Gloucester Cathedral, is a long trough in the north cloister walk, with a cupboard for towels near by. The other type was more elaborate, consisting of a circular or polygonal base and trough supplied through a circle of taps from a central supply, all set within an attractive structure. This might be attached to the main buildings or stand free in the cloister (Godfrey 1952). One such was described in the *Rites of Durham*:

> within the cloister garth over against the Frater-house door was a fair laver or conduit for the monks to wash their hands and faces at, being made in form round covered with lead and all of marble saving the very outermost walls. Within the walls you may walk round about the laver of marble having many little conduits or spouts of brass with 24 cocks of brass round about it, having in it 7 fair windows of stonework, and in the top of it a fair dovecot. (Fowler 1903)

Nearby hung a bell used to call the monks to wash and dine. On either side of the refectory door were cupboards in which 'sweet and clean' towels were kept. An earlier lavatory was found in excavations at Durham set into the south-west angle of the first cloister garth (Hope 1903). It was square in plan with a circular basin. The basin was replaced in 1432–3 with a new basin of Eggleston marble, now preserved in the cloister garth.

The remains of the octagonal lavatory in the cloister garth at Wenlock Priory (Cluniac, Shropshire) show the quality of embellishment that such a structure might receive (figure 51). Two late-twelfth-century panels survive, one of which has Christ on the Lake. They are a reminder that washing before meals was not simply a matter of hygiene; for the brethren it was more importantly an affirmation of spiritual cleanliness and purity. This explains the prominence given to what might otherwise be considered a

Figure 51. The lavatorium in the cloister of Wenlock Priory, Shropshire; late-twelfth-century panel representing Christ walking on the water.
Photograph by Patrick Greene.

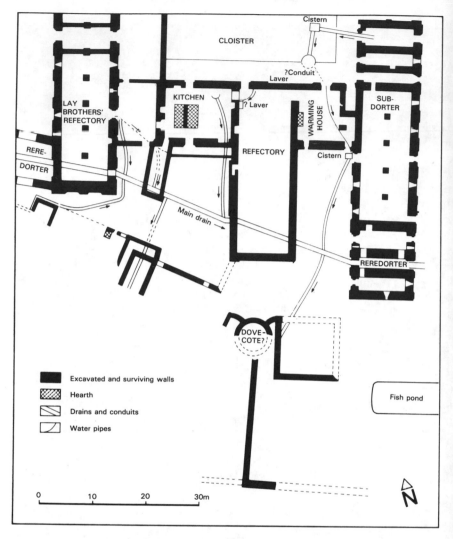

Figure 52. Plan of the water-supply system, Kirkstall Abbey. The complexity of supplying water, and providing drainage, is illustrated by this plan of the arrangements that existed in the thirteenth and fourteenth centuries in the buildings on the south side of the cloister.

Plan supplied by West Yorkshire Archaeology Service.

utilitarian facility. The lavatorium at Mellifont Abbey in Co. Louth shows the attention it might get even at a Cistercian house that had, in theory, denounced unnecessary decoration (Stalley 1980).

Other buildings requiring piped water

Another destination of the piped water system was the kitchen. A convenient and plentiful supply was required for the preparation and cooking of food. Likewise, the brewhouse and bakehouse would have been incorporated in the distribution system. Excavation over a period of four decades at Kirkstall Abbey (Cistercian, Yorkshire) has revealed something of the complexity of the piped water-supply system (Moorhouse and Wrathmell 1987) (figure 52). Within the cloister garth a stone-lined structure was found that has been identified as a cistern. There were inlet and outlet conduits which held lead pipes. The cistern may have served the function of the 'susparails' chambers at Charterhouse (see above) – to avoid bursting problems due to air in the system, and as a silt trap. Nearby, close to the lavatory in the south cloister walk, was a deep, circular stone-lined structure that might be a well. Wells at Reading Abbey (Berkshire), Lewes Priory (Sussex) and Durham Cathedral Priory in a similar position appear to have served as emergency sources of water when pipes became blocked. Water could be drawn from the well and poured into the top of a vertical column linked to the pipe network, thus maintaining some pressure in the system. Another pipe extended from the lavatory basin in the south cloister walk to the area south of the meat kitchen. It terminated in a cistern, stone-built with steps on its west side. An outlet, a stone-lined conduit, extended further south. The refectory also had a supply which seems to have served a wash-basin near the entrance from the cloister. The pipe had been sealed off when construction of a staircase necessitated the removal of the laver; two bronze taps were found in the filling. There were fragments of a lead pipe in the scullery next to the kitchen.

The guest house at Kirkstall was also supplied with a piped water supply (Wrathmell 1987). Substantial lengths of lead piping that had been installed in the thirteenth century were found *in situ*. The pipes were about 25 mm. in diameter. Their joints had been reinforced with lead collars and wads of clay to minimise the danger of leaks (figure 53). A sink in the scullery and wash-basins in the hall were supplied with water. A branch also skirted the guesthouse to supply buildings to the north-west. As the buildings were enlarged, and their functions changed, the system of pipes was modified.

At some sites, for example Kirkham Priory (North Yorkshire), ceramic instead of lead pipes were used for the distribution system. The most impressive ceramic system to have been found in an excavation is at the Cistercian abbey of Glenluce (Dumfries and Galloway). Some of the pipes have been left *in situ*, and components are also displayed in the site museum. The pipes had marks inscribed in the wet clay before being fired to facilitate assembly on site. Ceramic junction boxes of globular form had a removable top to allow sediment to be removed.

The latrines

Monastic latrines, also known by the medieval euphemism 'necessarium' and the nineteenth-century invented term 'reredorter', were built alongside the dormitory range. Like the dormitory itself, the actual latrines were at first-floor level. Very few dormitories have survived, and even fewer upper floors of latrine blocks. The visitor to a monastic site can get a misleading impression of sanitary arrangements, for it is easy to assume that the seats were

Figure 53. Lead piping, Kirkstall Abbey, installed in the early thirteenth century outside the east wall of the guesthouse. Pads of clay can be seen at intervals where extra sealing was required around the joints between sections of piping.
Photograph by West Yorkshire Archaeology Service.

mmediately above the monastic drain. In fact they were as much as seven
netres above it. What evidence there is suggests that the arrangement was
a series of cubicles in a line, separated by screens (figure 2). In many
nonastic houses there were sufficient cubicles to cater for every monk
ndividually, so where a latrine block has been enlarged it is safe to assume
:hat it was in response to an increase in the size of the community.

The inmates of a monastery usually had superior toilet accommodation to
:hat endured by their secular benefactors, as comparison with the
arrangements in most castles and manor houses shows. The benefits to a
monastic community were considerable. A group of people living perma-
nently in close proximity to each other is particularly susceptible to disease.
An efficient sanitation system can lower the risks of transmission of those
illnesses, diseases and parasites associated with faecal matter. There must
have been a universal recognition of this fact amongst all the religious
orders, however imperfectly the actual mechanisms of contagion were
understood.

In the case of Cistercian houses in which the upper floor of the west range
was usually the lay brothers' dormitory, an additional latrine was required.
Excavations at Valle Crucis (Clwyd) found the remains of a latrine attached
to the west side of the lay brothers' range (Butler 1976). Its foundations were
of slight construction, suggesting that the upper floor may have been timber-
framed. The monks' latrine was situated at the southern end of the
dormitory (figure 2).

The flow of water down the drain was often regulated by a sluice gate.
This allowed the latrines to be flushed periodically, by releasing a rush of
water. It was not always possible to provide a constant supply of water to
the latrines if there was no convenient stream or spring. The deficiency could
be remedied, at least in part, by ensuring that roof water, and waste or
excess from the supply system, was directed to the drain. This was the solution adopted at Canterbury as described previously, and at many other
urban monasteries. Battle Abbey (figure 5) faced this problem to an even
greater degree as a result of its hilltop location.

As well as the reredorter, latrines were to be found in other buildings,
notably the infirmary. Often this was placed to take advantage of the main
drain. The guesthouse latrines might feed directly into the main drain, or
might be served by a branch drain. At Kirkstall Abbey the guesthouse had
two sets of latrines (figure 54) on the ground floor in the thirteenth century
(Wrathmell 1987). They were served by the main drain, which was fed by
a stream, perhaps from the abbey millpond. The drain ran south to serve the
guesthouse, then swung east to pass beneath the lay brothers' latrines (a
distinctive requirement in the drainage arrangements of Cistercian houses)
and the monks' latrines (figure 52) before discharging into the River Aire.

The main drain of a monastery was often a magnificently built structure
with a paved base, masonry sides and a top made of stone slabs. The drain
at Melrose Abbey (Borders) was 1.2 m. wide, 1.5 m. deep and 450 m. in
length. The sides were built of stone, the base was cobbled, and it was
roofed with lintels except where it passed beneath buildings where it was
arched (Richardson, Wood and Tabraham 1989, 22). The accidental
discovery of drains in later centuries probably explains why 'secret passages'

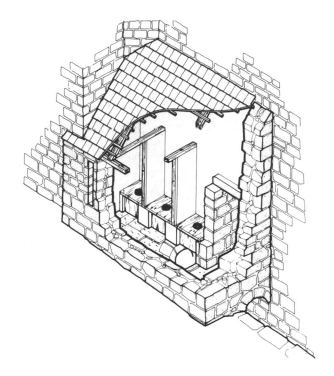

Figure 54. Reconstruction drawing of the guesthouse latrine, Kirkstall Abbey. The latrine, which was attached to the chambers (see figure 71), had three cubicles with wooden seats set over the main drain.

   Drawing supplied by West Yorkshire Archaeology Service.

are commonly believed to run from so many monastic sites. Not all drains were as impressive. A small, relatively poor house such as the nunnery at Polesworth (West Midlands) had a latrine served by a drain, but it was on a much more modest scale (Mytum 1979, 81). Garderobes with individual cess-pits or soakaways might serve particular rooms. An example was excavated at Bristol Greyfriars in the east range of the Franciscan Friary (Ponsford 1973).

Drainage of rainwater

Getting water to a monastery was one challenge. Removing unwanted water was another. The greatest problem was the drainage of the cloister. Rain falling on the roofs that faced into the cloister – the church, dormitory, refectory and west ranges as well as the roofs of the cloister-walks – was concentrated on the cloister garth. Heavy rain would result in large volumes of water flowing into this area. It is likely that every monastery had a drain around the perimeter of the cloister garth. As well as roof water, some other drains (especially the waste from the wash-basin) emptied into the cloister drain. Because so few cloisters have been excavated to a satisfactory standard it is difficult to know how most monasteries tackled the problem of removing the water from the cloister drain. Two options existed – to carry it by a drain beneath adjacent buildings to a point where it could empty into the main monastic drain, or to take it beneath whichever building enabled the water to flow away from the site most easily. Many other subsidiary drains took roof water from individual buildings, often joining to form a complex drainage system. A substantial drain was often required to serve the church on the side opposite the cloister. Like all aspects of the monastic complex, the drainage system evolved over time and required modifications whenever substantial changes to buildings took place.

Another important drain served the kitchens. It usually emptied into the main monastic drain. The direction of flow of water down the main drain was usually arranged in such a way that the kitchens were served before the latrines, but this was not always possible. On well-drained sites, soakaways could assist in the drainage of the monastery. A special location for a soakaway was at the eastern end of the church where it served the piscina – the basin near the altar where the vessels used during the Eucharist were rinsed.

Moats

A number of monastic houses were surrounded by moats. They had two principal functions. One was drainage – on a low-lying site, the digging of a moat could lower the water table when linked to a ditch carrying excess water away. The second function was that of security, where the moat took the place of a precinct wall. Examples of monastic houses with moats are Ulverscroft Priory (Augustinian, Leicestershire) and Michelham Priory (Augustinian, Sussex). For both, security was the main consideration behind their construction (Knowles and St Joseph, 1952, 228–9 and 220–1). Unlike most moats that were dug in clay soils and which were filled by natural seepage, Michelham was supplied by a contour leat that carried water from the Cuckmere River 400 m. upstream. Moats might provide part of the precinct boundary, with a wall around the remainder. The Gilbertine priory at Shouldham in Norfolk (figures 13 and 14) had a partially-moated precinct. Moats might be of considerable dimensions. The moat of Abingdon Abbey (Oxfordshire) has been excavated recently (Allen 1990). It was 10 m. wide and required a timber bridge, the trestle supports of which were discovered. Moats are very difficult to date because they were usually cleaned out on a regular basis. The Abingdon moat could date from the refoundation of the abbey in 959, or alternatively it may have been a response to riots in 1327, or it could be unconnected with either event. The bridge, however, was dated by dendrochronology to the beginning of the sixteenth century. Some of the small monasteries that acquired moats may have done so as much for prestige as for security, at a time when members of the lesser gentry were building moated manor houses.

Fishponds

The consumption of fish was a feature of the diet of members of the medieval upper classes. For monastic communities, with restrictions on meat-eating (albeit varying from order to order and tending to become less strictly applied with time), the availability of fish was of particular importance. Fresh fish might be obtained from river or coastal fisheries. Dried and salted fish were purchased for the monastic stores. The third source, adopted by very many monastic houses, was to rear fish in ponds designed for the purpose. Fishponds were not peculiar to monasteries, however. Many secular landowners constructed fishpond systems to serve manor houses and castles (Aston 1988). One of the first references to a monastic fishpond is a writ of Henry I dated 1115–28 noting the possession by the Benedictine monks of Selby Abbey (Yorkshire) of the fishpond 'which existed when the abbey was founded' by William I (Currie 1989, 147). This was clearly the grant of a secular fishpond to the monastery as a part of its endowment.

The quantities of fish that a monastery might require has been calculated (Currie 1989, 154, converted here to approximate metric equivalents). A monastery would have about 175 fish days a year. Each monk might be expected to consume about 200 g. at a sitting, so annual consumption would be 35 kg. a year per person. Thus a small house of ten brethren would need 350 kg. of fish a year, and a large house of forty monks would consume 1,400 kg., to which must be added the consumption by guests and their entourages, servants, and alms for the poor. As the content of fishponds would be of the order of 100 kg. per 500 square metres of water, and as only one fifth of this total could be harvested each year to ensure regeneration of the stock, it is clear that the ponds could only supply part of the monastery's needs. It is likely that fresh fish from fishponds were eaten on feast days, with dried and salted fish used on other occasions. Where a monastery had access to river fisheries, the availability of fresh fish was less of a problem, so fishponds could be regarded as a reserve for occasions of particularly high demand.

The earthworks of many fishpond systems have been surveyed, including those on the estates of Evesham Abbey in Worcestershire (Bond 1973; Aston and Bond 1988). There has been relatively little excavation, although the fishponds belonging to Southwick Priory (Augustinian, Hampshire) have recently been excavated. The environmental potential of the sampling of fishpond deposits has been demonstrated in the case of Owston Abbey in Leicestershire (Shackley, Hayne and Wainwright 1988). This small Augustinian house was founded before 1161 and was dissolved in 1536. It had a group of four fishponds arranged so that water would have flowed through each in sequence (figure 55). A system of breeding and cropping would have been possible. Samples from a section cut into the silt of one of the ponds provided evidence of flora, invertebrates and fish remains (mainly scales and teeth). Six species were identified – perch, rudd, bream, roach, pike and chub. All but the last were edible.

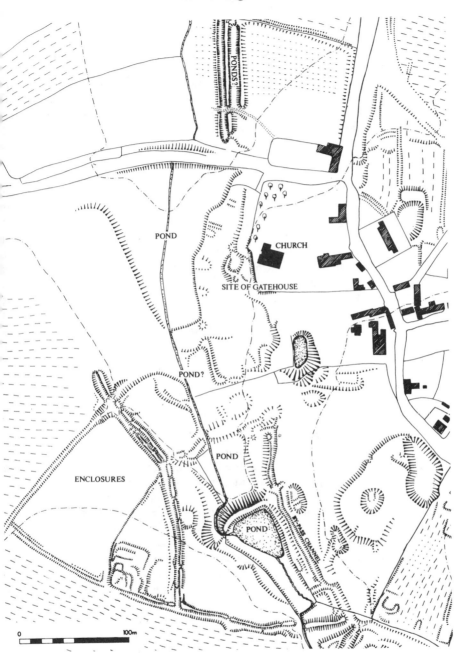

Figure 55. Plan of the fishponds, Owston Abbey, Leicestershire. The site of the monastic buildings is small compared to the area occupied by the earthworks of the fishponds, which run in a sequence along the valley. Beyond is the ridge-and-furrow of open fields, shown as dashed lines.

Drawing supplied by Leicestershire Museums.

Watermills

Wherever it was possible, monastic complexes incorporated a watermill in which grain for consumption by the community was ground. Frequently it also served as the manorial mill where tenants would have to bring their grain. The Cistercian statutes recommended that abbeys should be located where it was possible to harness a stream to power a mill, thereby reducing the amount of manual labour that the brethren would have to engage in. That at Fountains Abbey (Yorkshire) is the best surviving example in Britain (Bond 1989, 102). It is 7.16 m. wide and was originally over 30 m. long, the earliest parts predating the fire of 1147 (see Chapter 3). There were probably two undershot wheels in the basement. The building was still being used as a corn mill in 1937 (Coppack 1990, 115–17). Another mill has recently been recognised at the Benedictine abbey at Abbotsbury in Dorset (Graham 1986). It measured 17.5 m. by 5.5 m. internally and originally had two overshot wheels side by side driving two sets of stones. These were later replaced by a smaller wheel driving a single set of stones. This may have been a response to water shortages.

Byland Abbey (Cistercian, Yorkshire) had a corn mill and a fulling mill at the Dissolution. Although no trace of these has been found, there are extensive earthwork remains of the dams and ponds (McDonnell and Harrison 1978). Fulling mills harnessed water power to operate trip hammers to beat woollen cloth to remove oils from the fabric and 'felt' the cloth. At Fountains a water wheel was added to the wool house when its function changed from storage alone, to the finishing of cloth as well, in the first half of the thirteenth century (Coppack 1986). A culvert was built to take water from a stream that ran down the hillside to the building. It was originally lined with timber and sheets of lead. A sluice controlled the flow of water. The channel on the west side of the building seems to have powered a small undershot wheel that operated machinery in the building, possibly for fulling. In the late thirteenth century a massive masonry base incorporating two ashlar-lined vats was constructed. It appears to be the base of a fulling mill with hammers powered by an undershot wheel driven by water in the leat to the west (figure 56). A further change to the function of the building took place in the first half of the fourteenth century, but it continued to be the abbey's focus for wool processing. The fulling vats were partly demolished to make way for tanks and furnaces. Lead pipes fed water to coppers placed on the furnaces, and further pipes took the heated water to parts of the building including the tanks that are likely to have been used for dying wool. In the fifteenth century the building was used for metal working.

At Bordesley Abbey (Hereford and Worcester), earthworks which are the product of a complex series of water management measures cover an area of 36 ha. (Aston 1972; Rahtz and Hirst 1976). A large triangular area bounded by earthwork banks was identified as a millpond. Remains of a mill (figure 57) have been excavated at the apex of the triangular pond. It has revealed the best preserved, and earliest, evidence for water-powered metalworking in Britain (Astill 1989). The head-race had a timber framework which funnelled water on to the undershot wheel. Two sluice gates controlled the flow. The tail-race was a timber-lined channel with

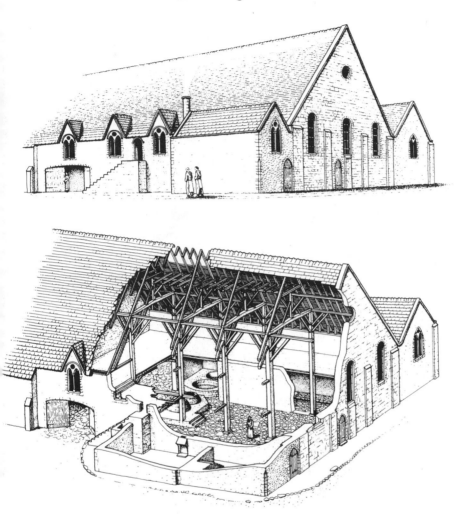

Figure 56. Reconstruction drawing of the wool house, Fountains Abbey, North Yorkshire, in the fifteenth century. The lower drawing shows the interior of the aisled building, originally built as a store for wool, adapted as a fulling mill and then for metal working.

Drawing supplied by Glyn Coppack, English Heritage.

surviving base planks 5.23 m. long. The mill building had earth-fast timbers, and hearths near the wheel pit. Gear-pegs and part of a wooden wheel that was part of the mechanism that transmitted the power to trip hammers or bellows were found. After the abandonment of the first mill (built in the late twelfth century), three other mills were constructed in sequence on the same site. In the late fourteenth century the mill was abandoned, possibly in response to the silting of the millpond. There also seems to have been a deterioration in the management of the water systems that led to widespread flooding of the precinct.

Figure 57. The excavated remains of the watermill, Bordesley Abbey. The head race is at the top: the timbers of two sets of sluice gates that directed the flow of water on to the wheel are visible embedded in the clay. The shallow wheel-pit (for an undershot wheel) is in the middle; in the foreground is the timber channel of the tail-race. The mill building stood to the right.
  Photograph supplied by Bordesley Abbey Project.

Even urban monasteries sometimes contrived to have watermills. Of the nine watermills in thirteenth-century Winchester, four served religious houses and were located in the precincts of the Cathedral, St Mary's Abbey, Hyde Abbey and St Cross Hospital (Keene 1985, 61).

Land reclamation and sea defences

The channelling of the River Arrow by Bordesley Abbey had the effect of making the valley usable for a variety of purposes. The diversion of natural watercourses was carried out by a number of monasteries. At Byland Abbey ditches were dug to drain marshland, and the headwaters of two streams were diverted along an embanked and canalised channel towards the Vale of York. The scheme may have been carried out by the Cistercian monastery in co-operation with the neighbouring Augustinian Newburgh Priory (Bond 1989, 97). The diversion of the Rye by Rievaulx Abbey has been described (Chapter 3). St Bees Priory (Cumbria) transferred water from one valley to another to create a mill leat with a greater head of water (Todd 1985).

Large monasteries had the resources to undertake major drainage enterprises that represented a long-term investment in the abbey estates. On the south bank of the River Mersey in Cheshire, St Werburgh's Abbey (Chester) engaged in drainage of marshland in co-operation with the royal manor of Frodsham. Further upstream Norton Priory brought marshland into cultivation. The rich agricultural land required protection from flooding by high tides in the estuary by means of embankments and sluices to prevent inflow of water back up the drainage ditches (Greene 1989, 31). In Lincolnshire, abbeys such as Ramsey, Spalding, Ely, Peterborough and Crowland all undertook drainage schemes. Maintenance of the drainage system was vital. In 1285 extensive flooding occurred on Ely's land as a result of the neglect of those whose duty it was to repair the banks and ditches (Taylor, 1973, 111). Glastonbury Abbey was active in the reclamation of parts of the Somerset Levels (Platt 1984, 73).

The progress of marshland drainage can be followed by landscape analysis and field survey. Drainage ditches by their nature tend to be enduring landscape features. Embankments can often be traced. It would be interesting to know more about the detail of drainage systems, such as the design and materials used in the construction of sluices. There are good chances that substantial remains of such structures survive in the waterlogged conditions of abandoned ditches and may therefore be capable of location and excavation. The examination of pollen and sediments from the Pevensey Levels in Sussex has provided information on the gains and setbacks experienced by Battle Abbey in its drainage works (Moffat 1986).

A case study: Norton Priory

Excavation at the Augustinian priory at Norton, Cheshire (Greene 1989) has shown how it was possible for a monastery to have a fully-integrated water management system. It developed in a number of stages. The temporary timber buildings of the twelfth century were provided with open drainage ditches. Within the original latrine block the drain was lined with a hollowed, half-sectioned elm trunk. Presumably its rounded profile helped to prevent the accumulation of waste. A large drain lined with unmortared, roughly-shaped stones, was built immediately to the north of the church, presumably to carry away roof water and ground water.

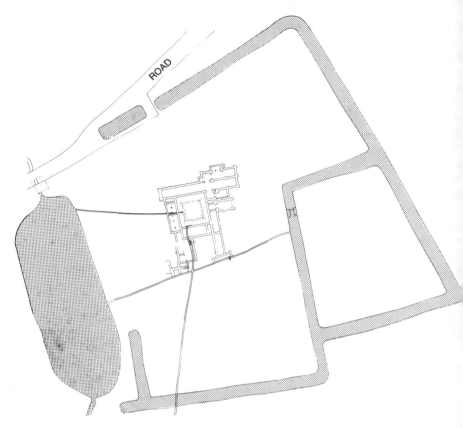

Figure 58. Plan of the water management system, Norton Priory. The monastic buildings occupy the centre of a large precinct bounded by moats, with the mill pond to the west. The monastic drain is supplied with water from the eastern moat; drinking water is piped from a spring to the south. Another drain takes water from the cloister towards the mill pond.

Drawing by Patrick Greene, reproduced by permission of Norton Priory Museum Trust.

At the end of the twelfth century a permanent drainage system was installed as part of the general building campaigns of the fast-expanding priory. By the late thirteenth century (possibly earlier), all the elements were in place (figure 58). The priory was surrounded by an extensive system of moats. They have been located by a combination of map evidence, geophysical survey and excavation. They measured 8 m. to 10 m. wide and 2 m. deep and defined the precinct on the south, east and part of its northern side. The remainder of the northern boundary was protected by a wall in which the outer gatehouse was set. On the west was a very large millpond. Water entered the system from springs at the south-east corner. The south-eastern portion of the precinct was separated from the remainder by a return of the boundary moat. On the western side of the inner moat, a stanks system was found. It consisted of two masonry abutments which narrowed the moat. They incorporated a slot into which large timbers could be fitted, forming a dam. Water backed up behind the dam to a level at which it would flow down the main monastic drain, which took all its supply from the moat. Presumably a timber dam was preferred because it could be dismantled periodically to drain the moat for maintenance. The abutments also supported a bridge which gave access to the inner moated area. A horizontal timber with mortise holes provided a base for the central supports of the bridge. The area reached by the bridge may have been the 'Infirmary Orchard' referred to in the sixteenth century.

The main drain comprised a flagstone base with ashlar sides and slab top, set in a trench cut through the boulder clay. The frame of a wooden sluice gate was set into the masonry of the drain immediately before it entered the latrine building, to perform the flushing function referred to earlier. The excavation revealed evidence of two distinct phases in the part of the drain that emerged from the latrines. Originally it had continued with a flat base and vertical sides. In the fourteenth century a new drain structure was built on a slightly different alignment. This had base-blocks of sandstone cut to a semi-circular section. The sides consisted of two courses of ashlar, above which a corbelled course supported capstones. As well as a number of minor side-drains carrying roof-water from buildings on the south side of the cloister, the kitchen drain fed into the main drain. The new drain may have been installed to counteract problems caused by a relatively small flow of water from the moat. The rounded base and increased fall of the new drain will have improved its self-scouring performance.

To the west the drain emptied into the millpond created by damming a brook. Excess water from the moats flowed into the pond. An eighteenth-century drawing shows a watermill with an undershot wheel at its northern end. It is referred to in medieval documents, and operated as a corn mill and briefly as a fulling mill.

Another drain served the cloister, which underwent a number of rebuildings. In each phase, from the thirteenth century, water was collected in a drain which lined the four sides of the cloister garden. It then flowed beneath the west range, originally continuing in an open ditch towards the millpond. A stone-lined drain was subsequently set into the ditch. The final modification to the cloister in the sixteenth century produced an elaborate arrangement of projecting bays, with the drain becoming a 'water feature'.

Water supply to the priory came from springs to the south, carried through lead pipes. There was a settling tank midway along the route of the pipework. In the kitchens, a pipe discharged into circular masonry cisterns to provide a ready supply of fresh water. The overflow led into the kitchen drain. A branch of the piped system led to the wash-basin in the south cloister walk. The outflow from the basin led through a small stone drain into the cloister drain.

The tail-race of the mill joined the brook that flowed northwards to the River Mersey. Here it passed through the reclaimed marshland, where drainage channels emptied into the brook. There must have been a sluice where it entered the river, to prevent high tides flowing through the embankment and flooding the land behind. The embankment followed the south bank of the Mersey. 'Diverse operations against the sea' were costing seven pounds a year at the time of the Dissolution. In the fourteenth and fifteenth centuries there were episodes of serious flooding which damaged the income of the priory.

The creation of a water management system on the scale of that at Norton required considerable investment. It has been calculated (Greene 1989, 35) that the moats alone would have taken a team of forty labourers three years to complete. The mill-pool dam and the embankment on the estuary would also have involved a major investment in labour. The rewards were considerable. Providing it was adequately maintained, the priory had a system that gave it a secure boundary, drainage of the surrounding area, a source of water to clean the latrines, a means of removing latrine and kitchen waste and roof water, fresh piped water supplied under pressure, a source of energy for grinding cereals, areas of water which could double as fishponds, and rich grazing and arable land where there had once been marshes. Fish-weirs on the Mersey provided an additional source of fresh fish.

Norton Priory's exploitation of water was matched by many other monastic houses. The extensive nature of the earthworks of Marton and Moxby Priories in Yorkshire, both small houses, reflects the extent of investment in water management that they were prepared to make (figures 19 and 20). The investigation of systems of monastic water management is a fruitful area for further study. Research designs need to take account of the disparate elements of systems; the opportunities presented by field survey of earthworks; the location of leats, ditches, ponds, pipe-runs, etc. by geophysical methods; aerial photography and map evidence; and excavation, including the likelihood of recovering environmentally-rich waterlogged deposits.

6 Food and drink, hospitality and health

The primary function of the inmates of a religious house may have been the work of God, but the constant round of prayer, contemplation and worship required sustenance for the body. The obligation to provide hospitality for travellers meant that guests needed to be fed. Alms for the poor were usually provided in the form of food and drink (though often these consisted of the left-overs from the refectory or the guest quarters). Many monasteries sold corrodies – agreements whereby aged persons would be accommodated within the monastery in exchange for an advance payment. The agreements usually specified the amount of bread and beer that the corrodians would receive on a daily basis. Servants living in the monastery also ate there. Even a monastery of modest size had many mouths to feed. The main source of foodstuffs for a monastery or a nunnery was its own lands. Friaries were established on the basis that the necessities of life would be obtained by begging, but this gradually became converted to the acquisition of alms in the form of money, used to purchase foodstuffs and other goods at markets. Although they did not own land, friaries often had gardens and orchards, and sometimes mills and fisheries.

Land ownership

The grants of land by benefactors, and tithes obtained directly by gift or as part of the benefits from the ownership of a parish church, provided the basis for a monastery's food supply. Rights to river fisheries, gifts of deer from hunting parks, and grants of ownership of mills were other valuable gifts that a benefactor might bestow. Surplus production could be sold to produce an income to support other activities. The efficient management of its lands and productive properties was therefore essential for the survival and growth of a monastery.

The initial grants of land by benefactors rarely came in the form of compact, easily-administered units. A founder or benefactor of the eleventh or twelfth century would be likely to possess properties scattered across many counties. Those that were most inconvenient to administer because they were small or distant were often given to monasteries as part of their endowment. Thus the landowner obtained the benefits of rationalisation whilst anticipating spiritual grace.

The consequence for a monastery was that its possessions were often at a considerable distance. This was particularly so for Augustinian and Cistercian houses; eleventh-century Benedictine establishments frequently obtained complete manors (often in the form of a confirmation of pre-Conquest monastic properties), but by the twelfth century landowners were more reluctant to part with large blocks of land. The location of a religious house could also determine the manner in which its possessions were distributed. Augustinian Nostell Priory in West Yorkshire had property in at least sixty-four villages in twelve counties ranging from the Scottish border to near London (Burrows 1985). Outside the West Riding, much of the land was in poor areas and its distance must have made effective exploitation almost impossible. Bridlington Priory, also Augustinian but on the Yorkshire coast, was in an area where there was less competition from rival monasteries for benefactors' gifts. This enabled it to develop larger and more concentrated possessions than Nostell.

Houses of the reformed orders often engaged in a gradual process of exchange, purchase, sale, rental and clearance of waste to augment holdings that might be enlarged into viable manors. Thus in the late twelfth and the thirteenth centuries, Nostell made acquisitions in the West Riding and contracted its holdings outside Yorkshire. Despite such rationalisation, the distribution of monastic properties continued to be wide. Even at the time of the Dissolution, half of the manors owned by Augustinian houses were more than 15 kilometres distant (Robinson 1980, 317). Of these, half were over 30 kilometres away from the monastery. The distribution of Augustinian-appropriated churches was very similar; the ownership of rectories usually brought with it parcels of glebe land.

The scattered nature of monastic holdings was one of the reasons why most religious houses had rented out the bulk of their lands by the fifteenth century. It was far easier to collect cash payments, and income was known in advance, thus facilitating the financial management of the monastery. The movement towards rentals had gathered pace in the latter half of the four-teenth century as the countryside suffered labour shortages as a result of the Black Death. Prior to this, much monastic land had been administered directly by the monastery. By the Dissolution this often applied to just one manor – usually that closest to the monastery.

Manors and granges

Many manors owned by monasteries were virtually indistinguishable from their lay counterparts. The abbot occupied the role of lord of the manor, with all the rights and privileges that pertained to the position. Peasants owed the same types of duties to the abbey in exchange for their land holdings as they did on secular estates. The duties included an obligation to provide services on the monastery's directly-farmed lands (known as the demesne lands).

The exploitation of demesne land was one of the characteristics of the monastic economy. Although the creation of extensive sheep runs by the Cistercians is one of the best-known examples of such enterprise, all orders of monks and canons participated in land improvement. As perpetual corporations they could take a long view of their investment in land. The drainage of marshland is one example (see Chapter 5). The clearance of waste and sometimes woodland was widely practised. Farms (often called granges) were established on demesne land. Cistercian granges were staffed

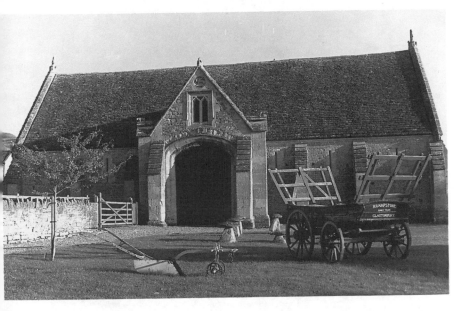

Figure 59. The north side of the Abbey Barn, Glastonbury, built in the mid
fourteenth century.
Photograph supplied by Somerset County Museums Service.

(prior to the fourteenth century) by lay brothers and labourers. Other orders
employed a steward or bailiff to manage a grange and its labourers. The
Cistercians depopulated some settlements in order to establish granges in the
early years of their isolationist fervour (Donkin 1978, 44).

A combination of documentary and archaeological study has shown the
range of buildings that was required for a grange (Platt 1969). Their scale
varied considerably. Barns on the granges of rich houses could be very large.
At Great Coxwell, a grange of Cistercian Beaulieu Abbey (Hampshire), a
magnificent barn still survives (Horn and Born 1965). It is 43.6 m. (144 ft.)
in length and 11.5 m. (38 ft.) wide internally, with a height of 14.5 m.
(48 ft.) to the ridge. The grange seems to have served as a centre for a
number of estates owned by Beaulieu. It had an oratory for the private use
of the abbot and convent, so must have had a subsidiary function as a place
of rest and recuperation. A rebuilding of the grange shortly before the
Dissolution resulted in an elaborate set of apartments – a new hall set over
a wine cellar, several adjoining chambers, one of which had a vaulted undercroft, and a chapel. Many impressive medieval barns have survived,
including those at Bradford-on-Avon (Wiltshire) which was owned by the
nuns of Sherborne in Dorset, Abbotsbury (Dorset), and Glastonbury in
Somerset (figure 59).

A thorough survey of the buildings of the grange owned by the Augustinian priory Llanthony II (Gloucestershire) at Duleek in County Meath was
carried out on 26 June 1381 (Platt 1969, 32). It provides a picture of the
components of a medium-sized grange. The buildings were arranged about

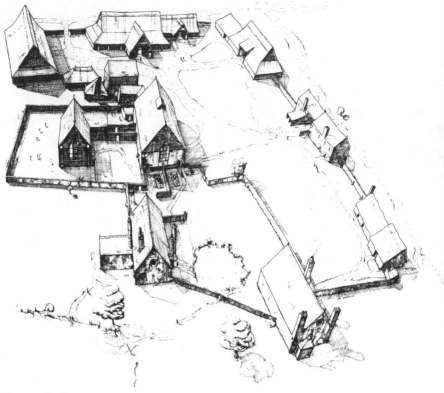

Figure 60. Reconstruction drawing of the complex of buildings at South Witham Templar preceptory, Lincolnshire.
Drawing by Jake Goodband supplied by Philip Mayes and English Heritage.

a large court, flanked by gardens and a stream. On the east were the chapel, great hall, a kitchen, a thatched dairy, a tile-roofed stable, a long chamber with a latrine and the 'knight's chamber' – both on undercrofts, one of which was a pantry for bread and ale, the other a larder. On the south was a bakery and a brewhouse with a malt loft. Next to these were a small threshing-barn, a trough for preparing the malt, and another bakehouse with a pigsty at one end. In the south-west corner was a stone gatehouse with a thatched chamber above. As well as the gatehouse, the west range comprised a tiled granary over a pigsty and a long, thatched ox-house, used for bullocks and cows. The north side of the court was lined with a sheep-house, a long, thatched stable, a stone gatehouse with an upper chamber, a guest chamber above the gate-keeper's lodge, and a stone wall linked the the kitchens at the west end of the hall. Nearby were two dovecotes, a watermill, and a shed to store wheat and hay.

Duleek corresponds with the components of many other granges for which records and occasionally buildings exist. The excavation of the Templar preceptory at South Witham (Mayes forthcoming) uncovered a complex of buildings which was both a religious house and a grange (figure 60). The

Figure 61. Excavated remains of one of the South Witham barns, with the foundations of the walls and of the aisle posts clearly visible, and a cobbled area outside the large entrance in the side wall.

Photograph supplied by Philip Mayes and English Heritage.

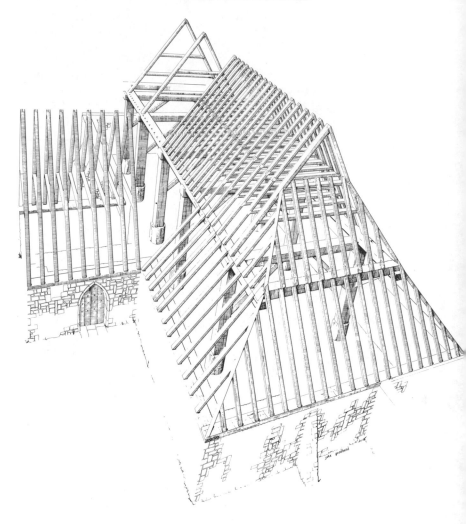

Figure 62. Reconstruction drawing of one of the South Witham barns showing how the timber roof could have been supported by the masonry walls and wooden aisle posts.

Drawing by Jake Goodband supplied by Philip Mayes and English Heritage.

complex grew from a first phase comprising an aisled hall, two small ancillary buildings, and a watermill which formed part of the donation to the Templars at the end of the twelfth century. Between about 1220 and 1240, the preceptory was enlarged by the replacement of all the first-phase buildings except the mill. The core consisted of a chapel, greater hall, lesser hall and kitchens. Arranged around the courtyard were a granary, five other barns, a workshop, a blacksmith's shop, a forge, animal houses, a brewhouse and dairy, and gatehouses. Figure 61 is a photograph of one of the barns, and figure 62 is a reconstruction of its possible appearance based on the evidence of the excavation.

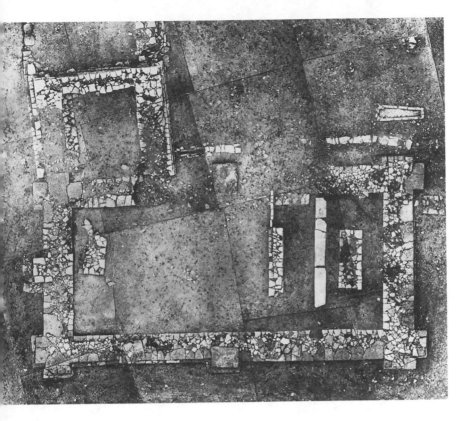

Figure 63. The chapel, South Witham preceptory. In the rectangular building the altar can be seen within a chancel at its eastern end.
Photograph supplied by Philip Mayes and English Heritage.

The chapel measured 12.8 m. by 5.0 m. internally; it was built of limestone blocks, and both the chancel step and the altar base survived (figure 63). A number of burials were excavated outside the chapel. The site declined later in the thirteenth century, and South Witham may have ceased to be a preceptory by the time the Templars were arrested in 1308 and suppressed four years later. South Witham, although a religious house in which the seven services of Divine Office would have been celebrated by the brothers in the chapel every day, was in essence a grange, and similar buildings are likely to be found on other grange sites.

The remains of Monknash Grange (South Glamorgan) are impressive (figures 64 and 65). The grange, which was the property of Neath Abbey, was 310 ha. (840 acres) in extent, with the buildings enclosed in a polygonal earthwork enclosure 8 ha. (20 acres) in area (Williams 1990). Remains of the granary, 64 m. (211 ft.) long, still survive, as does the dovecote. There was a grange chapel, three watermills and a windmill on the estate.

The range of buildings that might be found on a grange is also similar to

Figure 64. Aerial photograph of the site of Monknash Grange, South Glamorgan. The enclosure is bounded by roads and earthworks; the dovecote casts a long shadow towards the centre, and the remains of a barn can be seen near the lower road.

Reproduced with permission of the Cambridge University Collection of Air Photographs.

those found in many monasteries' outer courtyards, which often performed the role of a home farm. For rural monasteries, agriculture and religion were close neighbours. That continued to be the case right up to the Dissolution, as Augmentations Office surveys demonstrate. The layout of the precinct of Rievaulx Abbey (Yorkshire) has been reconstructed on the basis of such a survey (Coppack 1986). Saighton Grange, Cheshire (figure 66) is an example of a grange that also functioned as a rural retreat for the abbot.

In addition to granges, other buildings were needed for specialised functions on demesne lands. Out-stations included *vaccaria* (cattle ranches), *bercaria* (sheep ranches) and mineral-working complexes (Moorhouse 1989).

Figure 65. Plan of the surface remains of Monknash Grange. Rectangular platforms to the north of the dovecote mark the sites of buildings. Two lines of boundary earthworks define the north and west sides of the enclosure.

Drawing supplied by the Royal Commission on Ancient and Historical Monuments in Wales, Crown Copyright.

Large expanses of grazing land were mainly in upland areas, but low-lying marshland was also used. A combination of changes to the climate and agricultural practices has left upland relatively unaffected by later development. There is, therefore, considerable potential for archaeological fieldwork to study the remains of monastic activities in these areas, combined with the study of documents, maps and aerial photographs. A deserted site

Figure 66. Saighton Grange, Cheshire: the gatehouse of the Abbot of Chester's manor, built in the late fifteenth century on a site that had been in monastic ownership from before the Conquest. The splendour of the structure shows that monastic granges could have other functions than agriculture; in this case the complex was more akin to a country house.

Photograph by Patrick Greene.

Figure 67. The excavation of the farmhouse, Roystone Grange, Derbyshire.
Photograph by the Peak National Park photographer, Ray Manley.

that has been the subject of detailed drawn survey is on Abbot Hills above
Malham, North Yorkshire, once owned by the Augustinian canons of Bolton
Priory (Abramson 1987). Another, on Levisham Moor in North Yorkshire,
belonged to the Gilbertine canons of Malton Priory (Moorhouse 1986). Sites
of buildings, enclosures and boundary systems are complex and extensive.
They are also likely to have undergone numerous changes over several
centuries of occupation.

It was possible to trace the grange boundary in the form of a wall of
Grange near Ashbourne in Derbyshire, however, has formed part of an
extensive study of the evolution of the landscape from its prehistoric roots
(Hodges, Poulter and Wildgoose 1982; Wildgoose 1987; Hodges 1991). The
grange belonged to Garendon Abbey (Leicestershire), which was founded as
a daughter of the first English Cistercian house, Waverley, in 1133. Records
of the grange occur from the early thirteenth century. Sheep farming was the
predominant activity, with a capacity to graze 720 animals. Three major
buildings constituting a manorial complex were located in a valley bottom.
The largest, which measured 20 m. across with finely-coursed masonry and
a carved stone entrance, must have been the grange farmhouse (figure 67).
Analysis of the thousand sherds of pottery showed that the majority were
from jugs, with few cooking pots represented, confirming the high status of
the site.

It was possible to trace the grange boundary in the form of a wall of
limestone boulders enclosing an area of 154 hectares (figure 68). Medieval
sheep pens were identified, also with boulder walls. They came to light as

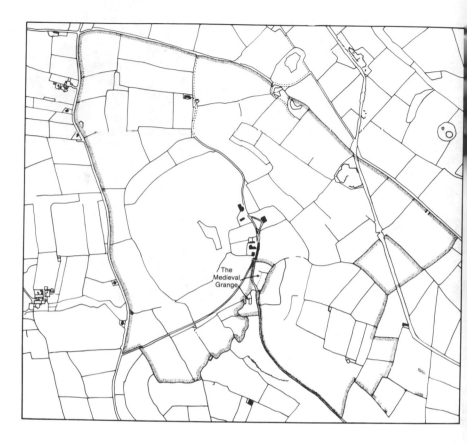

Figure 68. The boundaries of Roystone Grange, shown with a stippled outline. Drawing by Richard Hodges supplied by the Peak National Park.

a result of a complete survey of 60 km. of field boundaries in the valley (Wildgoose 1987). A sequence was worked out on the basis of method of construction, details of intersections and other factors.

Monasteries required specialised buildings for the trade in wool. The need for regional studies, rather than a concentration on the practices of an individual monastery, and an awareness of different practices between orders, has been stressed (Moorhouse 1989, 49). Whereas the Gilbertines collected their wool at their priories, Cistercian houses established collecting centres near to areas of production. The sites of wool-houses may be located, and also drove-roads used to move flocks between grazing lands. Where a grange was fragmented, a monastery had to negotiate with neighbouring landowners rights-of-way between the various parcels of land in order for livestock or crops to be moved.

Fish production on monastic estates

The construction of fishponds as part of the management of water by monasteries was described in Chapter 5. Where a source of fish was at a distance from the monastery, at a lake or a river fishery, means were needed to preserve the catch. Buildings for the collection and processing of fish were established on some monastic estates. The Abbot of Glastonbury's fish-house at Mere in Somerset is a well-preserved example. A combined fish-smoking house and equipment store was excavated next to one of the large fishponds belonging to Byland Abbey in Yorkshire (Kemp 1984). A large number of weights for nets, some made of baked clay and others of lead, were found.

Mills

Watermills used for grinding corn, fulling cloth, and metal-working were features of many monastic estates (Chapter 5). Grinding corn, as a manorial monopoly, was also a useful source of revenue, so mills might feature in a monastery's endowment even in places where it possessed no land. Often they were leased to provide a money income. Windmills were built on monastic estates. Whereas the sites of watermills can often be found relatively easily by examining water-courses for traces of leats and dams, windmills can prove more elusive. Place-name evidence can help, especially as many windmills continued to function on the same site after the Dissolution. Sites will often be found on the crests of hills or on slopes facing the prevailing wind. They may appear on aerial photographs as soil or crop-marks with the characteristic 'hot cross bun' appearance of a circular area (the mound) containing a cross left by the positions of the post-mill's horizontal anchoring timbers.

Mineral extraction

Monasteries did not only use their lands for agricultural production. In Chapter 3 the opening of quarries to produce building stone was described. Where chalk or limestone occurred on a monastery's lands, it could be burnt in kilns to make lime for mortar. Sand was also required for mortar and this might be found on the estates, for example in pockets within alluvial clay, or obtained from estuaries and coastlines. Geological examination of mortars can help to identify the likely sources.

Other types of minerals might also be exploited. Furness Abbey in Cumbria was in receipt of grants which imply that it was engaged in water-powered iron-working as early as 1160. Although iron was important to Furness, its wealth came primarily from the production of wool on its sixteen granges with their extensive upland grazing lands. The wool was transported by land and water, using a series of staging posts, to Boston in Lincolnshire for export to the Continent (Donkin 1978, 142).

Iron-working required more than deposits of ore. Grants from benefactors were designed to provide other necessities such as furnace and forge sites, woodland for the production of charcoal, and rights-of-way (Moorhouse 1989, 51). For archaeologists investigating monastic iron-working sites, as with other forms of mineral extraction such as quarrying and coal mining, post-medieval activity often obscures or has removed evidence. One example of this is Bentley Grange in Yorkshire, where Byland Abbey was involved in iron-working from the thirteenth century. An area covered by heaps of spoil surrounding shafts made a dramatic subject for an aerial photograph taken in 1953 (Beresford and St Joseph 1979, 257). Recent excavation in advance of the laying of a pipeline produced late-sixteenth-century pottery beneath one of the mounds, which must therefore belong to the phase of mining which took place in the 1580s (Moorhouse 1989, 52). Beneath the mounds, however, are remains of ridge-and-furrow and other medieval earthwork, which relate to the iron-working grange. Medieval coal mining has left traces of its activities, also in the form of shafts and spoil, but as with iron mining, its study is complicated by later extraction.

Salt

Salt production was carried out extensively on coastal sites. Holm Cultram, a Cistercian abbey in Cumbria, had salt pans on both sides of the Solway estuary (Donkin 1979, 120). The extraction of salt from brine springs took place in Northwich and Nantwich in Cheshire and Droitwich in Worcestershire. Monasteries often owned salt works in these towns – for example, the Cheshire houses of Combermere, Vale Royal, Norton and Chester. A salt works which revealed detailed evidence of medieval practices has been excavated in Nantwich (McNeil 1983).

Wood

Woodland was an important resource in the medieval landscape. It was managed to supply many needs. Coppicing of hazel and pollarding of willows provided a crop of wood on a cycle of production, for making charcoal and as wattles for use as building materials and in hurdles (Rackham 1976). The need for timbers for construction of monastic buildings, mills, weirs, etc. might be met from a monastery's own lands, but frequently gifts of trees were made by benefactors. Often the trees were taken from woodland that formed a deer park owned by the Crown or by a magnate. In 1269 Furness Abbey was granted ten oaks annually from royal forests for the construction and repair of one of its granges (Donkin 1969, 124). The Abbey of St Thomas the Martyr, near Dublin, was given twenty oaks from the forest of Glencree by Edward I to reconstruct buildings 'lately burnt down by misfortune' (Elliott 1990, 63). These are typical of grants that benefited many religious houses. Other forest products could be the subject of grant. Holm Cultram Abbey was entitled to take bark from the forest of Inglewood for use in tanning. It was also allowed to establish a vaccary for forty cows and a horse pen with rights of grazing in Inglewood (Donkin 1969, 133). Rights that enabled a monastery to send its pigs into the woods

f neighbouring landowners to forage for acorns and mast feature in many
harters.

Food in the monastery

The sources of information on monastic diet are varied. The rules and
observances of religious orders provide some information on dietary regulations. Documentary evidence includes cellarers' accounts and manorial
records. The strictures that followed visitations that found shortcomings
can reveal the nature of the departure from expected standards. Excavation
can provide evidence drawn from a range of food remains. The examination of the excavated skeletons of the inmates of a religious house can
produce information on the health, and some of the effects of diet, on
individuals.

Strict adherence to the Rule of St Benedict by the Cistercians meant that
consumption of flesh-meat was prohibited except to the sick in the infirmary
until the fourteenth century. Gradual departures from such firm regulation
extended meat-eating in the infirmary to monks who were not infirm, to the
abbot's lodgings, and eventually, in some monasteries, to the 'misericord', a
room adjoining the refectory in which meat might be eaten. In contrast, the
Augustinians took a more relaxed view of meat-eating. Their regulations
were more concerned to identify days on which it was banned. Regulation
of diet was not therefore a simple matter about which generalisations can be
made, for it varied between orders and over time.

The extent to which the diet of a religious house might depart from the
original regulations is illustrated by Cistercian Whalley Abbey (Lancashire).
The ascetic ideals of the twelfth century stand in stark contrast to the
sixteenth-century situation in which two-thirds of Whalley's considerable
income was being expended on food and drink – £640 out of a total income
of £895 in 1520 (Ashmore 1962). There were about twenty monks to feed,
with about forty servants, twenty members of the abbot's household and
twenty-four old men who were accommodated as a charitable deed. In addition, there were guests to entertain. The biggest items in the accounts were
staples such as wheat and barley malt. Meat included beef, mutton, veal,
pork, young pigs, lamb, wild geese and fowl, red and white herrings, dried
and salted fish and eels, and sturgeon. Wine was purchased in quantity, and
exotic items included figs, raisins, currants, almonds, pepper, saffron,
ginger, nuts, rice, nutmeg, spices, cloves, liquorice, cinnamon, dates, olive
oil, cakes, treacle, sugar and sugar-candy.

The members of a monastic community took their meals in the refectory,
which was almost always located on the side of the cloister opposite the
church. In the case of most orders its long axis ran parallel to the side of
the cloister. In Cistercian abbeys the refectory was often built with a north–
south axis in consequence of the extra space required by the presence of lay
brothers in the west range, although in their earliest form the refectory might
have the standard east–west orientation. From the fourteenth century, when
lay brothers no longer featured in Cistercian houses, new and rebuilt refectories were sometimes constructed in the same way as other orders.

Refectories were usually placed above an undercroft, but sometimes they took the form of a ground-floor hall. It has been suggested that the placing of the refectory on the upper floor was symbolic of the room in which the Last Supper took place. If so, its significance was not so strong as to make the planning of refectories on the ground floor untenable.

In all orders, the favoured position of the kitchens was in the corner next to the refectory and the west range. Foodstuffs could be brought into the outer courtyard to be stored on the ground floor of the west range, and then the stores could be drawn on as required by the kitchen staff under the watchful eye of the cellarer. Cooked dishes were passed through a serving hatch into the refectory (and in the case of Cistercian houses, the lay brothers could also be supplied from the same kitchens). Likewise bread, eggs and other foods produced on a daily basis in the buildings of the outer courtyard could be taken into the kitchens for preparation and serving. The kitchens might also prepare meals for the guest quarters and for corrodians. Cooked foods could therefore be taken across the outer courtyard to supply the guesthouse and corrodians' lodgings. The kitchens of St Gregory's Priory in Canterbury contained a large bread oven in the west corner, a central oven built of limestone blocks, and a work area to the east (Hicks and Tatton-Brown 1991, 103).

Within the refectory, the internal arrangements and the manner of taking meals differed little between orders. The abbot, abbess or prior sat on a raised dais at one end of the hall, sometimes accompanied by officers of the monastery or important guests. The other inmates sat at long tables in the body of the hall. Silence was obligatory, and regulations such as the Barnwell Observances (Clark 1897) specify how, for example, salt was to be requested without speaking, as well as many other matters of manners and etiquette. During meals, one member of the community would read aloud from a pulpit passages of the scriptures. The pulpit was usually incorporated in the side wall of the refectory towards the dais end.

In Carthusian monasteries, instead of the brethren gathering in a refectory, they took most of their meals in their cells, each of which had a serving hatch facing on to the cloister walk through which food could be passed. The supply of water to individual cells allowed the monks to wash their hands before meals – an adaptation of the standard pattern in which monks were obliged to wash at the basin in the cloister before entering the refectory (see Chapter 5).

Vessels

The preparation and serving of food on such a highly organised and standardised basis has left its mark in the archaeological record. Compared to secular occupation sites, fragments of ceramic cooking pots are underrepresented at monasteries, presumably because institutional catering required large metal cauldrons. Fragments of ceramic jugs, however, are very common, from tripod pitchers of the eleventh and twelfth centuries to glazed and decorated jugs of later centuries. This corresponds closely to the injunctions, in documents such as the Barnwell Observances, to those responsible

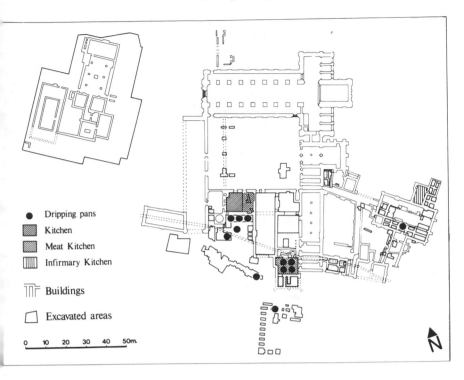

● Dripping pans

▨ Kitchen

▧ Meat Kitchen

▥ Infirmary Kitchen

〒〒 Buildings

◻ Excavated areas

0 10 20 30 40 50m.

Figure 69. Find-spots of dripping-pan fragments, Kirkstall Abbey, all found close to the buildings in which they were used.
Plan supplied by West Yorkshire Archaeology Service.

for laying the refectory tables to ensure the provision of jugs of beer. Wine featured in feast-days, and the common discovery of jugs with polychrome birds, foliage and shields from the Saintonge region of western France testifies to its widespread consumption in monastic refectories. Staves from wine casks and barrels are also sometimes found in waterlogged deposits on monastic sites. Some monasteries in southern England had their own vineyards, such as the ones shown on the water-supply plan of Canterbury Cathedral (Chapter 5). However, the climatic deterioration that occurred in the fourteenth century may have depressed average temperatures below the level required for viniculture (Lamb 1966).

In the late fifteenth and early sixteenth centuries, another range of pottery vessels makes its appearance on monastic sites. Drinking vessels, the designs of which often imitate their metal precursors, are found in a number of regional fabric-types and styles. In the north of England they have characteristically a thick, dark brown or black glossy glaze, sometimes with decoration in the form of applied white clay. Confusingly, this type of pottery is often given the name 'Cistercian Ware' but although it is found on the sites of monasteries of that order, it is certainly not peculiar to them, and indeed it was made in largest quantities after the Dissolution. Imported stoneware pottery found on many monastic sites includes both jugs and drinking vessels from Langerwehe, Sieburg and Raeren.

The nature of a monastic site, with the clear functional distinctions of the different parts of the complex, results in an uneven distribution of fragments of ceramic vessels. The site of the church, dormitory range and cloister may prove on excavation to be virtually aceramic, with the kitchens as the focus of the greatest density of ceramic material. There can be a close correlation between the find-spots of vessels with specialised functions and the buildings in which they were used. For example, pottery dripping-pan fragments found at Kirkstall Abbey (Cistercian, Yorkshire) were found in close proximity to the three kitchens on the site – the main kitchen, the meat kitchen and the infirmary kitchen (Moorhouse and Wrathmell 1987, 107) (figure 69). Similarly, globular vessels known as 'Jordans' were used as urinals, and are most frequently found in the area of the latrines and dormitory. It follows therefore, that specialised pottery types can assist in the identification of the functions of buildings.

On a large, stratigraphically complex site such as a monastery, the matching of fragments of the same vessel from a number of locations can suggest relationships between archaeological contexts that may be spatially separate. Providing such linkages can contribute to the construction of an overall sequence of the events that have left their mark on the stratigraphical record. However, other difficulties remain in getting an overall picture of pottery use on a site, as survivals tend to be fragments casually discarded, or otherwise deliberately dumped into disused features such as cisterns or drains. Most pottery was doubtless removed from the site, along with other rubbish, and spread on gardens and fields.

Other types of food vessel may also be found. Waterlogged conditions, through the exclusion of oxygen, can result in the survival of wooden vessels. Lathe-turned bowls are frequently found, and platters less commonly. These are doubtless the kind of bowls that are referred to in the Barnwell Observances as the receptacles for fruit. Each monk or canon would carry his own knife and whetstone attached to his belt. Knives are sometimes found on monastic sites, and pendant whetstones are common. Metal vessels are underrepresented because they had scrap value, but were doubtless common articles especially in the richer monasteries.

Other objects found on monastic sites that were used in the provision of food and drink include hand-mills for grinding grain and strainers for skimming froth off beer and other liquids. Another type of object probably associated with refectories is an open panel of lead measuring about 150 mm. square, or strips about 70 mm. wide. They were cast with attractive geometric or foliage details. The most likely explanation of their function is that they were incorporated into refectory windows as a means of ventilation and the removal of the smell of food.

Details of the day-to-day diet of a monastery is hard to come by as documentation is inevitably limited, and may not in any case reflect changes in diet over time. Excavation is capable of providing an additional source of information of a very different nature through the recovery of food remains. Those that are capable of survival include grains, seeds, fruit pips and stones, mammal and bird bones, and fish bones and scales. In addition, pollen grains can provide information on types of plants growing in the locality.

One of the first scientific studies of animal bones from a monastic site examined remains from Cistercian Kirkstall Abbey, Yorkshire (Ryder, 1958, 1959, 1960; summarised in Moorhouse and Wrathmell 1987, 39 and 152). Immediately outside the meat kitchen, a dump of bones represented about 5,000 animals. The meat kitchen had been built in the fifteenth century to supply the misericord which had been created on the ground floor of the refectory building. Most of the bones had been chopped, but some were apparently sawn. Ox bones predominated, mainly from old animals, and there were also pigs, sheep, fowl; red, roe and fallow deer, wild duck, rabbit, fish and shellfish. As this kitchen was established specifically to supply food to the misericord, there can be no doubt that the sample reflects patterns of consumption by the monks in the half-century prior to the Dissolution. It is not always so certain who the consumers of food remains on monastic sites actually were. Where a kitchen supplied guest quarters as well as the refectory, the remains will result from a wider population than the monks alone. It would be wrong, therefore, to infer from the presence of animal bones in deposits relating to phases when meat-eating was prohibited that the regulations were being flouted. It could simply be a case of the monks not inflicting on their guests the restrictions to which they themselves were subject.

At Norton Priory (Augustinian, Cheshire), two substantial groups of animal bones were examined, one from the later part of the monastic occupation of the site and the other from the post-Dissolution manor house in the sixteenth and seventeenth centuries (Greene 1989, 49–54). The fish eaten at the priory included cod, oysters, mussels, and cockles, and bird bones from fowl, geese, mallard, teal, wood pigeon, rook, jackdaw and woodcock were found. In terms of numbers of individual animals, the distribution between sheep, cattle and pigs was 47, 30 and 23 per cent respectively. The majority of sheep were slaughtered when aged two or three years, with the large number of tibiae and humeri indicating a preference for legs of mutton. In terms of meat yield, cattle accounted for 68 per cent of the meat eaten. Most were killed when aged four years or over, but veterinary evidence showed that they were not worn-out draught animals (which would be expected to show severe arthritis in about 30 per cent of a sample). Shoulder, fore-leg, rump and hind-leg cuts were consumed in preference to inferior joints. There was remarkable continuity between the pre- and post-Dissolution groups in terms of predominance of cattle meat (93 per cent after the Dissolution), the types of joints selected, and the average age of slaughter. Spanning from medieval to post-medieval cattle was a minor, non-pathological congenital abnormality at a significant level. Not only did the Tudor owners of the priory have a diet similar to that of the medieval occupants of Norton, but it seems that the herds of cattle continued to be drawn from the same stock.

The Norton canons had a preference for young and sucking pigs – most bones were from animals killed in their first or second years. Bones from fallow and red deer were doubtless the result of the annual grant of two animals each year at the Feast of the Assumption from the neighbouring deer

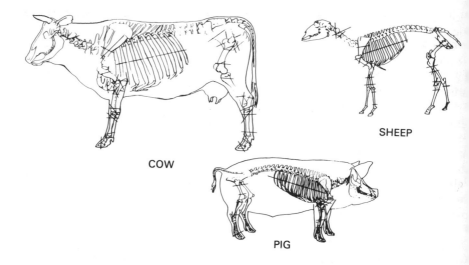

SHEEP

COW

PIG

Figure 70. Main butchery points of animals eaten at the Chester Dominican Friary. The lines represent the principal cuts to the carcasses, as shown by the examination of excavated bones.
Drawing supplied by City of Chester Cultural Services.

park of the Baron of Halton. Only three horse bones were found, consistent with a general pattern of aversion to the eating of horse-flesh amongst the higher social classes. Rabbits and hares were surprisingly rare, as the existence of a warren on the priory lands is known from place-name evidence. The bones of hares were amongst the remains of animals found in the excavation of the Dominican Friary at Chester (Ward 1990 178–90). As at Norton, cattle provided by far the biggest proportion of the meat eaten at the friary, in a county where cattle-rearing has always predominated. Study of the Chester bones revealed information on the butchery practices (figure 70).

The recovery of tiny bones from rabbits, rodents and birds is a particular challenge to excavators. Fish bones and scales are similarly difficult to recognise by conventional means during the course of excavation. Special techniques have been developed to ensure that a more representative sample can be obtained for study (Jones 1989). Since the mid-1970s, selective sieving has been introduced on some sites, and a much more accurate series of samples of biological remains has been recovered. The most promising deposits to sample are those which are known to be rubbish from kitchens. Fish bones, as well as seeds of fruit, fragments of bran, and eggs of parasites, can survive in human excrement, so latrine deposits may be worthy of study. Fishponds may also yield small quantities of bones which can show the species with which they were stocked (Shackley, Hayne and Wainwright 1988).

The range of fish enjoyed by the Benedictine monks of Westminster Abbey in the twelfth century has been shown by the analysis of deposits from the misericord (Jones 1976). More than twenty species were identified, including sole, plaice, flounder, gurnard, mackerel, bass, ling, haddock, cod, whiting, conger eel, common eel, cyprinids (i.e. fresh water fish such as chub and roach), pike, herring, shad, thorn-back ray, sturgeon, John Dory and turbot. The Augustinian Friars at Leicester ate at least eleven kinds of fish, of which nine were marine; they must have been brought either dried or salted to this inland site (Thawley 1981).

There is great potential for increasing knowledge of monastic diet and health through rigorous programmes of sampling on future excavations. There also needs to be thorough recovery of material from closely-dated deposits in order to understand differences over time and between orders. The potential is illustrated by the analysis of bones recovered from a well in the garden of the London Greyfriars dated to the period 1480–1500 (Armitage and West 1985). The Friars-minor moved to the site in 1225 and established the large garden to the east of the church. 4,939 fragments and complete bones of large mammals were recovered, of which 1,638 were capable of recognition. In terms of meat yield, cattle exceeded sheep, and pigs were comparatively rare. There were small numbers of fallow deer and rabbit bones. The forty-one bird bones included fowl, goose, rock-dove, robin, skylark, song- and mistle-thrushes, ringed plover, grey plover, snipe, jackdaw, green sandpiper and garden warbler. The fish bones included common eel, conger eel, herring, sprat, smelt, dace, roach, cod, haddock, whiting, hake, gurnard and plaice. The nature of the garden was revealed by a study of the bones of small mammals and amphibians that had fallen into the well. By identifying the niche-requirements of different species, a rich variety of habitats was revealed, including grassland, water-filled ditches or ponds, and scrub. The Greyfriars' garden was clearly not the carefully-tended haven that the concept of the monastic garden brings to mind.

Botanical remains

Under suitable conditions a great range of botanical material can survive on a monastic site. This is particularly true of waterlogged deposits which, given the siting of monasteries near sources of water and with the invariable presence of drains and ditches, will usually be present. The potential of the microscopic remains of plants has been illustrated by a study carried out at the Augustinian priory of Jedburgh in the Borders Region by Dr Brian Moffat. A nearby Observant friary was also examined. Samples were obtained from ditches and pits which had contained sewage. A heavy presence of pollen from the plant tormantil, of the species *Potentilla*, suggests its use in combatting infestation of whipworm in animals and humans. The pollen had probably been carried into the body adhering to fragments of the plant, including flower heads, used as an astringent. Another study by Dr Moffat concerned a sample of organic material from a pit at Waltham Abbey, the Augustinian house in Essex. Of 486 seeds and fruits in the sample, all but seven were from hemlock (31) and black henbane (448). Both plants are poisonous, and their growth as wild plants in the monastic precinct where they might be eaten by grazing animals is unlikely. However, they were cultivated in medieval gardens for medical purposes, and both feature in herbals that would have been found in monastic libraries. They were used in preparations intended to be anaesthetic and analgesic, but with warnings of the risks involved in using such poisonous plants. Alternatively, the seeds may have been incorporated in a poultice.

Guesthouses

One of the duties of a monastic house was the provision of accommodation for travellers. For monastic houses on well-used routes, the burden could be considerable. Birkenhead Priory, a small and relatively poor Benedictine house on the banks of the River Mersey close to the ferry-crossing, found itself used with such frequency by travellers that it had to ask to be spared some of its obligations for hospitality. Indeed, the monks were licensed by the Crown in 1317 to build lodgings near the ferry and to sell food to passengers (Kettle 1980, 129).

Two comprehensive excavations of guesthouses have recently been undertaken. Both are on the sites of Cistercian houses, Kirkstall in Yorkshire (Wrathmell 1987) and Tintern in Gwent (Courtney 1989). The first guesthouse at Kirkstall was built in the early years of the thirteenth century. It consisted of an aisled hall of five bays, with a partition enclosing the northern bay to form chambers, and the southernmost bay built as services. Nearby were a bakehouse and a kitchen. Over three centuries the guesthouse underwent a series of modifications, including the construction of a subsidiary hall to the west. Both halls had hearths in the centre; smoke from fires would have escaped through louvres set in the ridge of the roof of each building. The main hall would have been used by prominent guests such as the abbey's benefactors and even royalty with their extensive retinues of courtiers and servants (who probably slept in the lesser hall). The main hall was similar in its facilities to a substantial manor house. In its final form (figures 71 and 72) it consisted of the chamber block of two storeys at the north end, with latrines supplied with running water and drainage; the main hall occupying the central portion of the building; and services on the south with yard, scullery, bakehouse and kitchens. The lesser hall was converted into a smithy and stables. The complex was provided with a piped water supply (see Chapter 5). The main hall had a brief interruption to its normal function when it was used as the site for casting a bell in the fifteenth century. The casting pit was dug where the hearth was usually placed.

At Tintern Abbey, similar facilities for guests were built in the thirteenth century. Like those at Kirkstall, they underwent a series of modifications over three centuries. At the heart of the complex, which was situated on the outer courtyard due west of the church, was an aisled hall. It was of four bays, the northernmost of which was divided off with a narrow cross-wall with a central door to form the service bay containing the buttery and pantry. The central hearth consisted of a pair of millstones set in the floor. A building to the north with flagged floors, and platforms which showed the effects of heat, may have been a brewhouse. The west range was of two

Figure 71. Excavation of the guesthouse, Kirkstall Abbey, looking south. In the foreground is the chamber block, with the latrine (see figure 54) and the main drain on the right. In the middle is the hall, with supports for the aisle posts and a central hearth. Beyond is the complex of service buildings, including kitchens, bakehouse and scullery.

Drawing supplied by West Yorkshire Archaeology Service.

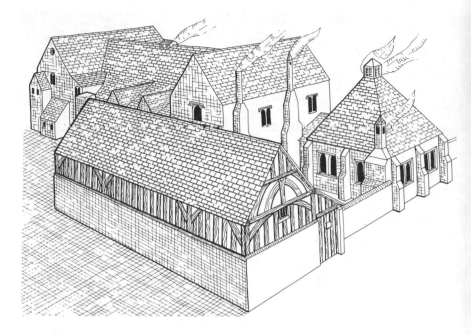

Figure 72. Reconstruction drawing of the guesthouse, Kirkstall Abbey, in its final form in the fifteenth century. The building in the foreground served as stables and a smithy. The kitchens are to the right. Beyond is the great hall with the chamber block at the far end.
Drawing supplied by West Yorkshire Archaeology Service.

phases, the first of which was associated with smithing activities. The second phase was a rebuilding with more massive walls. The two-storey building had a chimney stack serving a fireplace on the upper floor, and two latrines linked to a drain. It probably contained chambers.

The hall eventually went out of use as guest quarters. A series of bowl hearths were found cut into the floor. They may have been used in the process of cupellation – the extraction of silver from lead. Another may have been used for melting copper-alloy scrap. In the south-east corner of the hall was a kiln-like structure that had been used for casting a bell (see Chapter 3). In its final phase, after the period of industrial use, the site of the hall seems to have become an open courtyard.

The two guesthouses at Kirkstall and Tintern show similarities of plan in their early phases but subsequent diverging histories under the influence of local circumstances. The presence of metal-working, and particularly bell-casting, on both sites is a surprising development in this location. The abbeys would have retained an obligation to provide hospitality, so at Tintern guests must have been accommodated elsewhere. Possible locations might be the upper floor of the west range where lay brothers had originally been housed, or in an annexe to the abbot's house. The provision of chambers for guests formed part of the changes at Valle Crucis Abbey

Figure 73. Part of the outer courtyard of Thornholme Priory, Lincolnshire, including the porter's lodge attached to the gatehouse and the precinct wall in the foreground, seen from the north.
    Photograph supplied by Glyn Coppack, English Heritage.

(Clwyd) in which the upper floor of the east range was converted into the abbot's house (figure 47).

Service buildings of the outer courtyard

Buildings such as the brewhouse and the bakehouse were situated in the outer courtyard. Few brewhouses and bakehouses have survived, and even fewer have been excavated owing to the small number of investigations of outer courtyards. At Thornholme Priory (Lincolnshire), a small Augustinian house founded in the mid twelfth century, the potential of the excavation of monastic outer courts has been demonstrated (Coppack 1989 and 1990). The sheer complexity of successive developments and changes of use of the buildings demonstrates the dynamism of this part of the monastic complex in response to the changing requirements and circumstances of the priory. No fewer than eleven superimposed phases were identified, albeit on an island site in a peat fen which restricted opportunities for lateral expansion.

The earliest masonry building that was built on this part of the Thornholme site was a guesthouse near the entrance road. A gatehouse was then built astride the road, with a porter's lodge on its north side (figure 73). A staircase gave access to the upper floors of both buildings. A group of buildings, including a wagon shed facing on to a yard, was added near the lodge. All these developments were completed within half a century of the foundation. Early in the thirteenth century, however, the guesthouse was converted into a bakery. An oven was built into what had been a mural fireplace. Numerous other changes were followed in the fourteenth century by the replacement of the gatehouse with a new structure. After a short period of operation it too was demolished to make way for another gatehouse that made use of the footings of its predecessor. The bakehouse, however, continued, though provided with a new floor and oven.

At the end of the fourteenth century an almonry was built outside the gatehouse. It consisted of a hall with a cross-passage, central hearth, wall-benches and an oven. To the south of the passage were two small chambers enclosed by a timber screen. To the north of the hall was a room that may have served as a lay infirmary, equipped with a latrine. Nearby, another building was converted into a chapel with a raised altar platform. A crucifix made of jet was found here. The bakehouse was dismantled and a grain drier built in its place. Subsequently another grain drier was built in what had been the lay infirmary.

A second area was excavated to the south. Here a dovecote was found, built in the late twelfth century. It was plastered and had a hipped tile roof. Another building may have been the hall of the steward, replaced in the next phase by a substantial manor house-like building. In the early thirteenth century this in turn was replaced by a ground-level hall for the steward. His previous abode was drastically altered to become a brewhouse. Subsidence led to two further rebuildings of the steward's house. In the late fourteenth century, however, it was partly demolished and converted into a granary. The brewhouse was remodelled as a malt kiln. The dovecote underwent repairs. In the early sixteenth century a great aisled timber barn was erected.

The excavation at Thornholme Priory has demonstrated the enormous potential of outer courtyards as sources of information about the ancillary buildings that a monastery required. They included security (gatehouse, precinct walls and ditches); administration (steward's house); storage (wagon shed, barn); food (dovecote, granary, grain drier, bakehouse); drink (brewhouse, malt kiln); hospitality (guesthouse, chapel); and charitable activity (almonry, lay infirmary).

Infirmaries

The usual location for infirmaries was to the south-east of the claustral buildings. They were used for brethren who were ill or aged, and for the periodic bleeding in which monks had their veins opened for supposed medical and religious benefits. Elderly lay people (from benefactor families) might also be accommodated in the infirmary. At Kelso Abbey (Borders), an infirmary was found in the south-east part of the site (Tabraham 1984). It was built towards the close of the twelfth century on an area that had previously been used as the construction yard by the builders of the abbey, which belonged to the order of Tiron. The infirmary consisted of a large hall with its long axis aligned north–south. It had an arcade of alternating round and octagonal columns, providing a single aisle in which the beds of the inmates would have been placed. An altar will have been placed in the nave or in an adjoining chapel. At Kirkstall a twelfth-century infirmary was found; it was a large timber hall with screen walls (figure 3). It was replaced by a masonry infirmary that incorporated a lodging for visiting abbots (Moorhouse and Wrathmell 1987, 51–6). Three phases of growth were detected in the infirmary of Cluniac Bermondsey Priory, all arranged to make use of a large drain that discharged into the Thames. The final phase consisted of a hall 28 m. by 16 m. with four small rooms attached (Beard 1986).

Burials

Documents, food remains, vessels and buildings are not the only sources of information on medieval diet and conditions of health. An additional field of study concerns the skeletal remains of those who consumed the food and drink. Although many monastic excavations have resulted in the discovery of graves with skeletons, few reports have yet been published on the scientific examination of the bones. The potential, however, is enormous.

In assessing indicators of health and diet as revealed by skeletons from a monastic site, it is essential to understand the types of people who were likely to be buried there. It would be quite wrong to assume that all burials are those of the inmates. Lay people, especially members of benefactor families, were often buried in the church and its chapels. They may be identified as such by the presence in a group of burials of children and (in a male house) of some skeletons of women. There may also be grave-slabs bearing symbols such as swords or articles of trade that indicate the status of the person buried beneath. In broad terms, burials of different groups occur in four main zones. Benefactors were buried in the nave, aisles, transepts and transept chapels of the church. The head of a religious house might be buried in the choir, chapter house or cloister walk (figure 74). Other monks, canons, nuns or friars would be buried in a graveyard to the east of the church. Ordinary lay people such as servants and tenants of the abbey would be buried outside the church on the far side from the cloister. None of these were hard-and-fast rules, however, and they vary between orders and over time. Information can be obtained on three distinct groups that can be compared on an identical chronological scale. Samples of the size of that excavated from the lay cemetery at Whithorn, where 1,600 skeletons are being studied, are particularly valuable.

The type of data that can be obtained is clearly related to the nature of the material, for it has to be capable of leaving a trace in the skeleton. The fusing of vertebrae as a result of arthritis, syphilitic lesions, tubercular decay of vertebrae and Paget's disease (thickening and weakening of the skull) were all found in skeletons of benefactors of Norton Priory, Cheshire, by Liverpool University Human Anatomy Department. A poignant discovery was that of a woman who had probably died in childbirth, with the tiny bones of the baby found in the pelvic region. Medical practice may be revealed in the form of mended fractures. One of the Norton skeletons was that of an

Figure 74. Effigy of one of the abbots of Dundrennan Abbey, Dumfries and Galloway, which once covered a tomb-chest. He is shown wearing his habit and holding a pastoral staff. Between the staff and his right hand a dagger penetrates the figure in the region of the heart; it has been suggested that the abbot had suffered a violent death and that the effigy commemorates this.

Photograph by Patrick Greene.

adult male whose femur had broken and been successfully set. A contributory cause of the fracture was revealed by X-ray examination, which showed a lesion within the femur that had weakened it. The condition of teeth is partly related to diet, and the increasing incidence of dental caries in the later medieval period, found in a number of studies, has been linked to the greater use of sugar. Stature may also be a function of diet. It is an oft-repeated myth that medieval people were shorter than the present-day population. The sample from Norton Priory of males who had reached adulthood showed that their distribution of heights was little different to the modern population. The essential factor was that benefactors and canons were drawn from social classes that had the advantage of a plentiful and diverse diet. A contemporary group of peasants from Rhuddlan in Clwyd studied by the Liverpool University team provided a contrast to the Norton sample. Their life expectancy, stature and other indicators of health were all considerably lower. They were the victims of restricted diet and the periodic famines that followed crop failures. In terms of stature, they had been unable to fulfil their full genetic potential for dietary reasons.

7 Monasteries and towns

Introduction

The archaeology of urban monasteries has received considerable attention since the 1960s as rescue excavations have taken place in advance of development. However, there are particular problems associated with the archaeological study of monasteries in towns. The intensity of occupation has usually resulted in far greater damage to sites compared to rural monasteries. The excavation of the Franciscan friary in Northampton (Williams 1972) illustrates the problem. Although the scale of the development made excavation of a large area possible, the information that could be recovered was limited due to the considerable damage caused by the construction of the cellars of Victorian buildings. The excavator concluded that 'it was impossible to reconstruct anything like the complete plan of the friary' (*ibid.*, 96). Often the areas available for excavation are much smaller than that at Northampton, and are determined by the strategies of development rather than the priorities of archaeological research. This, combined with the fact that even small urban monasteries established on constricted sites nonetheless covered substantial areas, means that the majority of excavations produce very limited information. Other archaeological techniques such as geophysical survey are difficult to apply on urban sites due to the extent of disturbance caused by post-medieval activity, and the presence of disruptive modern features such as pipe-runs and electricity cables. Finally, standing remains of monastic buildings are less likely to survive than those of rural monasteries due to their convenience to townspeople as a source of building materials.

Monasteries in Chester

Chester, in the north-west of England, is an example of a town in which a number of religious houses have been subject to archaeological investigation since the 1960s (Ward 1990). The monasteries were established over several centuries. A church of secular canons dedicated to St Werburgh may have been founded as early as 907 when Aethelflaed, sister of Edward the Elder, organised the refortification of Chester (Kettle 1980, 132). In 1092 the first earl of Chester, Hugh d'Avranches, sought the help of Anselm, the archbishop of Canterbury, in effecting the transformation of the house of secular canons into a Benedictine monastery. The first abbot came from Bec in Normandy. Of the monastic buildings that were erected during his abbacy, only part of the north transept of the church remains, although foundations of the apsed choir aisles have also been traced by excavation. The rebuilt church has survived largely intact as a result of its conversion to a cathedral by Henry VIII. The cloister and domestic ranges are also well preserved.

Figure 75. Plan of late medieval Chester, with its monastic precincts shown stippled. 4 is St Werburgh's Abbey; 6 the Franciscan friary; 10 the Dominican friary; 11 the Carmelite friary; 16 the collegiate church of St John; and 17 the Benedictine nunnery. Other numbers represent hospitals and parish churches (many of which were also owned by monasteries in Cheshire).

Drawing supplied by City of Chester Cultural Services.

The limits of the monastic precinct must have been defined at an early stage (figure 75). On the north and east the boundary was provided by the town walls which followed the course of the defences of the north-east part of the Roman legionary fortress. The west side coincided with Northgate Street, and to the south lay the burgage plots that fronted on to Eastgate Street. The monks defined the western and southern sides of their precinct with boundary walls, within which were set two gatehouses. The south transept was accessible to townspeople, however, for it served as the parish church.

The occupation by the abbey of six hectares of the town, enclosed by strong walls and gatehouses, inevitably became a source of antagonism between monks and townspeople. The insertion of a postern gate into the town wall in 1275, to enable the monks to take a short cut to the vegetable garden, was resented by the mayor and corporation because it reduced their control of the defences (Burne 1962, 62). In the fifteenth century there were repeated clashes between monks and townspeople. In 1480, for example, the abbot and twelve monks were bound over to keep the peace after brawling with tradesmen (Kettle 1980, 142). The efficacy of the precinct boundary is called into question in some visitation records. Difficulties were experienced in excluding lay people, and the walls failed to prevent the monks from going out into the town to frequent taverns and consort with prostitutes. Other large urban monasteries had similar problems of conflict between the strictures of the Rule and the temptations of urban life. More damaging, however, was resentment over a monastery's commercial privileges and property rights.

The refoundation of the dissolved abbey as one of the new cathedrals in 1541 perpetuated its physical presence in the city. The precinct was transferred to the dean and chapter in its entirety, and it remains to this day as a distinct, intact urban enclosure. Likewise, the abbey church still dominates the skyline.

In the middle of the twelfth century Ranulph II, earl of Chester, granted some crofts near his castle to a group of Benedictine nuns who were to build their conventual buildings and a church dedicated to St Mary there (*ibid.* 146). Their precinct occupied an area in the south-western part of the town, the buildings visible from the residence of their benefactor. Their fate is more typical of the mass of urban monasteries than that of the abbey. The nunnery became a secular dwelling after the Dissolution. The buildings were pillaged during the Civil War in 1643 and were left in ruins. Early in the nineteenth century the castle became the site of the new Shire Hall, and the few remnants of the nunnery were cleared away to improve the approaches to it.

The nunnery site was the subject of a hurried excavation in 1964 in advance of the construction of the new police headquarters. The results (Ward 1990, 3–22) are an illustration of just how difficult it is to interpret a site of this size from the results of trenching, which was all that the excavators could manage with limited time and resources. Nonetheless, in combination with a remarkable sketch plan drawn in the latter half of the sixteenth century (BL Harleian Ms 2073 fol. 87) the excavations permit a partial reconstruction of the nuns' precinct (figure 75). On the south side were the castle defences, and to the west the town walls were built. A boundary wall separated the nunnery from the town on the north and east. Within the precinct was the variety of buildings that would be expected on any monastic site. At the heart of the complex was the church – a modest structure with chancel and single-aisled nave. The internal measurements of the church were 20.5 m. by 11.5 m. The cloister lay to the south, and to the north was the outer courtyard. This formed the basis of the post-Dissolution house. The nunnery was reached by a lane from the east, probably guarded by a gatehouse. The various enclosures within the precinct included a graveyard to the east of the church, and a kitchen yard containing the well from which the nuns obtained their supply of water. Other enclosures were doubtless gardens and orchards.

During the thirteenth century the abbey and nunnery were joined by four other religious houses, all of them friaries. The Dominicans arrived in 1236 and acquired a block of land immediately north of the nunnery. Within two years the Franciscans had established themselves in another substantial precinct a little further north. By 1277 the Carmelites had acquired a small plot of land to the east of the Dominicans, and this they managed to enlarge by purchases in the fourteenth century.

Chester therefore had five monastic precincts – the abbey, the nunnery, and three friaries. Together they took up no less than a quarter of the medieval town (figure 75). In many other towns, religious houses occupied a similar proportion of the total area. The nunnery, Dominican friary and Franciscan friary dominated the western side of medieval Chester. It had lain outside the Roman walls; the medieval town walls were constructed in the late twelfth century to enclose the area, but it was not built up. The fact that it was occupied by crofts (mainly gardens and orchards) made it ideal for the sites of the new religious houses. Excavation on the site of the Dominican friary showed that a collapsed Roman building was still available as a source of materials. The builders of the friary found Roman ashlar facing-stones and pilae tiles from a hypocaust particularly useful.

The areas available to the archaeologists were frustratingly constricted, but valuable information was obtained on the form of the friars' church, and the complexity of its development. There were five phases in which the church was converted from an aisleless structure to one with a broad nave incorporating two aisles (figure 76). It therefore corresponded to the most common form of friars' churches, in which a premium was placed on the capacity of the nave for preaching. The plan can be compared with those of Dominican houses in Oxford (see Chapter 1), Newcastle-upon-Tyne (Chapter 8), Norwich, Ipswich and Cardiff. In its third phase the church also acquired a tower over the crossing – another common feature of friaries. In the fifth phase the entire nave was demolished and foundation trenches were dug for a new, and presumably even bigger structure. Work came to a stop for some reason and the Dissolution in 1538 prevented its resumption. The site was sold, and the remaining structures were levelled in the seventeenth century. The friars solved the universal problem of urban monasteries, the supply of water, by laying a lead pipe to springs 1.25 km. outside the town.

The Franciscan and Carmelite friaries in Chester have not been the subject of recent excavations, but information about them has been brought together

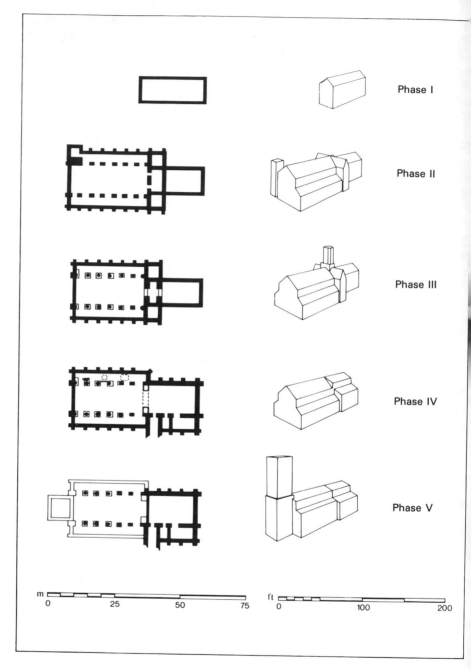

Phase I

Phase II

Phase III

Phase IV

Phase V

Figure 76. The development of the plan of the Dominican friary, Chester, with perspective reconstructions of the church.
Drawing supplied by City of Chester Cultural Services.

rom documentary records and chance discoveries made over the years Ward 1990, 197–209). The Franciscan friary had an aisled nave and to the north was the cloister, with a lesser cloister incorporating the infirmary further to the north. By 1528 the nave had become disused for worship. It was being used by the sailors and merchants of Chester, who were responsible for its repair, for the storage of sails. Little is known about the Carmelites' buildings.

There are many aspects of the pattern of monastic settlement in Chester that are common to towns throughout the British Isles. As expensive institutions to found and to maintain, the fortunes of the monastic houses tended to reflect those of the town itself. The size of their precincts often dominated the layout of a town, and even the smaller friaries occupied significant blocks of land. To undertake a comprehensive investigation of an urban monastery is therefore very difficult, unless (like the Benedictine Abbey at Chester) it has buildings adapted to alternative uses at the Dissolution and still surviving. This means that only the very largest (and most destructive) development projects are likely to enable access for excavation over a sufficiently wide area for worthwhile results to be obtained. Often the strategy has instead to be one of gradual accumulation of information as opportunities present themselves.

Special characteristics of friaries

Two distinctive aspects of the orders of friars were the commitment to a mendicant life (reliance on begging for their sustenance), and the mission to preach salvation to the poor. They were also members of international organisations in which mobility of individuals was common. The friars were therefore markedly different in their activities to the orders of canons and monks, whose lives were dedicated to an unending round of religious devotion. Although it was possible for a friary to be established in the country, the vast majority of houses of friars were in towns where the poor were numerous, but also where the brethren might expect to find sufficient numbers of people prepared to support them with alms. Friaries are therefore predominantly an urban phenomenon in England, Scotland and Wales, although some Irish friaries were established at a distance from the nearest settlement. This was particularly true of the Observant Franciscans (a reformed order that sought to return to the original simplicity of St Francis) who settled in remote places, particularly in the west of Ireland, from the mid fifteenth century onwards (Mould 1976, 81) (figure 78).

The two major orders of friars became established throughout the British Isles in the decade from 1221. Following the arrival of the Dominicans (black friars) in England in 1221 at Canterbury, the Franciscans (grey friars) chose the same town for their first house in 1224. During that year both orders founded friaries in Ireland. In 1230 the first Dominican friary in Scotland was founded, followed a year later by the Franciscans. The rate of expansion was dramatic, and by 1240 friaries were to be found in all the major centres of power (Butler 1984, 123–5). The Carmelites (white friars), introduced to England in 1240, differed from the black friars and the grey friars in that they were originally a hermit order. Their first English houses at Hulne (Northumberland) and Aylesford (Kent) were in rural locations. However, it was not long before they too became part of the urban scene. The fourth order of friars to establish itself in the British Isles, and which like the Carmelites began as a hermit order, followed the Rule of St Augustine (sometimes known as the Austin friars). Both orders began to spread in the mid thirteenth century and came to resemble closely the Franciscans and Dominicans in their mendicant lifestyle and evangelical mission.

In thirteen English boroughs (Boston, Bristol, Cambridge, King's Lynn, Lincoln, London, Newcastle-upon-Tyne, Northampton, Norwich, Oxford, Stamford, Winchester and York) all four orders of friars settled, and often became involved in competition for the alms upon which they all depended. Indeed, this may explain why it was not uncommon for friaries to transfer their locations from the outskirts of a town to the busy, populous centre where alms might be solicited more successfully (Dobson 1984, 112). The Carmelites of York, for example, migrated from the suburbs to a site in the city. The Augustinian friars at Winchester attempted to move to a location within the walls from the southern suburbs where they and the Carmelites were established (Keene 1985, 130). They were unsuccessful, and remained outside the walls. Competition was particularly intense in Winchester. It is remarkable that the four orders of friars succeeded in gaining a foothold in a city that already had the Cathedral Priory, St Mary's Abbey, Hyde Abbey, the hospital of Holy Cross, and about fifty-five parish churches. The Franciscan and Dominican friaries were built close to the working population of Winchester, in the part of the city where leather trades and cloth manufacture were located. However, 'whatever may have been their intention in their first choice of sites . . . the friar's main appeal was to leading citizens and the country gentry rather than the urban poor' (*ibid.* 131).

It is sometimes asserted that friaries, as relatively late arrivals on the scene, were relegated to poor, damp sites on floodplains of rivers, outside the town walls. It is certainly true that the period of greatest growth of friaries occurred in the thirteenth century when the population of medieval Britain reached its peak, and the pressure on space within towns was at its most intense. However, the description of the friars' precincts in Chester should serve to emphasise the fact that friaries were frequently located on extensive sites within the defences of towns. Some friaries, such as the Augustinian house at Leicester (Mellor and Pearce 1981), were built on undeniably wet riverside locations. It should not be assumed, however, that this was a result of a lack of choice. As has been described in previous chapters, the majority of monastic houses of all kinds selected sites that permitted efficient water supply and drainage, which were clearly much more easily achieved by the channelling of streams and rivers than through the laborious and organisationally complex construction of a piped water supply into a town. In acquiring sites, the friars were in fact remarkably successful in attracting the support of individuals of wealth and influence, including royalty. Thus, in York the Dominicans occupied a three-acre (1.2-hectare) site just within the walls, given to them by Henry III in 1227 (Dobson 1984, 113). He also supported the grey friars, whose precinct was immediately adjacent to the royal castle in York. Like their brethren in Oxford (see Chapter 1), the York

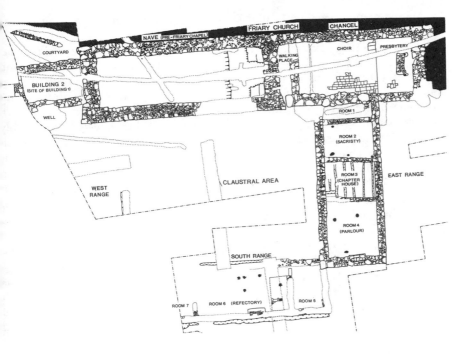

Figure 77. Plan of the buildings of Linlithgow Friary, Lothian Region. The simple arrangement of this small friary contains the basic ingredients of the standard monastic plan – a church of nave, choir and chancel on the north, a sacristy, chapter house (with slots for floor joists) and parlour on the east, and the refectory range on the south. The graveyard lies to the north and east of the church.

Drawing supplied by Historic Scotland.

Franciscans expanded their holding by encroaching on existing defences – in the case of York, as excavation has shown, across the ditch and into the outer bailey of the castle (Ottaway 1981).

The techniques of archaeology can make a particular contribution to the study of friaries. Their written records have not survived to anything like the same extent as those relating to the houses of the monastic orders. In terms of the survival of buildings they have also suffered particularly badly, except in Ireland which still possesses a remarkable assemblage of friary structures. Only fifteen friaries in England and Wales have left substantial buildings from a total of around 270 houses, and in Scotland out of fifty-four friaries only six have visible remains (Butler 1984, 126). Four Scottish Carmelite houses have recently been the subject of archaeological investigation, including Linlithgow which revealed considerable information about the layout of its claustral buildings (figure 77) (Stones 1989). Ireland has over 100 friary sites with buildings surviving above ground, some almost complete. The total includes 57 Franciscan houses out of 110 foundations, 28 Dominican friaries (out of 43), 13 Carmelite houses (out of 28), and

16 Augustinian friaries with at least some of the masonry standing on the
22 sites (Mould 1976).

One topic that excavation at sites such as Oxford Greyfriars has
illuminated is the tension between a commitment to poverty of lifestyle and
the popularity that self-denial on the part of the friars generated in their
supporters. The original friary buildings at Oxford were very simple, and
when the first church was built it consisted of a long choir and a nave with
a single aisle. As the friars' reputation grew, the church was considerably
expanded, with an extended preaching nave and a long transept on the north
containing ten chapels (figure 10). The followers of the teaching of St Francis
were now inhabiting a building of considerable grandeur – a contradiction
that applied to many communities of friars, especially in large towns, which
attracted hostile comment from contemporaries. In the 1530s one writer of
a tract, Simon Fish, complained of the 'infinite number of begging friars',
calculating that at the rate of four pence in alms from each person in the
realm, the friars had an annual income of £43,333. The only thing 'these
sturdy, idle, holy thieves' did was seduce a hundred thousand wives
(Knowles 1976, 84). The exaggeration was absurd, but the resentment was
real. The friars were caught in the trap in which other ascetic orders such
as the Cistercians had already found themselves. The wealthy inhabitants of
towns, hearing the friars preach the virtues of a life of poverty, and
anticipating the spiritual benefits that would accrue to the donors of alms,
gave generously to support friaries. But the more successfully the friars
enabled the wealthy to gain spiritual grace through the vicarious experience
of poverty, the less it became a reality for the friars themselves.

Many excavations, albeit often on a small scale, have shown that there are
general characteristics that are shared by many friaries (Butler 1984). As at
Chester Dominican Friary, the church often developed from a simple two-
cell structure to become a building with a broad nave and aisles to accommodate large numbers of people attracted by the friars' reputation as
preachers. The chancel, containing the choir and high altar, often remained
relatively small. Separating it from the nave was the 'walking space' beneath
a tower (at first friaries were only supposed to have a simple belfry).
However, it was far from inevitable that a friary church would grow to this
extent. The simple church of the Gloucester Blackfriars (Rackham, Blair and
Munby 1978, 106), with its nave, choir, narrow nave aisles and small
transepts, is possibly more typical of the generality of friaries.

An additional function of friary churches was as places of burial. If the
founder was a magnate with an existing religious house acting as the family
mausoleum, the tradition was rarely broken in favour of the new foundation. Thus Ranulph Blunderville, earl of Chester, was interred not in the
Franciscan friary he had founded in Coventry, but with his ancestors in St
Werburgh's Abbey in Chester, although his heart was buried separately at his
Cistercian foundation at Dieulacres (Ormrod 1985, 73). The friaries did,
however, provide an opportunity for people of lesser rank to be buried in
religious houses in return for their financial support. By the sixteenth century
the performance of masses for the dead had become a prime activity for the
friars. No less than 40 per cent of people making wills in York in the last
decade before the Suppression included the friaries as beneficiaries (Dobson

16). The large naves and aisles of friary churches had therefore the additional virtue of providing plentiful space in which the graves, tombs and chantry chapels of benefactors might be accommodated.

Friary cloisters as places of peace and contemplation must have taken on an increased value compared to those of the monastic orders in view of the role of the church as a focus for preaching and meetings. Sometimes, as a means of increasing the degree of privacy, the cloister-walk closest to the nave was separated from it by a small open court as at the Franciscan friary at Walsingham (Norfolk) and the Dominican friary at Norwich (Butler 1984, 132). The three cloister ranges commonly consisted of separate two-storey blocks. Whereas the standard monastic plan had the dormitory in the east range and the refectory on the south, not all friaries followed this pattern. Careful excavation of the internal spaces to detect diagnostic features and objects associated with the use of the buildings could provide information on the use to which they were put. Other buildings that may be found on friary sites include scriptoria (rooms for writing), guesthouses and infirmaries. The remaining building of the Franciscan friary at Lincoln (now the home of the City and County Museum) has been identified as an infirmary hall built in the thirteenth century and remodelled to provide accommodation on two floors (Stocker 1984).

Sometimes the cloister-walk was incorporated within the ranges rather than having the lean-to roof or stone vault of most abbeys and priories. In this arrangement the upper floors projected over the cloister walk, which became, in effect, an internal passage on the three sides of the cloister apart from the church. Possibly this originated as a means of making the most of constricted urban sites. However, the paucity of standing domestic buildings of friaries makes generalisation hazardous, and the interpretation of what are often no more than robbed foundations in terms of the structures they once supported is fraught with difficulties. Some standing buildings that have survived, for example Gloucester Blackfriars and Newcastle-upon-Tyne Blackfriars, show evidence of once having had lean-to cloister roofs.

Cloisters and their buildings survive in a substantially complete state at a number of Irish friaries, such as Ennis and Quin (County Clare), Moyne (County Mayo), Adare and Askeaton (County Limerick), Sligo (County Sligo) and Sherkin Island (County Cork) (figure 78). Most friaries in Ireland have the cloister to the north of the church. There does not seem to be any explanation for northern cloisters. Some impressive Irish sites have survived which give an insight into the appearance of friaries in other parts of the British Isles. At Ennis Franciscan Friary (County Clare), the church and cloister still exist in ruined condition, with the tower rising above the choir. Details such as a carved figure of St Francis showing the stigmata, a beautifully ornamented screen, and superb tombs are a reminder of what has been lost on so many sites.

Urban properties

The influence of monastic houses on towns was not restricted to the presence of religious houses within them. Monasteries often owned urban properties.

Figure 78. Sherkin Island Franciscan Friary, Co. Cork, seen from the north-west. Founded in the late fifteenth century, Sherkin is an example of the isolated locations favoured by the Friars of Strict Observance. The church is dominated by a large tower; the claustral buildings are in the foreground.
  Photograph by Con Brogan, Office of Public Works.

Buildings were acquired through benefaction or purchase as investments yielding an income from rents. Augustinian Holy Trinity, Aldgate owned property in no fewer than eighty-seven London parishes. By 1300, one-fifth of the properties of Oxford were in the ownership of four of its monasteries (Robinson 1980, 333, 335). Monasteries might also have houses in towns where the abbot, prior or other officials were regularly required to be present, for example, to attend court or to act as an official of the secular administration. Their function is illustrated by arrangements made by the abbot of the Tironensian abbey at Arbroath (Tayside) in the fourteenth century (Mackie and Cruden 1954, 2). Houses belonging to the abbey in a number of Scottish burghs were leased to laymen on condition that the lessees provided facilities for anyone from Arbroath Abbey visiting the burgh. Their requirements included a hall in which they could eat in comfort, with a table, trestles, etc., a pantry and a buttery, a sitting room, a kitchen, and a stable for their horses. The tenant also had to provide fuel, candles, beds (presumably placed in the hall or sitting room), salt, but not food.

Figure 79. Drawing, based on evidence from excavation and used in the interpretation of the site to visitors, showing the location of the graveyard of Whithorn Priory, Dumfries and Galloway. It lies to the south of the monastery, and is crossed by paths taking pilgrims to the church.
Drawing supplied by the Whithorn Trust.

Ownership of towns

Some towns were established as a result of the presence of a monastery, and others were stimulated to growth. Twenty-five English boroughs were actually owned by religious houses, twenty of them Benedictine and five Augustinian (Trenholme 1927). The Augustinian canons of the wealthy house in Cirencester purchased the town from Richard I and controlled its trade.

Major shrines were capable of attracting large numbers of pilgrims, thus creating a market which stimulated economic activity. Excavation at Whithorn Priory (Hill 1988, 1990) has demonstrated the phenomenon in the case of the longest-established religious settlement in Scotland. Pilgrims from northern Britain and Ireland were attracted to the shrine of St Ninian, where he had established his 'Candida Casa' (shining house) church in the early fifth century. A settlement grew up to cater for their needs, becoming an important trading centre in the kingdom of Northumbria, and subsequently a place where Norse craftspeople and merchants settled, in about 1000 AD. The king of the medieval kingdom of Galloway established a cathedral priory served by Premonstratensian canons in the late twelfth century. Their church had a small nave, but developed an elaborate eastern part consisting of transepts, aisled chancel, and chapels set above three vaulted crypts. The focus of the entire building was the shrine of St Ninian in the eastern part

The settlement on the slope immediately south of the priory died out in the thirteenth century, and the area became a graveyard (figure 79). With pilgrimage flourishing, the focus of the town moved a little further south where buildings grew up alongside a broad street where markets were held The town became an ecclesiastical burgh in 1325 and a royal burgh in 1511 The excavators found that in the fifteenth century the surface of the graveyard was dug away and a broad roadway leading from the town to the church was constructed. The road was cobbled and was lined by stone and timber buildings that doubtless catered for the needs of pilgrims. A lead pilgrim badge showing the figure of a bishop, presumably Ninian, was found nearby. To this day, the layout of Whithorn reflects its origins as a place of veneration and commerce.

Bury St Edmunds in Suffolk is an example of a town to a large extent created by an abbey that was determined to benefit to the maximum from sources of urban income. The town was developed on planned lines by the great abbey soon after the Conquest. Pilgrims were attracted from throughout the land to the shrine of St Edmund. The grid layout of the streets, which survives to the present day, was aligned on the monastic complex. When Bury's burgesses became too powerful for the abbot's liking, he abolished the gild merchant. Tensions between the burgesses and the abbey were never far from the surface. In 1327 serious rioting caused great damage to the abbey. One of the responses by the abbey was to strengthen its precinct boundary which became less a means of ensuring the peaceful pursuit of religious life than a defence against the oppressed townspeople. Although the abbey is now reduced to little more than the stumps of flint and mortar wall cores, the town retains its medieval grid arrangement, and the walls and gatehouses built to protect the monks' privileges still stand. They comprise a fine Romanesque gatehouse, and a fourteenth-century gatehouse with portcullis and arrow slits betraying the defensive intentions of its builders.

Bury is an example of seigneurial planning by an abbey on a considerable scale. More typical is a development, on a much more modest basis, by the Augustinian canons of Royston in Hertfordshire (Taylor 1979, 130). Royston Priory was situated in an empty area on the boundary of two counties where five parishes met. Its major advantage was that it was at the junction of two roads – one from London to the north, the other from the south-west to East Anglia. The priory was thus in a position to benefit from passing trade, and to that end obtained the right to hold a market and fair in 1189. A small town was laid out to fit the existing route pattern. The London road was widened to create an elongated market place on both sides of the cross-roads with plots for houses and shops alongside it. Success quickly followed, with further grants of fairs made in 1213 and 1243. A second market place was required when permanent shops were built within the first market place.

The importance of capturing passing trade was appreciated by Ramsey Abbey in Cambridgeshire. One of its possessions, the village of Slepe, was situated on the river Ouse in the vicinity of roads from Ramsey, Ely and

London. Downstream of the ford, which was the crossing point for north–south traffic, a huge causeway was constructed across the floodplain leading to a bridge that fed travellers directly into a new market place. In 1110 the abbey obtained a licence to hold a fair during Easter week. The abbey made a series of grants that allowed tenants to build houses on the frontages of the market place. The fair became one of the greatest in medieval England, with traders coming from throughout the country and from France to buy and sell, amongst other goods, fine cloth and wine. The settlement lost the name Slepe and adopted St Ives. It never became a borough – the abbey retained tight control of its profitable enterprise. The area of the market place is still discernible in the present-day layout of St Ives. The causeway and a masonry bridge, built in 1414 to replace its wooden predecessor, still survive (Beresford and St Joseph 1979, 180–3).

The canons of Royston and the monks of Ramsey were little different to secular landowners in promoting their new towns for the benefit of the rents and tolls that would accrue to them from fairs and markets. However, the advantage that monastic houses had over lay promoters of towns was the religious element itself. The fostering of pilgrimage by the acquisition of relics with popular appeal increased the numbers of people drawn to the town. There was also the potential of creating fairs linked to festivals celebrating the monastery's holy days, particularly that of the patron saint.

Not every attempt by a monastery to create a new town was successful. If it was not in the right place to attract trade, a new settlement was never likely to grow to the size intended by the founder. The Knights Templar established the village of Bruer in Lincolnshire at the site of their preceptory, founded in the mid twelfth century (Beresford and St Joseph 1979, 161–4). The Templars required a labour-force for their lands, but also had greater ambitions for their settlement. A weekly market was established, but Temple Bruer never developed into a town as it was too far away from important routes. All that remains of the village is an extensive area of soil-marks, and a farm with the tower of the preceptory standing in it. The site of the precinct was excavated in the early years of this century (Hope 1908).

Where the fortunes of an abbey were bound up with those of the town, it was in the interests of a monastery to carry out works that facilitated trade. The abbot of Arbroath Abbey agreed in 1394 to construct a safe harbour for the town which had suffered 'innumerable losses and many vexations' (Mackie and Cruden 1954, 10). In return the burgesses were to contribute the labour and some of the tools, and in future pay double their rent. A monastery, as a permanent institution with substantial assets, was in a strong position to act as the agency to fund and organise improvement works of this kind.

Reading Abbey (Berkshire) made use of its waterfront location to engage in trade. The Cluniac monastery was established in 1121 by Henry I, who also promoted Reading as a town that the monks dominated throughout the medieval period. When he died, his body was brought up the River Kennet to be buried in front of the high altar. Recent excavations on the waterfront (Fasham 1984) have shown how wharves were built to serve the abbey. For the first two centuries of the abbey's existence the wharf consisted of a large dump of clay supported by timberwork (figure 80). In the early fourteenth

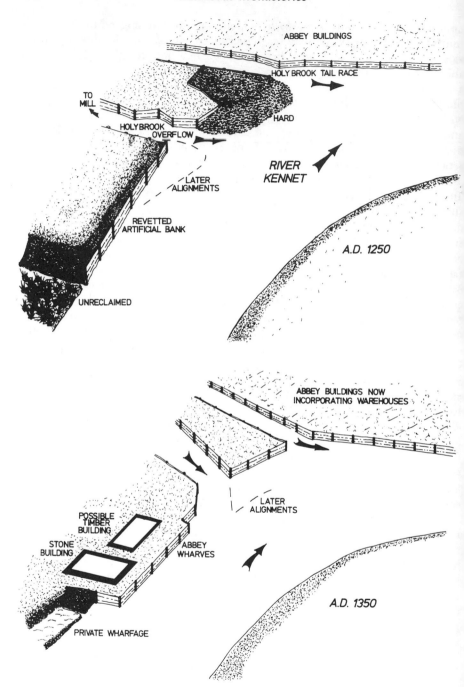

Figure 80. The development of the waterfront of Reading Abbey, Berkshire, in the thirteenth and fourteenth centuries.

Drawings supplied by Wessex Archaeology.

entury the waterfront was remodelled. A permanent quay was built, with
stout facing of oak posts and planks. On the bank the excavators
uncovered the foundations of a large rectangular building, presumably a
warehouse.

New settlements

There is evidence of monastic planning at work in settlements that were
never designed to develop into towns. One circumstance that might lead to
the establishment of a new village was the removal of an existing settlement
if it was considered that it was in the wrong place. When the Cistercian
abbey that ultimately developed at Byland was established in Ryedale at the
site that proved to be too close to Rievaulx Abbey, the monks moved an
existing village that occupied the spot where they intended to build. The new
village, about 2 kilometres away, was planned with the houses set round a
green (Beresford and St Joseph 1979, 159). To this day it is known as Old
Byland – old only in relation to the site where Byland Abbey was subsequently built. Villages were sometimes removed to make way for granges.
Byland appears to have depopulated the village of Mershaw for this purpose
(Faull and Moorhouse 1981, 796). The Cistercian abbey at Valle Crucis
required the removal of the inhabitants of the settlement of Llanegwestl to
Stansty to the north-east (Evans 1987, 2). Norton Priory in Cheshire did not
need to move an existing settlement, but it is possible that the nearby village
of Norton was re-established by the canons on a planned basis in the form
of a street village (Greene 1989, 41).

8 The Dissolution

The Dissolution of the monasteries in England and Wales was a campaign by the Crown that had a dramatic and rapid impact throughout the two countries from its beginning in 1536. In Scotland and Ireland monastic life was not extinguished in the five years that it took in England and Wales but nonetheless by the close of the sixteenth century it was in terminal decline. The impact of the closure of monastic houses was far-reaching affecting individuals, institutions, buildings and the landscape. It led to the most radical redistribution of land and property that had occurred at any time since the Conquest and which has not been exceeded since. The physical consequences of the Dissolution are capable of investigation using the range of techniques available to archaeologists. The religious and political circumstances that led to Dissolution and which were consequent upon it have been dealt with by other writers (of which the most authoritative and highly readable account is Knowles 1976).

Although 1536 was the date of the Act of Suppression which permitted the closure of all religious houses with fewer than twelve inmates or with an annual income below £200, there were precedents for Henry VIII and Thomas Cromwell, his chancellor, to copy. In the case of the Knights Templar, all members of the order were arrested and their estates were sequestrated in 1308, followed by heresy trials and suppression by papal decree in 1312. During the Hundred Years War, 'alien houses' – monasteries dependent on a mother house in France – were closed, or they swiftly severed their continental links. In the sixteenth century there were closures of houses that were in difficulties as a result of dwindling numbers or escalating debts. One group of twenty-seven monasteries was suppressed by Cardinal Wolsey between 1524 and 1529 for the purpose of founding and endowing colleges at Oxford and Ipswich. The Oxford college was established in the suppressed Augustinian priory of St Frideswide. Work to convert the monastic buildings into Cardinal College took place between 1525 and Wolsey's fall in 1529. The college was eventually completed as Christ Church, and the canons' church became Oxford Cathedral in 1545. Archaeological work has illuminated some of the aspects of the conversion of St Frideswide's to a college and cathedral, especially the changing plans for the accommodation of the bells (Blair 1990). The priory's great tower and spire were restored in 1545-6, having been partly demolished, to house not only the St Frideswide bells but also those from Oseney Abbey.

The Benedictine priory at Sandwell in the West Midlands was one of Wolsey's victims. It had never been large, but by the time of its demise it only had two monks (Hodder 1989). Like many of the monasteries suppressed two decades later, Sandwell was converted into a dwelling (called Priory House). The Augustinian canons of Holy Trinity, Christchurch in London suddenly surrendered their house to the king in 1532, overwhelmed by debt resulting from poor administration (Knowles 1976, 85). The canons were dispersed to other houses, the foundation was suppressed, and much of the property went to Audley, the new chancellor. He set about converting the buildings into a palace (Schofield 1984, 145–8). In 1534 the houses of the Franciscan Observants were closed, with many of the friars taken into custody for opposing the royal supremacy.

In 1535 commissioners were appointed to carry out a survey of monastic income and property, ostensibly as a basis for a tax assessment. The survey, known as the *Valor Ecclesiasticus*, provided an indispensable source of information for the Crown. It is highly valued today for its wealth of information on the state of religious houses on the eve of the Dissolution (for example, Robinson 1980). At the time of their suppression, monasteries were subject to a further detailed survey by commissioners appointed by the Court of Augmentations. The Court had been set up by an Act of Parliament in 1536 to organise the Crown's management, rental and sale of monastic properties. The surveys provide an invaluable source of information that can be used in conjunction with the *Valor*.

Events moved rapidly once the Act of Suppression had been passed. In April 1536 the commissioners appointed by the Court of Augmentations in the English and Welsh counties began to visit each of the smaller houses that fell below the size limits of the Act and accepted their surrender, or in some cases recommended that they should continue. Their survey included an assessment of the value of the lead, bells and other structural components that might be broken up before the sale of the buildings and lands took place. When the sites of dissolved monasteries were sold, the bells and lead were reserved by the Crown. In the event, about eighty of the smaller houses were allowed to continue, including the majority of nunneries. A large fee was charged, in the region of the house's annual income, for it to be refounded 'in perpetuity' by the king. In reality, this perpetual dispensation bought no more than three years' precarious survival.

In the autumn of 1536, the process of suppression provided the spark to ignite a popular uprising in the northern counties of England where social and economic grievances were already deeply felt. The Pilgrimage of Grace, as it is known, was in fact a number of more or less simultaneous revolts that had as one common concern the reversal of the process of dissolution of the monasteries. In Lincolnshire the uprising was marked by violence, but elsewhere it was mainly peaceful. There was often a reluctance by the religious themselves to be drawn into the fray, and in Lincolnshire and elsewhere there were instances of congregations being forced by threats to join the rebels. There was a greater degree of participation in some of the monasteries of the north-west. The brethren of Holm Cultram, Furness and Salley became actively involved. The king ordered the earl of Derby to hang the abbot of Salley and some of the other monks from the church tower. Neighbouring Whalley Abbey, in contrast, refused to open its gates to the insurgents until they threatened to burn it down. Salley had already been suppressed but Whalley, a much richer Cistercian house, was doubtless hoping to survive.

Retribution was swift. The king ordered the duke of Norfolk to 'cause dreadful execution upon a good number of the inhabitants, hanging them on trees, quartering them, and setting their heads and quarters in every town . . . cause all the monks and canons that be in any ways faulty, to be tied

up, without further delay or ceremony, to the terrible example of others
(Knowles 1976, 216). The monasteries of Salley, Hexham, Newminster
Lanercost and St Agatha (Easby) were specified, as well as 'all other such
places that have made any manner of resistance, or in any way conspired
or kept their houses with any force'. Summary execution of some of the
rebels took place, but monks and canons seem to have had the opportunity
to defend themselves in court. The abbots of Salley and Whalley were both
executed on the grounds of treason in March 1537. Despite being one of the
larger houses unaffected by the Act of Suppression, Whalley was closed and
taken into royal ownership. Furness was surrendered to the Crown by means
of a deed signed by the abbot and all the monks – a precedent for a course
of action which would lead to the 'voluntary' closure of the major houses
over the following four years. The fear that the larger houses were under
threat was clearly felt by some abbots. The abbot of Barlings Abbey in
Lincolnshire was accused of advising his monks to hide and sell the plate and
ornaments of the house. His defence was that he anticipated the larger
houses would soon go the way of the smaller ones. His explanation failed
to save him from execution at Tyburn on 29 March 1537.

In November 1537 the closure of the greater houses began. The first to
go was the wealthy Cluniac house at Lewes in Sussex, quickly followed by
its daughter house, Castle Acre Priory in Norfolk. Premonstratensian
Titchfield Abbey (Hampshire) was surrendered a few days later. By January
1538 the process was being speeded by a series of visitations by Cromwell's
agents designed to persuade and coerce communities into surrender. At the
same time shrines came under attack. 5,000 marks' (£3,300) worth of gold,
silver and precious stones were stripped from the tomb of St Edmund at the
great Benedictine abbey of Bury St Edmunds. The commissioners wrote to
Cromwell that it was 'a rich shrine which was very cumbrous to deface'
(Cook 1965, 114). Several wagonloads of precious metals and jewels were
sent to the king from the shrine of St Thomas Becket at Canterbury.

From February 1538 efforts began to bring about the closure of friaries,
which had been excluded from the Act of Suppression. The process was
similar to that for abbeys and priories, with the friars 'voluntarily' surrender-
ing their houses into the hands of the king. In May 1539 an Act of Parliament was passed which regularised the continuing campaign of surrenders by
vesting in the Crown all monastic possessions from houses that closed.

As the closures continued, some houses anticipated their demise by selling
their possessions. In Oxford the various houses of friars had been felling
trees, selling jewels and plate, and the Franciscans had even gone so far as
to dig up and melt down the lead pipes of their conduit (Knowles 1976,
247). Nonetheless, there was little violence or other signs of defiance from
the demoralised communities when the end came. The religious accepted
their pensions, and in numerous cases found livings as parish priests, clerks,
or even bishops.

Scotland

The closure of Scottish monasteries did not take place with the speed of the Dissolution in England and Wales. It might have done had James V heeded the advice of his uncle, Henry VIII, who wrote to him in 1540 recommending tactics that would enable the wealth of the Scottish houses to benefit the royal exchequer (Knowles 1976, 88). Instead, monasteries declined over a period of half a century, hastened by a number of factors. Foremost of these was the practice which had begun in the late fifteenth century whereby 'commendators' were appointed as abbots or priors. They were usually kinsmen of the king or of powerful lords who could use their influence to secure for their relatives the dignities and income of the abbacy without any of the duties. Thus in 1514 James Stewart, Earl of Moray, an illegitimate son of James IV, became commendator of the Tironensian abbey of Arbroath (Tayside Region) at the age of fifteen (Mackie and Cruden 1954). A later commendator, who was also Archbishop of St Andrew's, made liberal grants of Arbroath's lands to his mistress in the 1540s. The path of departure from monasticism continued through the sixteenth century. Despite being a protestant, the marquess of Hamilton still used the title of Abbot of Arbroath. Not until 1608 was a charter confirming Arbroath's dissolution granted by King James VI. The abbot's house became a dwelling, and the lady chapel served for a few years as a protestant church, until in 1590 the parishioners moved into a new church built from the stones and timber of the monastic dormitory.

The lingering death of monasticism in Scotland was hastened in the case of Borders monasteries by attacks by English forces. Dryburgh Abbey suffered so badly in 1544 that the monastery was never rebuilt, although it continued in name until the last of the Premonstratensian canons died at the end of the century (Richardson and Wood 1948).

Ireland

The Act of Suppression of 1536 applied to all religious houses in Ireland, but those in the Gaelic West were beyond the effective power of the Crown. The monasteries within the Pale were therefore the first to be closed. There was little opposition and no violence. The priority of the Crown in England was the maximisation of finance for the Exchequer. The relative poverty of most Irish houses made financial gain less important, but seizure of their lands provided an opportunity to attract English immigrants that could buttress the authority of the Dublin colonial administration (Stalley 1987, 28). The Anglo-Irish houses were dissolved within a similar time-frame as their English and Welsh equivalents. The two largest Cistercian abbeys, St Mary's in Dublin and Mellifont (Co. Louth), surrendered in July and October 1539. St Mary's was rapidly converted to become an arsenal for the royal army. As early as 1540 the roof timbers of Bective Abbey (Co. Meath) were being used for the repair of the king's mills. Christchurch Cathedral in Dublin was dissolved as an Augustinian priory in 1539, but it continued as a cathedral under a dean and chapter.

Bective Abbey was sold to Thomas Agard, vice-treasurer of the Dublin Mint, who used the buildings to establish a short-lived weaving enterprise (Stalley 1987, 227). Eventually he adapted the monastic buildings as a fortified mansion. An external staircase was built on to the south front to give access to the refectory which became the great hall.

Beyond the Pale the fate of the monasteries resembled those in Scotland more than England. Monks continued to occupy the buildings, but their numbers gradually dwindled and ownership passed into lay hands. Holycross Abbey (Co. Tipperary) had a particularly protracted decline. By the late sixteenth century it was continuing with a bizarre combination of 'relics, pilgrimage, a Cistercian monk and Protestant prayer books' (*ibid.* 29). In the seventeenth century there was an attempt to revive the Cistercian order by the 'abbot' of Holycross who also established houses at Drogheda and Dublin. The venture was ended abruptly during Oliver Cromwell's savage campaigns of 1649–50. At Mellifont the last person to style himself 'Abbot' died in 1719, long after the medieval buildings had been converted to a secular residence.

The friaries that had spread throughout Ireland, and which had experienced a surge of popularity in the fifteenth century, clung tenaciously to a form of continued existence in the West. The Franciscan friary in Ennis (Co. Clare) was reformed in 1550 and became the last school of Catholic theology in Ireland. It became a parish church in 1615, and the last of the friars died in 1617. In 1628, however, a few friars returned. In 1651 Cromwell's forces expelled the friars, but again they returned. It was not until the end of the seventeenth century that Ennis Friary was finally deserted. The preservation of a form of monastic life in turn led to the survival of friary buildings for, in the case of Ennis, a century and a half longer than in England. In consequence, Irish friaries are often in a much better state of preservation than those in other parts of the British Isles. The Dominican Friary at Athenry (Co. Galway) was even rebuilt following the return of friars under the patronage of merchants of Galway, and it achieved the status of a university in 1644. Six years later, however, the Cromwellians evicted the friars.

Destruction

The Pilgrimage of Grace, with the demands for the restitution of suppressed houses and instances of the actual return of brethren as at Salley Abbey, made it imperative that the closed monasteries should be made uninhabitable. Commissioners were instructed to 'pull down to the ground all the walls of the churches, steeples, cloisters, fraters, dorters, chapter houses, with all other houses, saving them that may be necessary for the farmer' (Platt 1984, 229). By farmer was meant the person appointed as interim custodian of the site. In some cases professional demolition gangs were employed. Giovanni Portinari's team of twenty-five men were hired in London to demolish Lewes Priory; five months after its surrender most of the buildings had been destroyed. Masonry and columns were undercut and shored with timber, which was then set alight to bring the structure crashing down. Gunpowder was also used (Knowles 1976, 267). Portinari's evident pride in his destructive expertise is shown in a letter written to Cromwell in March 1538: 'I told your lordship of a vault on the right side of the high altar, that was borne up with four great pillars, having about it five chapels, which be compassed in with the walls 70 steps in length, that is 200 feet. All this is down on Thursday and Friday last. Now we are plucking down a higher vault, borne up by four thick and gross pillars' (Cook 1965, 138).

Chertsey Abbey in Surrey surrendered on 6 July 1537. The lands were used to endow an entirely new monastery at Bisham, founded by the king at the suppressed Augustinian priory. The abbot and fourteen monks moved from Chertsey with instructions to pray for the king and Jane Seymour. Henry's abbey had a short life, but the vacated buildings at Chertsey lasted even less time. They were demolished to provide stone for the king's new manor house at Oatlands in Surrey. Only the foundations and lower courses of the walls were left, to be rediscovered in a number of diggings and excavations (Poulton 1988) (figure 17). Indeed, it was to extract further stone to use in building a house that a Mr Groombridge purchased the site and employed workmen to dig for masonry, leading to the discovery of the superb series of tiles for which Chertsey is renowned (Eames 1980, 141). Large quantities of mouldings from the monastic buildings were found in excavations at the king's house at Oatlands (Cook 1969).

Although the instructions to the commissioners envisaged wholesale demolition of the buildings of the cloister, it was rare for destruction to be as thorough as at Lewes and Chertsey. The sheer cost was prohibitive, so it usually sufficed to strip the roofs from the church and the chapter house, thus making religious life impossible should attempts be made to reoccupy the site. In addition, it seems probable that the dormitory was made uninhabitable as a further deterrent to reoccupation. This would account for the small number of dormitory buildings to survive to the present day.

The extent to which a monastic house was dismantled was largely a matter of chance. Two factors were the suitability of the buildings for conversion to alternative uses, and the value of the components as building materials. Conversion led to the survival of medieval buildings at least in part. Their use as a source of stone and timber, on the other hand, could result in thorough demolition. The determining factor was the location of the monastery. If it was in a place where there was a plentiful supply of building stone and timber, it was far less likely that the buildings would be used as a quarry. If, on the other hand, it was situated in an area that lacked good building stone, the value of reused material was far higher, justifying the expense of demolition. There is a considerable contrast between the rate of survival of monastic remains in Yorkshire, with its plentiful supplies of good building stones, and Lincolnshire where so few monasteries have substantial above-ground remains. The thoroughness with which a monastery might be demolished is well illustrated by Shouldham Priory in Norfolk (figures 13 and 14).

The examination of individual monastic houses can provide an indication of the value placed upon different types of stone. At Tintern Abbey (Gwent), the removal of stones was only worthwhile from positions in the building where it was relatively easy. Thus, the buttresses on the church have had

Figure 81. Buttresses of the south aisle of the church, Tintern Abbey, showing robbing of the quoin blocks only to a height that could be easily reached from the ground. Putlog holes where timber scaffolding was attached during construction can also be seen on the aisle and clerestory wall faces.
  Photograph by Patrick Greene.

blocks of ashlar facing-stone removed to a height that it was possible to reach from the ground, but no higher (figure 81). At Glenluce Abbey (Dumfries and Galloway) the walls consist mainly of slate rubble with sandstone ashlar facing to doorways and windows, and quoins at the corners of buildings. The squared sandstone blocks were attractive for reuse and have therefore been removed in places, but the slate rubble was of little worth (figure 30).

  The other factor that determined the extent of survival of monastic buildings was their location in relation to centres of population. A monastery in an isolated spot in the country was far less likely to be used as a source of stone than one within or close to a town. Thus, to take the example of Yorkshire again, there is a marked contrast between the surviving structures at country sites such as Byland, Rievaulx, Fountains and Mount Grace, and the urban monasteries of York. Of the friaries practically nothing now remains except for part of the Franciscan precinct wall. The Gilbertine priory of St Andrew's, founded outside the walls of the city in 1202, has been excavated (Kemp 1987). It was found to have been demolished and thoroughly robbed in the years following the Dissolution. A large limekiln was built into the centre of the cloister where the demolition team had reduced the less valuable pieces of limestone, such as window mouldings and other carved embellishments, to quick-lime for mortar used in building activities in the city. St Mary's Abbey was closed in 1539 and the abbot's house was converted into the 'King's Manor', the headquarters of the Council of the North. In 1568–70 the building was remodelled and extended, with the south nave aisle of the church converted to house domestic quarters of two storeys. In excavations in 1829 (figure 16) a wall was found that had been built as part of the remodelling, and which consisted of reused pieces of medieval masonry. At a depth of about 2 metres, seven life-size sculpted figures of prophets and apostles were found lying face-down where they had been placed as a base for the foundations (Wilson 1983, 100). The casual way in which such magnificent religious subjects were treated, simply used as foundation rubble, is an eloquent reminder of the extent to which beliefs had changed by the later sixteenth century.

Lead and bellmetal

The reservation by the Crown of lead and bellmetal usually entailed its removal in advance of the sale or lease of the site, presumably because such valuable metals were vulnerable to theft. At Rievaulx Abbey in Yorkshire, four lead ingots were found during clearance of the west end of the nave by the Department of Works under Sir Charles Peers in 1920 (Dunning 1952). Each was 'canoe-shaped', having been made by pouring molten lead into a trough scooped in the ground. They weighed about 9 hundredweight (c. 450 kg.) each. A crowned rose denoting royal ownership had been stamped on the upper surface of each. There was also a hole for prising the ingot out of the mould using an iron bar. The Rievaulx ingots are consistent with a commissioner's letter to Thomas Cromwell in August 1537 about another Yorkshire house, Jervaulx Abbey. The writer says he had 'received his letter ordering him to have the leads . . . melted into sows and marked with the king's mark'. The stripping of the Jervaulx cloister took five days, and that was just the beginning. Altogether the buildings produced lead valued at £1,000 over a period of three months. By this time it was impossible to move it, as another letter to Cromwell explained: 'the ways of the county are so foul and deep that no carriage can pass in winter'. The lead weighed 399½ fother. A fother was 19½ hundredweight (almost 1 tonne), so two ingots of the kind found at Rievaulx constituted one fother. Amongst Yorkshire abbeys, Rievaulx produced 140 fother; Byland 100; Kirkham Priory 30; Northallerton Friary 15, and Richmond Friary 12. Amidst the destruction of the roof of the great church at Rievaulx, it is understandable that four of the ingots should be mislaid. Another ingot that failed to be delivered to the Crown, and which is now displayed in the parish church, came from the Augustinian abbey at Kenilworth (Warwickshire).

On most sites, the lead from windows was treated no differently from other structural lead. Heaps of window glass are frequently found in demolition deposits, dumped after the lead cames had been melted down. Occasionally, however, windows were removed for reuse elsewhere. Bradwell Abbey, a small Benedictine house in Buckinghamshire, was one of the monasteries closed by Wolsey. A survey of 1526 referred to windows in the

0   400mm

Figure 82. Reconstruction drawing of the window from Bradwell Abbey, Buckinghamshire, found in Dissolution layers, showing the painted glass and lead-work.

Drawing supplied by Buckinghamshire County Council.

church and chancel 'which would be taken down and saved for the mending of divers Chancels etc' (Croft and Mynard 1986). During the excavation of the abbey, a leaded panel of a late-thirteenth-century window was found within a sixteenth-century layer of dumped clay roof-tiles and limestone rubble outside the north wall of the church. Careful lifting and treatment of the glass and the lead frame enabled the design to be reconstructed – a beautiful geometric and foliage panel flanked by borders of birds alternating with six-petalled flowers on a stylised vine (figure 82). The Bradwell Abbey window, and the hundreds of glass quarries that are found in the destruction levels of monastic sites, testify to the extent of the losses of this particularly fragile component of medieval monasteries.

There is less information on the use of the bellmetal. A typical monastery might produce two or three tonnes of the valuable copper alloy. Because its melting point is much higher than that of lead, it was less practicable to build furnaces to melt it down on site (although specialist bell-makers had often constructed furnaces of appropriate design for casting the bells). The four bells from Neath Abbey (Glamorgan) were transported to Bristol to be melted down (Butler 1976, 12). The seven bells from Monk Bretton Priory were sent to London (Graham and Gilyard-Beer 1966, 5). It is not certain to what use the metal was then put, but the Crown did have a use for bronze. The canon for ships such as the *Mary Rose*, and for the coastal forts that Henry VIII built as a protection against invasion from the continent, may have been cast from monastic bellmetal, the antithesis of turning swords into plough-shares.

The sale and rental of land and buildings

The greatest resource for the Court of Augmentations was the monastic buildings and lands. Although Cromwell's original intention was to keep the properties of dissolved monasteries in hand, the policy was rapidly overtaken by the need of the royal Exchequer for large sums of money, and by the voracious appetite of the Tudor gentry for land acquisition. A small proportion of the total were given away to individuals to whom Henry owed some favours, but the vast majority were sold at the market rate or leased (usually for terms of twenty-one years). Individuals who had entered into rental agreements with monasteries prior to the Dissolution had their contracts honoured.

Conversion of buildings

The fate of the monastic buildings varied. Demolition carried out with the thoroughness that occurred at Lewes and Chertsey was rare, for the structures themselves had a potential for adaptation. The most common fate was conversion into a residence for the new owner. The remains that stand as the most potent symbol of the new order are those of the gatehouse range of Thomas Wriothesley's new mansion at Titchfield. The nave of the priory church provided the basic structure for the immense, dramatic statement of

Wriothesley's power and wealth. The transepts, chancel and western part of the nave were levelled. No feelings of sacrilege seem to have troubled Wriothesley.

Whereas the gatehouse range at Titchfield was a new structure, the gatehouses of monasteries frequently continued to stand after the Dissolution as residences. They usually had chambers on the first floor and often lodges and other buildings attached to them. They had been particularly appropriate places in which to provide accommodation for corrodians, as they were situated on the fringes of the monastic precinct. In the late medieval period some gatehouses were built on an ambitious scale. That erected in the 1380s at the Augustinian house at Thornton in Lincolnshire is the most outstanding. Above the gateway passages were halls on the first and second floors, each with adjoining bedchambers equipped with fireplaces and toilets. It is not surprising that a gatehouse with the comfortable facilities of Thornton, or indeed much simpler structures containing more modest apartments, found an immediate use at the Dissolution, thus ensuring their long-term survival.

A considerable proportion of the medieval fabric survives in the mansion created at Lacock Abbey in Wiltshire. The Augustinian nunnery was unusually wealthy and underwent a major programme of rebuilding in the early fifteenth century. The arrangements for constructing a chapel are described in Chapter 3. The beautiful cloister and chapter house, built in a honey-coloured limestone, were incorporated into the house. The cloister became a major asset when Lacock was remodelled in Gothic Revival style by the architect Sanderson Miller in 1753. The outer courtyard, although apparently built by Sir William Sharington who acquired the nunnery following its suppression in 1539, had a range of buildings that are similar to those of a religious house. The brewhouse in particular, which still has its furnace, vats and cooling tanks, replicates its medieval predecessors. Although the cloister was retained, the church was comprehensively demolished: the excavator remarked that 'with the exception of the six westernmost bays of the north wall . . . the destruction had been so complete that the barest foundations alone were traceable, and in places even these were entirely removed' (Brakspear 1901).

At Newstead Abbey in Nottinghamshire the cloisters were, like those at Lacock, turned into corridors. Here the origins of the house as an Augustinian priory were made apparent to every visitor to the Byron household by the retention of the west front of the church as part of the facade of the mansion (figure 15). It would have been a simple matter to have demolished it along with the rest of the church, so it is clear that its incorporation was a conscious architectural and historical statement.

Not only was the west front of the church an asset to the Byrons. So too was the monastic water supply which continued in use, including the lead lavatorium cistern in the south cloister-walk (Girouard 1978, 247). Few medieval domestic houses had a piped water supply, but the new lay owners of many monastic sites adapted an existing system for their purposes.

Apart from those monasteries that became the cathedrals of Henry VIII's new dioceses (Bristol, Oxford, Gloucester, Peterborough and Chester) and those that continued in that role (Winchester, Worcester, Canterbury,

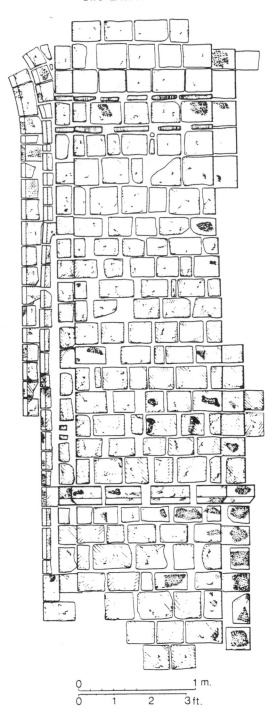

0 ———————————— 1 m.

0   1   2   3 ft.

Figure 83. Drawing of the reassembled wall of the presbytery of St Augustine's Abbey, Canterbury.
Drawing supplied by David Sherlock, English Heritage.

Rochester, Durham, Norwich, Ely and Carlisle), almost every site became a candidate for conversion to a house, including sites where the monastic church continued in parochial use. At Lanercost Priory (Cumbria), the nave of the Augustinian church was acquired by the parish, but the west range became a residence. It had been the prior's quarters, and included a tower-house built for defence as a result of the priory's exposed position near the border with Scotland.

The archaeological investigation of any monastic site should start from the assumption that traces of post-Dissolution occupation will be present. Occupation may have continued until the present day, or it may have lasted a few years in the mid sixteenth century. Evidence may be present in the form of earthworks or below-ground features, or standing structures. Collapsed masonry may be capable of reconstruction, at least on paper (figure 83), as at St Augustine's Abbey, Canterbury, where an entire length of walling was found where it had collapsed (Sherlock and Woods 1988).

Monastic remains hidden within later buildings

Post-Dissolution buildings may incorporate monastic structures, some of which remain to be found. The potential is dramatically illustrated by the case of Norton Priory in Cheshire, where the buildings of the outer court-yard were converted into a Tudor mansion, which in turn was replaced by a Georgian country house (Greene 1989). Removal of eighteenth-century brickwork revealed a late-twelfth-century passage with decorative arcading of the highest quality.

An impressive example of the capacity for medieval remains to survive unrecognised is provided by another Cheshire house, Vale Royal Abbey. It was acquired, with its lands, by one of the royal commissioners, Thomas Holcroft. In 1539 he wrote to the king reporting that he had 'plucked down' the church (*Letters and Patents Henry VIII* xiii (2), 123). It was widely assumed that all the monastic buildings had been demolished. The *History of the King's Works*, for example, states that 'nothing now remains above ground of one of the largest works of piety ever undertaken by a medieval English king' (Brown, Colvin and Taylor 1963, 257). Recent research has shown that, in fact, extensive elements of the west range, kitchens and refectory (figure 84) still remain encased within the existing structures (McNeil and Turner 1990). In particular, sets of roof trusses remain, still supporting the roofs of the two ranges but hidden away above later ceilings (figure 85). The timber-work showed that the refectory range of the Cistercian monastery occupied the southern side of the cloister with its axis aligned east–west. Dendrochronological sampling of the timbers gave a date in the second half of the fifteenth century for the reconstruction of the refectory in the form of a central hall of three bays, open to the roof, and flanked by a pair of single-bay rooms, all set above a masonry ground floor. Figure 85 is an isometric reconstruction of the refectory range as adapted after the Dissolution. The kitchens, of two bays, were immediately to the west of the refectory. Adjoining their north side was the west range. It appears to have been built in the late thirteenth or early fourteenth century in masonry to

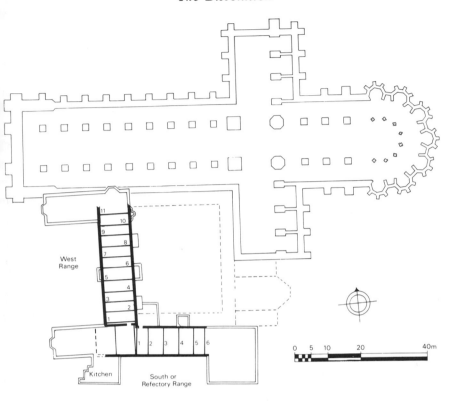

Figure 84. Plan of the buildings of Vale Royal Abbey. The location of surviving medieval fabric within the present house is shown in bold. The site was dominated by the enormous church with its chevet eastern end.

Drawing supplied by Robina McNeil.

eaves height. The timber roof showed three phases of medieval work, the earliest dating from the time when it covered the lay brothers' dormitory.

The examples of Norton and Vale Royal emphasise the importance of an awareness of the archaeological potential of buildings that occupy the sites of monasteries. The potential is most likely to be realised when building work is being carried out – at Vale Royal it was a proposal to convert the house into flats that precipitated the detailed study. The renewal of plaster, the modernisation of heating systems, the installation of damp-proofing, the repair of roofs are all the kinds of activities that may lead to the discovery of medieval features. In turn, the accumulation of information about the monastic origins of post-Dissolution houses can shed light on the ways in which their lay owners converted them to their new uses. The variety of options has been described in the case of Augustinian religious houses (Dickinson 1968).

The Tudor purchasers of dissolved monasteries were often looking for buildings that would form the basis of a country house surrounded by a ready-made estate. Urban friaries tended to be on restricted sites within

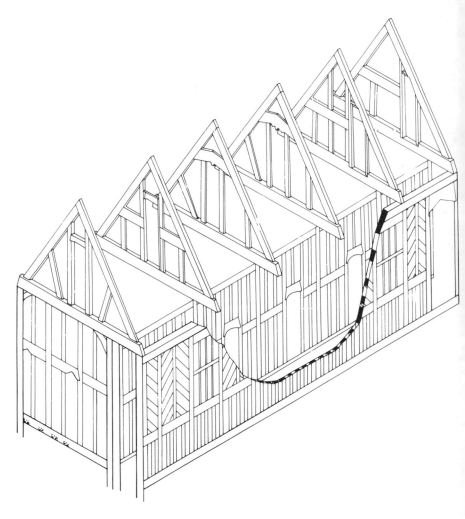

Figure 85. The refectory of Vale Royal Abbey, Cheshire, adapted as part of the secular mansion.
Drawing supplied by Robina McNeil.

towns or on their outskirts, and they lacked an endowment of land. They were therefore a much less attractive proposition for adaptation. The Dominican friary at Newcastle-upon-Tyne was, however, converted into accommodation for craft companies (figure 86). Some conversions of friaries to houses did take place, as happened at Hartlepool (Daniels 1983). The church of Gloucester Blackfriars was converted into a small mansion by Sir Thomas Bell in 1539. He inserted floors and windows in the church and put the cloister buildings to commercial·use. Despite experiencing various vicissitudes, the buildings have survived in reasonably complete form making it, with Norwich Blackfriars, one of only two English Dominican friaries still substantially complete. The roofs and floors of the Gloucester buildings have

Figure 86. The lavatorium built into the wall of the cellarer's range of the Dominican friary, Newcastle-upon-Tyne, close to the entrance to the refectory in the south range. The buildings were used as accommodation for the craft companies after the Dissolution.
    Photograph by Patrick Greene.

been the subject of detailed study (Rackham, Blair and Munby 1978). As well as conversion to houses and commercial premises such as workshops, other uses for friary buildings included schools, hospitals and guildhalls (Butler 1984, 134). The Carmelite friary at Coventry was divided at the Dissolution. The church was acquired by the corporation of the city, and the claustral buildings and land were purchased by one John Hales who adapted them as a house and grounds. A condition of the sale was that he should found a free grammar school, which he did in the church (Woodfield 1981). The magnificent east range survives, altered by Hales' work of conversion, but retaining the vaulted cloister walk, the chapter house and the dormitory extending above both on the first floor.

Monastic churches as parish churches

Monastic churches might find a post-Dissolution use no better than as farms and cowsheds (figure 87). However, a more dignified fate was possible, for some monastic churches were retained for parish use at the Dissolution. In some cases part of the church had already been in regular use by parishioners, but most retentions resulted from a swift offer of purchase

Figure 87. Buildwas Abbey, Shropshire. Watercolour painted by J.M.W. Turner in 1797 or 1798 showing the interior of the church, with the north transept converted into a barn and byre.

Reproduced by permission of the Whitworth Art Gallery, Manchester (accession number D.10.1887).

Figure 88. The refectory of Horsham St Faith Priory, Norfolk, converted into a farmhouse after the Dissolution, from the north. The round-headed doorway on the left led into a passage giving access to the cloister.
Photograph supplied by David Sherlock, English Heritage.

when the demolition of the building was threatened. The scale of the monastic church was often far greater than that required for parochial use. A common solution, as at Augustinian Bolton Priory in Yorkshire, was to build a wall across at the east end of the nave and abandon the eastern parts of the monastic church. The nave, although a conveniently-shaped rectangle, was not invariably the part that was retained. At Benedictine Pershore Abbey (Hereford and Worcester), the nave was demolished, leaving one of the transepts and choir as the parish church, which is now rather like a nose cone from which the rocket has separated. The parish church of Little Dunmow in Essex is the former lady chapel of the Augustinian priory. A refectory might be converted successfully into a secular residence, as at Horsham St Faith Priory in Norfolk (figure 88) (Sherlock 1976). At Beaulieu (Hampshire), however the refectory of the Cistercian abbey was acquired by the parishioners as their church. Friary churches of the Norwich Blackfriars, the Chichester Greyfriars, and Augustinian friars in London were given as churches for Protestant refugees from the Continent (Butler 1984, 134).

Parish churches that were once monastic have all the potential for archaeological investigation as churches that have always been parochial (Rodwell 1981). However, it is the presence of buildings of the cloister and beyond at once-monastic churches that make them particularly challenging (figure 21). As parish churches are usually surrounded by graveyards that are still in active use, the threat of piecemeal, unconscious destruction of archaeological information is considerable. Little survives the repeated digging of graves to the regulation depth of six feet. Where paths through the graveyard are of some antiquity, however, limited strips of undisturbed strata may survive, as at Porchester in Hampshire (Borg and Baker in Cunliffe 1977). It is in Ireland, however, that damage from modern gravedigging is at its most severe, as burials continue not only at those monasteries where the church is in use, but also amidst the ruins of long-abandoned monastic sites. In Scotland, too, there has been a tradition of continued burial at monastic sites. Dryburgh Abbey (Borders), for example, has the graves of Sir Walter Scott and Field Marshal Earl Haig.

Excavation of destruction levels

It is vital that post-Dissolution layers and features are excavated with as great a degree of care as earlier deposits on a monastic site. They are capable of yielding information on three main areas of study: the post-medieval use of the site; the process of demolition of buildings; and the form and character of medieval buildings as a result of the recovery of elements of their structures. Much excavation of monastic sites has simply involved the whole-scale clearance of rubble in an attempt to uncover masonry. The potential of careful excavation of Dissolution layers has now been demonstrated on a number of sites, including St Albans Abbey in Hertfordshire. The cellarer's range vaulting, with ribs in the form of a radiating star, had collapsed after the Dissolution and was found lying on the floor where it had fallen. This enabled its design to be accurately reconstructed.

The history of each site will determine the extent to which demolition layers survive. Norton Priory and Bordesley Abbey provide contrasting case-studies. At Norton the continued occupation of the site resulted in particularly destructive landscaping and gardening in the nineteenth century. Over much of the site there was a half-metre depth of rich black garden soil, with the tell-tale corrugations resulting from double-digging which penetrated into medieval layers. Few areas were immune from these activities, or the laying of drains, sewers, water pipes and foundations. The foundations, however, were a rich source of architectural fragments. Carved and moulded stones that were unsuitable for reuse as facing blocks were utilised as rubble.

At Bordesley Abbey, by comparison, considerable amounts of demolition rubble covered the site, little disturbed. Techniques of excavation and recording of the demolition layers were refined during the 1989 season of excavation (Astill, Hirst and Wright 1990). Work took place on the northern side of the church. Debris up to a metre in depth was banked up against the north and south faces of the north arcade. The excavation was gridded using the axes of the church. The main categories of building materials – stone, ceramic, window glass and lead – were recorded by context and grid unit in order to allow an assessment of their spatial distribution and significance for the demolished superstructure.

The sequence of demolition activities was revealed. Firstly the tile floors were stripped out, leaving only impressions in the screed, or areas of worn tiles. At the same time other fixtures and fittings were removed, such as the screens and the choir stall timber superstructure. A blocking wall behind the choir stalls was dismantled, opening up the choir and the east end of the church to the demolition team. Immediately above the floor screed in the northern aisle was a layer of trampled dirt containing fragments of window glass and lead scattered during the removal of the windows of the north aisle and the clerestory. The next step in the demolition campaign was the dismantling of the vault and roof of the north aisle. This was followed by the complete removal to foundation level of the north wall of the church – the upcast from the robber trench immediately sealed the layer of trampled dirt. This was the only wall to have been completely removed at the time of the Dissolution, and may have been demolished to ground level to facilitate access to the church and claustral area. Carts could then be brought into the north aisle to be loaded with stone.

Demolition then began in earnest. The excavators found layers of rubble and mortar that had built up against the lowest parts of the arcade piers. This suggests that stone was being selected for reusable pieces, with mortar left with material from the wall cores piled up in the church. Following a break in demolition, a second phase began which included the erection of scaffolding to enable the north arcade to be taken down. Broken pieces of mouldings and some intact carved stonework had been dumped, presumably having been rejected as unsuitable for reuse. After this intense period of demolition, soil accumulated in the hollow in the centre of the choir, and there was only small-scale robbing of stonework thereafter.

The evidence from the excavation is consistent with an account returned by John Scudamore, one of the commissioners for Worcestershire (Cook 1965, 180). It lists a series of sales of materials from the Bordesley buildings, including iron and glass from the windows on the north side of the cloister, paving tiles from the cloister-walks, and a stone buttress at the east end of the church (see Chapter 1). Analysis of the moulded stones from the Bordesley demolition layers will take several years, but it is clear that much can be learnt about the superstructure of the church. Details included a blind-arcaded fifteenth-century screen, and tracery from the clerestory windows.

Although the demolition of the church at Bordesley was carried out over a relatively short period, it cannot be assumed that the buildings of the cloister and outer courtyard were taken down at the same time, despite the sale of some materials at an early date. On any monastic site, the process of dismemberment is likely to have been complex, requiring considerable care to disentangle. Unfortunately the process of clearance to which so many monastic sites have been subjected has removed much potential information. However, evidence can survive, not only in the form of dumps of demolition debris, but also in the structures into which materials were incorporated. If the structures can be dated, then dates can be obtained for the dismantling of components of the monastic complex. Foundations of post-Dissolution buildings can prove particularly interesting, for moulded stonework is most likely to have been used here in the form of rubble. Most monastic sites had materials removed over a long period of time. Caution needs to exercised in interpreting the date of robber trenches, for these result only from the removal of the lowermost courses of masonry which may have taken place long after the demolition of the main superstructure.

Re-use of fixtures and fittings

Stories of the whole-scale reuse of elements of monastic buildings need to be treated with caution. There is no doubt that in some cases fittings were acquired at the Dissolution. The choir stalls of Whalley Abbey in Lancashire were moved into the neighbouring parish church where they remain to this day. However, legends abound of parish church roofs and screens that are said to have been brought from a nearby monastery. Few stand up to examination, for there seems to have been a temptation to ascribe any splendid piece of timberwork to a monastic origin. Comparison of dimensions is often sufficient to disprove the theory. The panelled roof of the nave and chancel of Witton church at Northwich in Cheshire is reputed to have been brought from Norton Priory at the Dissolution. However, not only does its span make this impossible, but the roof has the initials of William Venables, the lord of the manor of Witton, incorporated in a number of the carved bosses. Not all traditions of reuse of elements of a monastery are bogus, however. One well-attested case is that of Monk Bretton Priory in Yorkshire. Following the surrender of the priory in November 1538, Thomas Wentworth bought the north aisle of the nave with the pillars and arches to build a north aisle at Wentworth church. That church was demolished in 1877, but amongst the masonry were found four twelfth-century capitals from the priory church (Graham and Gilyard-Beer 1966, 9).

Fittings from dissolved monasteries could become scattered very quickly as a result of looting. Dr John London wrote in October 1538 to Cromwell about problems that he had encountered in Warwick (Cook 1965, 211): 'the poor people thoroughly in every place be so greedy upon these houses when they be suppressed, that by day and by night, not only of the towns but also of the country, they do continually resort as long as any door, window, iron, or glass, or loose lead remaineth in any of them.' The letter does provide an instance of the consideration of the reuse of a roof: 'The King's Grace hath a kitchen in building at Warwick Castle. There is one roof of 60 feet long and more at the friars would serve there, and the old tile is very good.'

9 Reawakening interest

During the eighteenth century, popular interest in the remains of former monasteries began to grow. On the one hand antiquarians engaged in writing the histories of monasteries, as described in Chapter 1. On the other, the ragged walls clad with ivy, sprouting grass, and tinged with mosses and lichens appealed to artists searching for inspiration in romantic ruins. This chapter will discuss the growth of awareness of monasteries amongst the general public, and the development of a widespread appreciation of the importance of monastic remains that led to measures to preserve and interpret them.

The artistic possibilities of classical antiquity attracted artists from the seventeenth century. Claude Gellée (Le Lorrain), 1600–1682, was foremost amongst those who portrayed a romanticised past of landscapes with classical temples and palaces. Sometimes, as with 'Seaport with the embarkation of the Queen of Sheba' (National Gallery, London, No. 14, painted 1648), correctly detailed classical buildings include one in ruins to emphasise the antiquity of the scene. The contrast between the mighty but decaying remains of a glorious past, and the apparently trivial preoccupations of the peasantry is a recurring theme of romantic painters. Often the descendants of temple-builders are shown engaged in nothing more exalted than washing their laundry in streams that flow past fallen columns and cornices.

By the beginning of the eighteenth century the Grand Tour had become established as part of the education of the aristocracy and the inspiration of artists. The sketch books filled on a single expedition with details of classical remains could provide the raw material for paintings for many years afterwards. J.M.W. Turner became familiar with classical landscape during the early part of his career when he was employed to copy drawings and paintings by established artists. He made his first actual visit to Rome in 1819. Amongst the many works resulting from the sketches he made on his tour is a large oil painting of the 'Forum Romanum, for Mr Soane's Museum' (Tate Gallery, London, N00504). It was exhibited in 1826, but proved too large for Mr Soane to accommodate. It exemplifies the kind of painting that is at first sight topographical, but is in fact charged with symbolism of past glories. It includes the Arch of Titus, the Basilica of Constantine and the Capitol, arranged with considerable licence, but accurate in detail. A human dimension is provided in the form of two women, one with bare shoulders sitting amidst fallen capitals, the other kneeling in supplication before a monk or friar in a brown habit who has been detained from a religious procession that is winding towards the Church of St Lorenzo (Temple of Antoninus and Faustina). The fallen women amidst the fallen masonry emphasise the painter's symbolic, moralistic intent.

At home in the British Isles, remains of the Roman era were not of a grandeur to compare with those that the traveller to Italy would encounter. There was nothing Roman in Britain capable of illustrating the fall of empires or the transience of human achievement. However, artists realised

Figure 89. Malvern Priory church and its gatehouse (Hereford and Worcester): watercolour by J.M.W. Turner, 1794. The picturesque qualities of the scene are enhanced by the contrast between the Gothic grandeur of the monastery, and the prosaic nature of the wagon in the gatehouse passage, the sawyers, and the cottage.
    Reproduced by permission of the Whitworth Art Gallery, Manchester (accession number D.2.1984).

that medieval ruins could provide a readily available alternative. Painters in the Romantic tradition of Claude and Poussin could use the decaying masonry of monasteries as the basis of atmospheric works. Italian peasants were substituted by farm workers and their animals.

A secondary influence was that of the topographical movement. The Buck brothers had worked with great energy between 1720 and 1753 to record 'the venerable remains of above 400 Castles, Monasteries, Palaces etc in England and Wales' (S. and N. Buck 1774) (figure 15). Their artistic quality may not have been of the highest standard, but they established the market that others of greater talent exploited, such as Samuel Hieronymous Grimm. Thomas Girtin (1775–1802) raised topographical painting to new heights with compositions such as 'Durham Cathedral and Bridge from the River Wear' (Whitworth Art Gallery, Manchester) which inspired contemporaries such as Turner and Cotman. Turner's early career included drawings, at the age of sixteen, of Malmesbury and Bath abbeys in 1791. The following year he visited Tintern Abbey, which had already been singled out for its picturesque qualities, for example in Revd. William Gilpin's *Observations on the River Wye* guidebook published in 1782: 'The splendid ruin, contrasted with

Figure 90. Netley Abbey, Hampshire: watercolour by Thomas Girtin, 1797. The majestic remains of the roofless abbey church rise above trees and undergrowth where a man collects firewood.
Reproduced by permission of the Whitworth Art Gallery, Manchester (accession number D.77.1924).

the objects of nature, and the elegant line formed by the summits of the hills which include the whole, make all together a very inchanting piece of scenery.' Tintern featured in many works by Turner in the 1790s, and other subjects in that decade included Westminster Abbey, Ewenny Priory, Christchurch Cathedral in Oxford, and Battle Abbey (Sussex). It was during this period that both he and Girtin were also employed making copies of works by Romantic painters such as John Robert Cozens, including scenes of Switzerland and Italy that were to influence their treatment of English subjects. Turner's watercolour of Malvern Abbey (Hereford and Worcester) contrasts the soaring grandeur of the monastic church with the prosaic labours of the sawyers in the foreground (figure 89). Girtin's portrayal of Netley Abbey (Hampshire) shows the church filled with undergrowth and even mature trees; a peasant gathers firewood in the foreground (figure 90).

By the end of the decade, Turner was in demand as an illustrator. In 1799 he visited Lancashire to draw Whalley Abbey for the engraved prints that were to illustrate a volume of local history (Whittaker 1801). The development of a market for prints of the paintings of artists such as Turner, in his *Liber Studiorum*, increased the availability of subjects that included monastic and ecclesiological scenes to people able to afford them. One of the out-standing engravings in the *Liber* is the 'Crypt of Kirkstall Abbey'. Amongst the finest engravings of Turner's paintings of monastic subjects were those of Easby Abbey and Eggleston Abbey, commissioned for Dr Whitaker's *History of Richmondshire* (Whitaker 1823). They bring together Turner's ability to portray monastic remains with a fully-developed landscape technique inspired by his visits to the Continent.

The industrious portrayal of religious houses by Turner and his contemporaries disseminated images of abbeys and priories throughout the homes of the art-buying public, gradually raising the consciousness of landowners to the importance of such remains as landscape features. As the nobility and gentry themselves bought tuition in the techniques of making pictures in pencil or watercolour, the remains of local monasteries provided convenient subjects for practice. There was therefore an incentive for landowners to stop using abbeys as quarries for the materials to build the walls and barns of country estates. Instead, they might be preserved as romantic ruins by their enlightened owners. The east end of the church of Gisborough Priory (Cleveland), with its impressive traceried window, was one of the first examples of a monastic ruin to be retained for its visual qualities. It could be viewed across formal gardens from the Georgian mansion (figure 91).

At Fountains Abbey (North Yorkshire), which was part of the Studley Royal estate, the monastic ruins were also utilised for their picturesque qualities. When John Aislabie, Chancellor of the Exchequer, retired in disgrace as a result of his involvement as a director of the South Sea Company, he sought solace in landscaping his estate. He began the task in about 1720, assisted by his head gardener William Fisher. The planting of trees on the rolling hills, the canalisation of the River Skell to create expanses of reflecting water, and the erection of obelisks, temples and statuary brought the idyllic world of the Romantic painting to life in the Yorkshire countryside. The ruins of the Cistercian abbey provided the ideal picturesque culmination of a walk or ride up the drive alongside the Skell. Where the form of the ruins lacked the appropriate Romantic content, however, they were the subject of partial demolition, and additions of new features.

During the period when Aislabie was at work, many other owners of monastic remains were demolishing medieval structures. Monastic ruins might look attractive in a parkland setting, but did not necessarily match up to the expectations of the gentry as places in which to live. Amongst the owners of mansions that had been adapted from monastic buildings at the Dissolution there was a widespread desire for country houses of classical design. The Brookes at Norton Priory in Cheshire demolished all but one of the buildings of the medieval outer courtyard that had formed the basis of their house for 200 years. The twelfth-century west range was left standing, but was encased in the rusticated stonework of the basement of the Georgian mansion (Greene 1989). At Stoneleigh Abbey (Warwickshire), the remains of the Cistercian monastery were incorporated into the post-Dissolution house, but this was swept away in the early eighteenth century when a classical house of palatial appearance was built on the site. Only the abbey gatehouse was left. The eighteenth century was therefore a period of rising interest in

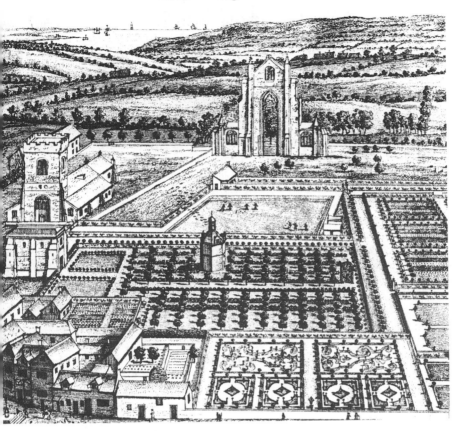

Figure 91. House, formal gardens and remains of church of Gisborough Priory by Johannes Kip.
Illustration provided by Cleveland County Council.

monastic remains, but also of destruction. If the monastery survived as ruins on the estate, its chances of survival were improved. If, however, it housed the landowner, it was in danger of being replaced by a Palladian mansion. Paradoxically, enthusiasm for classical buildings set in Romantic landscapes was the factor common to both situations.

By the nineteenth century, under the influences of the Gothic Revival and of antiquarianism, monastic remains were fashionable assets for the country house and its estate. The foremost influence on the taste for Gothic was William Beckford, who, with James Wyatt as architect, built the fantasy monastery Fonthill between 1796 and 1813 at a cost of £270,000 (Robinson 1979, 85). Like many medieval monasteries, Fonthill suffered a collapse of its tower (in 1800). Beckford employed Turner to produce drawings of the 'monastery' in course of construction, in a suitably picturesque setting; they were exhibited at the Royal Academy in 1800.

Where remains such as the west front of the canons' church at Newstead Abbey had survived, the owners were at a great advantage over those whose

ancestors had obliterated the monastic origins of their property (figure 15).
On occasions, however, the actions of the past could be reversed. The house
that occupied the site of Norton Priory was virtually turned upsidedown in
1868 to make the medieval undercroft the entrance. Previously visitors had
entered at the first floor, reached by flights of external stairs, unaware that
the basement contained medieval remains. Now they went in at ground level
through a porch containing a pair of Romanesque portals, one genuine and
the other a replica, into the restored twelfth-century undercroft equipped
with a 'medieval' fireplace, a new tiled floor, and stained glass windows.
Even the name was changed back from Norton Hall to Norton Priory. Some
owners were forced to reinvent monastic features to satisfy the enthusiasm
for medieval roots, or even, as in the case of Ashridge (Hertfordshire), to
sweep away the medieval buildings to replace them with a structure more in
tune with what its architect, James Wyatt, and patron, the Duke of
Bridgewater, thought the Middle Ages should have been like. Wyatt also
attempted a particularly unfortunate transformation of the seventeenth-
century classical Wilton House (Wiltshire) into a medieval abbey (Robinson
1979, 75).

The widening of interest

Whereas in the seventeenth and eighteenth centuries the remains of monastic
houses appeared in paintings and prints produced for the rich, in the nineteenth century the dissemination of images reached a wider audience.
Gradually, therefore, awareness of the beauty and the historic interest of
monastic remains grew. This was a necessary prerequisite for widespread
support for measures to secure their preservation. As well as paintings, prints
and books, the remains of monasteries began to appear in literature. Sir
Walter Scott's Waverley Novels had the greatest impact on the public's
awareness of castles and monasteries, which consequently became imbued
with qualities of romance and drama. *The Monastery* and *The Abbot*, both
published in 1820, were set in abbeys in the Scottish Borders. Both are
placed at the end of the Middle Ages, enabling the author to reflect Protestant attitudes to medieval monasticism whilst capitalising on their potential
as settings for historical fiction (Wilson 1989). It was fitting that Scott
should be buried within the remains of a particularly atmospheric
monastery, Dryburgh Abbey (Borders). The irony was that Scott's ancestors
had sold Dryburgh, and he had impoverished himself in building his own
'medieval' mansion whose name, Abbotsford, had echoes of a departed
monastic past. Other authors saw the possibilities of medieval themes for
their fiction. Books such as Barham's *Ingoldsby Legends* used illustrations of
actual medieval remains to sustain an illusion of historical fact within a work
of fiction (Bann 1988). The story 'Grey Dolphin' is bolstered by an engraving
such as might be found in a topographical volume, showing the effigy of Sir
Robert de Shurland in the abbey of Minster-in-Sheppey (Kent).
   The development of photography provided a further means of producing
and publishing images of monasteries. At Lacock Abbey (Wiltshire), Fox
Talbot took the first photograph in England in 1835. One of the first

Figure 92. Ivy-clad remains of the late-twelfth-century lady chapel of Glastonbury Abbey, photographed prior to the campaign of restoration of the ruins that took place in 1908–9.
Photograph supplied by Somerset County Museums Service.

markets for photography on a commercial basis was the sale of stereo images by Francis Frith and others. The picturesque qualities of monastic remains made them a popular subject (figure 92). For similar reasons, amateur photographic societies staged visits to monastic sites for their members, and abbeys frequently featured in annual exhibitions of photographs.

As photography increased as a medium for portraying monasteries, the interest of painters declined. The pre-Raphaelites found other aspects of the past to inspire them. Despite this, William Morris, as founding secretary of the Society for the Protection of Ancient Buildings, was a key figure in the movement to preserve their remains. Morris himself moved his manufacturing base to the site of Merton Abbey in 1881. One advantage was the proximity to the River Wandle. The waters that had been utilised by the medieval canons were equally valuable to Morris for the dyeing of cloth. The workshops also engaged in hand-loom weaving, embroidery, and hand-block printing of textiles. The ideal of craftsmanship was a direct result of Morris's interest in the Middle Ages, and he acknowledged the role of archaeologists in changing Victorian perceptions of it as a barbaric era to one in which the arts and crafts had flourished.

As the nineteenth century progressed, the public's appetite for images and histories of monasteries was fed by writers and publishers. An example is the two-volume *The Ruined Abbeys of Britain* (Ross 1882). It is illustrated with a full-page chromolithograph of each of the monasteries, supplemented by wood engravings in the text. The preface reveals the author's perceived market for the book:

> When an American visits his ancestral fatherland of England, his supreme desire is to look upon the cathedrals, the ancient castles, and the mutilated remains of the old abbeys, which lie scattered about so profusely over the length and breadth of our island. He has no abbey ruins in his own land, and, with a feeling of filial respect and veneration, longs to gaze upon those of England, which are the creation equally of his and our forefathers. Nor is this a sentiment peculiar to the Anglo-Saxon of the Transatlantic shore: it is shared by the denizens of every clime, where the descendants of the old castle and abbey builders are laying the foundations of new Anglian empires, with mighty futures before them, whose laws will be written in the same speech that was used by those builders of the past. At home, we who live in their midst are proud of them and are now, after centuries of neglect, doing our best, with tender care, to preserve and protect them from further decay. At the same time, every cultivated mind of other lands and peoples shares in our admiration of the architectural glories of the past, and long pilgrimages are made by them from far-distant countries, to worship at the shrines of Glastonbury, Fountains, Netley, Whitby, St Osyth, Byland, Malmesbury, Rievaulx, Jedburgh and Melrose.

It is interesting to note how monastic remains are portrayed, in the late-nineteenth century, as an essential part of the experience of American and colonial travellers in search of their roots. The Anglocentric stance of the writer (Jedburgh and Melrose are in Scotland!) and the use of the male gender alone may grate on the modern reader but would have gone unremarked in 1882. What does emerge, however, is that by that date people from Britain and abroad were visiting monasteries as tourists, and that measures were being taken to protect remains from decay.

As public interest in monasteries grew, increasing numbers of people travelled to visit the more outstanding sites. Some of these were in private ownership, but in the twentieth century, and especially following the Ancient Monuments Act of 1913, the state played an increasing role in ensuring the survival of key sites. They were seen as prime evidence of the country's history – in the words of Lord Curzon in 1913, 'documents just as valuable in reading records of the past as is any manuscript or parchment deed'. Sites such as Fountains Abbey and Bolton Priory in Yorkshire, Whalley Abbey in Lancashire and Furness Abbey in Cumbria provided an attractive day out for people in the industrial towns of northern England. Furness even had its own railway station. It did not attract universal approbation:

> A railway was made to violate the slumberous repose of the Valley of Nightshade, and that with every circumstance of Gothic ferocity to enhance the crime; its sleepers were laid down within a few feet of the spot where the mailed Barons of Kendal had hoped to find an undisturbed resting place; its engines made to whirl by the site of the high altar

(quoted in Ross 1882, 214, though he adds: 'the railway company, in the erection of the Furness Abbey Station and the adjoining hotel, have displayed

Figure 93. Visit by the drawing office staff of the Manchester locomotive builders Beyer, Peacock and Company to Whalley Abbey, Lancashire, July 1927.
Taken from 'Recreational News' in the Beyer, Peacock *Quarterly Review* volume 3, 1927, in the collection of the Museum of Science and Industry, Manchester.

great good taste in making them correspond architecturally with the ruins'). Expeditions to such abbey sites were organised by cycling and rambling clubs. They also featured in the programmes of factory social clubs (figure 93).

After the First World War the burgeoning enthusiasm for visits to historic sites encouraged publishers to produce books aimed at a mass market. In 1925 the Great Western Railway entered the field with a series of three volumes, *Cathedrals*, *Abbeys* and *Castles*. Priced at five shillings, they were 'obtainable from any bookseller, Great Western Station or Office, or direct, post-free, from the Stationery Superintendent, G.W.R.' The volume on abbeys was written by M.R. James, Provost of Eton, who is now better known for his ghost stories. In his preface he states: 'This is meant to be a popular book, and its object is to provide the traveller with an adequate explanation of the buildings he is to visit, and to bring out the importance, relative or individual, of the communities to which they belonged' (James 1925, v). He goes on to say in his introduction (page 13):

Of course I expect them to be interested, and think it worthwhile to come and see the place: that they are not merely to be unloaded for ten minutes from a charabanc and crammed into it again after wandering vaguely in and out. Visitors of that type will not be at the trouble of opening this book.

It is illustrated with photographs, drawings, plans and a map contained
within a pocket attached to the inside back cover. This at a glance reveal
what is not stated elsewhere in the book – that the monasteries selected fo
inclusion are only those that can be visited by using the GWR network! Thu
the monasteries of the East Midlands, East Anglia and the whole of northern
England and Scotland are rigorously excluded. The series is thus revealed a
another marketing tool in the bitter rivalry between the railway companies
That did not prevent it being popular with the public. The initial print-run
of 20,000 of the *Abbeys* volume sold out immediately, and a second impression of 20,000 appeared within six months. The companion volume
Cathedrals, sold 60,000 copies in two years.

The preservation movement

As awareness of the importance of monastic remains developed, preservation
became an issue when some outstanding sites came under threat. Usually it
was through the efforts of an individual, or a small group of people, that
sites were saved. Towards the end of the eighteenth century, Sweetheart
Abbey (Dumfries and Galloway) (figure 29) was purchased by two men with
the intention of using the site as a quarry (Richardson and Hume 1987). In
1779 a group of local lairds, ministers and supporters 'being desirous of
preserving the remainder of that building as an ornament to that part of the
country' bought the site from the quarrymen. The foundation of the
National Trust provided another vehicle for preserving monastic sites, such
as Hailes Abbey (Gloucestershire) and Mount Grace Priory (North
Yorkshire). In the case of Glastonbury, which had suffered greatly at the
hands of unsympathetic owners, the Church of England purchased the site
and placed it in the care of trustees.
   A succession of state organisations has been involved in the preservation
of monastic sites and their presentation to visitors. The Office of Works was
succeeded by the Ministry of Public Building and Works, and then the
Department of the Environment. Today responsibility is devolved to English
Heritage, Historic Scotland, Cadw, the Northern Ireland Office, and in the
Republic of Ireland the Office of Works is the government agency that cares
for ancient monuments. The increasing assumption of guardianship respon-
sibilities during the course of the century is illustrated by this sequence in
Wales (Robinson 1989, 327):

House	*Date of guardianship*
Tintern, Gwent	1901
Basingwerk, Clwyd	1923
Cymer, Gwynedd	1930
Strata Florida, Dyfed	1931
Talley, Dyfed	1933
St Dogmael's, Dyfed	1934
Penmon, Gwynedd	1940
Neath, West Glamorgan	1944
Ewenny, Mid Glamorgan	1949

Valle Crucis, Clwyd   1950
Llanthony, Gwent   1951
Haverfordwest, Dyfed   1982

The slow-down in acquisitions after 1951 is largely accounted for by the fact that by that date most of the significant monastic sites in Wales had been taken into care. Subsequently, however, other organisations have taken an increased responsibility for monastic sites. In the Welsh context, the outstanding example is Margam Abbey, where West Glamorgan County Council has restored the medieval and later buildings, and established a sculpture park.

Preserving monastic remains

To those charged with the preservation of monastic ruins it became clear that, without intervention, gradual decay would continue. Falls of masonry on important sites were alarming in themselves, but where large numbers of people were visiting there was also the risk of death and injury. One feature that made ruins particularly appealing artistically – the growth of plants on the stonework – accelerated decay. Ivy growing up the face of a wall could attain such a size that its weight could bring insecure masonry crashing down. Young trees becoming established on wall tops had a different effect. Their roots penetrated the cores of the walls, drawing sustenance from the lime mortar. As a tree grew, its roots thickened, detaching ashlar masonry from the core. The only solution was to clear vegetation from ruins and seal wall-tops to prevent plants gaining a foothold again. The result was masonry that looked much less romantic, but the life of which had been considerably extended. Sealing wall-tops with renewed mortar also enabled rain falling on them to be shed, slowing the weakening process of leaching lime from mortar, and reducing frost damage.

Following the passing of the Ancient Monuments Act in 1913, guardianship sites in the care of the State were the subject of campaigns of restoration in which many of the techniques of preservation in use today were developed (Thompson 1981). Unfortunately, while the quality of the repair of masonry attained a very high standard, it was often accompanied by drastic clearance of archaeological levels in and around the buildings (see Chapter 2). This led to the loss of a considerable amount of information that from a modern standpoint is to be greatly regretted. However, the survival of many buildings was ensured by repairs to the masonry.

The philosophy of restoration has changed considerably over the past century. No monastic site in the British Isles was subject to the kind of restoration that Viollet-le-Duc carried out on the twelfth-century kitchens at the monastery of Fontevrault l'Abbaye, near Saumur (Loire Valley) in France. The roofs of the kitchens appear today as an astonishing confection of cones topped by chimneys. However, although the octagonal, apsed plan of the building is genuine, it is now impossible to tell how much of the restoration of the roof was based on evidence found by the restorer, and how much was his imagination. The treatment by Victorian restorers of some of the monastic churches in Britain was as drastic as that of th Fontevrault kitchens, although rarely as attractive. St Albans Abbey was notable victim to over-enthusiastic improvement by Sir Edmund Beckett, ' very rich man who was unfortunately his own architect' (Clifton-Taylo 1967, 31). At the Dissolution it had become the largest parish church in England, but its size had exceeded the ability of the parishioners to maintain it. When the dilapidated building was raised to the rank of cathedral in 1877, Beckett was given a virtually free hand. It was one of the projects tha attracted the ire of the Society for the Protection of Ancient Buildings established to combat the destructive 'restorations' of churches. At the firs AGM of the society, held on 21 June 1878, Earl Cowper gave an example

> Now, with regard to the picturesque. The touch of time gives what nothing else can do, and beautifies in a way that nothing else can. If anyone wants to know what I mean, let him go to the cloisters of Canterbury Cathedral and look at one side of the moss-grown crumbling stone, and then let him look at the other side and see the modern reproduction and what a difference is there. To see this sort of thing going on is nearly enough to bring tears into the eyes.

The twelfth-century church of Augustinian canons at Brinkburn Priory in Northumberland was restored in a much more sympathetic manner. The church dates from the late twelfth and early thirteenth centuries and is a superb example of the transition from Romanesque to early Gothic architecture. At the Dissolution the south range became a house, and the church continued in parochial use until services lapsed in 1683. In 1825 the house was bought by the Cadogan family who commissioned the Newcastle architect Thomas Austin to prepare plans for the restoration. The building was reroofed and glazing was installed in the windows, all with great respect for the medieval building. Today it is in the care of English Heritage, and it provides an excellent example of the appearance of a medium-sized monastic church.

Until the 1970s there was, as well as the danger of the loss of stratigraphical information resulting from clearance, the problem of restoration to a 'correct' period. Although the organisers of a campaign of preservation work would acknowledge that monastic remains were likely to be the result of many phases of development, they were often ruthless in removing later material. Structures belonging to the post-Dissolution occupation of a site were demolished, usually without recording of any kind. As a result, valuable archaeological information about the process of conversion of monastic buildings to other uses has in many cases been lost. As far as medieval structures are concerned, however, the policy of 'treat as found' has left a reliable record capable of reinterpretation. In essence this policy, developed by the Ancient Monuments Board, means that the masonry of walls is repaired exactly as discovered without the replacement or addition of any stonework.

Occasionally it may prove possible to reassemble parts of a structure when a sufficient number of the components are recovered by excavation. The fragment of the cloister arcade at Rievaulx re-erected in the north-west corner is an example. Re-erection of this kind can only be justified where there is no doubt about the original design; otherwise it becomes very

Figure 94. Drawing of the re-erected fifteenth-century five-light east window of the church of Clontuskert Priory, Co. Galway. The difficulty of assembling a window of this complexity can be seen in the number of individual pieces of tracery. The entire window had collapsed; however, all but two of the pieces were recovered by excavation.

Drawing supplied by the Office of Public Works.

Figure 95. The restored cloister arcade, Holycross Abbey, Co. Tipperary. The elegant cusped arcade has been reassembled, and supports a lean-to roof. Photograph by Patrick Greene.

misleading. If the restoration programme is fully documented, the dangers of causing confusion for future archaeologists can be avoided. Re-erection has been successfully applied at a number of sites in Ireland. Excavation at Clontuskert Priory (County Galway), an Augustinian foundation, resulted in the recovery of carved stonework (Fanning 1976, 154). It proved possible to reconstruct the rood screen, parts of the cloister arcade, and the east window (figure 94).

There are cases where the long-term preservation of a building can be ensured by its conversion to an alternative use, whilst recognising that some archaeological damage will inevitably result. An excellent example is the restoration of the impressive fifteenth-century church of Holycross Abbey (County Tipperary). Parts of the church were roofless, as shown two centuries ago in the frontispiece to the *Antiquities of Ireland* (Grose 1794). Otherwise the church was largely intact, so it was a feasible proposition to bring it back into use for worship. The project, undertaken under the supervision of the Office of Works, was preceded by an archaeological excavation. Restoration began in 1971 with the intention that the project would become Ireland's main contribution to European Architectural Heritage Year 1975. Not only is the building restored, but internal features such as medieval tombs and wall paintings are protected from the elements (figure 95).

A contrasting scheme was carried out by the City of Newcastle upon Tyne on the buildings of the Dominican friary. It is one of very few monastic sites to have an account of its post-Dissolution history, including its recent restoration, published in detail (Harbottle and Fraser 1987). The friary was built within the town walls close to their north-west corner. Following the surrender in 1539, the royal visitor immediately began selling floor tiles and furnishings to the mayor. Soon, however, the mayor and burgesses made a successful offer for the entire site. The church seems to have been demolished quickly. The three domestic ranges were rented by the corporation to nine craft companies so that they might build their meeting halls within them. The bakers and brewers, butchers, skinners and glovers, cordwainers, saddlers, smiths, tailors, fullers and dyers, and tanners all benefited from this civic enterprise (figure 96). In the early eighteenth century, remodelling destroyed much of the medieval fabric on the upper storey. By the twentieth century Black Friars was surrounded by squalor and decay, and the buildings were suffering from vandalism. Proposals to rescue the site were first put forward in 1950, but there followed a succession of abortive schemes, including a proposal that part of the site should again be occupied by Dominican friars. Conversion to a record office was abandoned in 1967 as a result of restrictions on capital expenditure by local authorities. Another proposal came forward, in 1971, to treat the site as an open, roofless ruin. Fortunately, a financially viable alternative was devised in the same year to adapt the buildings to house a restaurant, studios, workshops, etc. Work began in 1975 on a rolling programme, preceded at every stage by archaeological excavation and recording. In 1985 the project was complete. The Black Friars Craftworkers Trust occupied the west range (figure 86), and in the south range was a restaurant and exhibition. The east range contained a tourist information centre, a small museum and an architecture

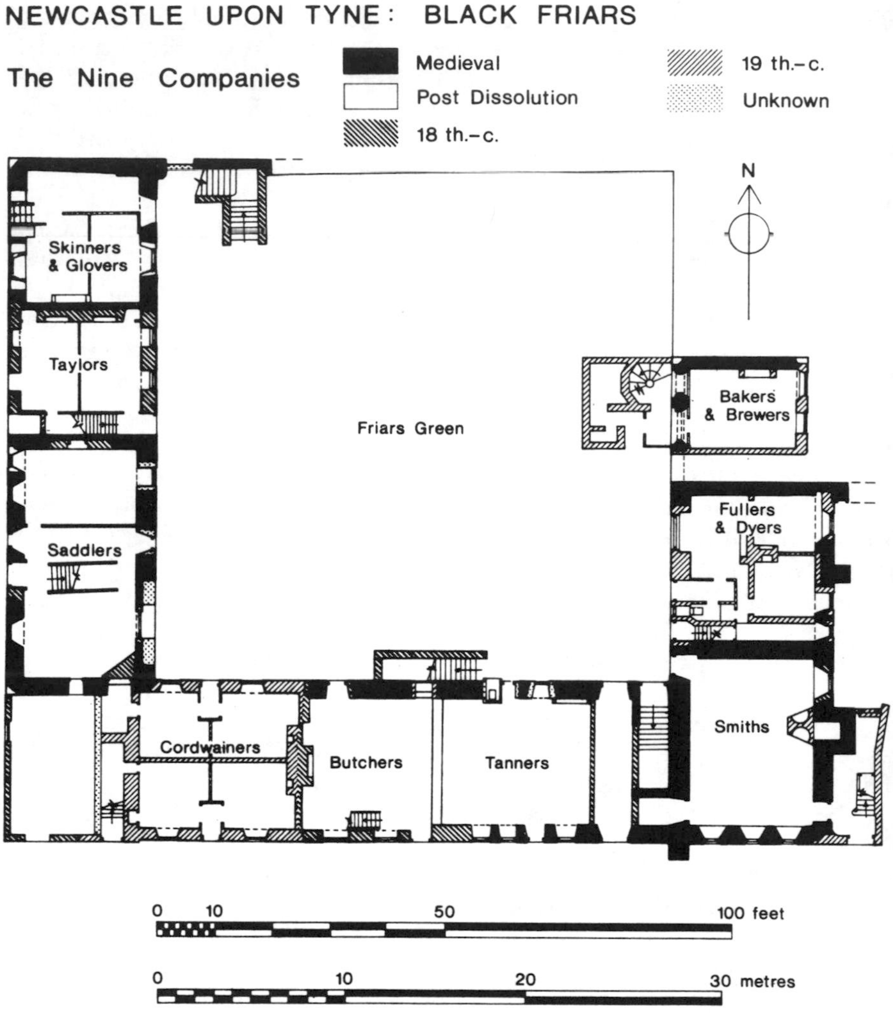

NEWCASTLE UPON TYNE: BLACK FRIARS

The Nine Companies

Medieval

Post Dissolution

18 th.–c.

19 th.–c.

Unknown

N

Skinners & Glovers

Taylors

Saddlers

Friars Green

Bakers & Brewers

Fullers & Dyers

Cordwainers

Butchers

Tanners

Smiths

0   10   50   100 feet

0   10   20   30 metres

Figure 96. Plan of the post-Dissolution arrangements of the ground-floor level of Newcastle-upon-Tyne Dominican Friary.

Drawing supplied by Barbara Harbottle, Development Department, Newcastle-upon-Tyne City Council.

workshop. The cloister was grassed and the excavated remains of the church outlined on the north side of the site (figure 97). Now the environs of the friary have been considerably improved and the whole scheme of regeneration can be considered a notable success.

Figure 97. The restored claustral buildings of Newcastle Black Friars, seen from the west end of the church (marked out in the foreground).
Photograph by Patrick Greene.

Interpretation

Until the 1970s, the methods used to make monastic sites intelligible to their visitors were minimal. At most monasteries in public guardianship, information was provided in two ways. Cast metal plaques fixed to walls, or set in the turf, acted as 'labels' bearing such legends as 'chapel', 'site of high altar' or, more obscurely, 'frater', 'dorter' and 'reredorter'. Blue-covered Official Guides published by HMSO were usually available, but the extent to which they helped visitors was questionable. They were written by experts such as Charles Clapham, A. Hamilton Thompson and Rose Graham, but although they were authoritative, they were difficult for the visitor to use and made few concessions in respect of language and terminology.

Since 1970, innovative means of conveying information for visitors have been developed (Greene 1989b). Medieval monasticism is far removed from the experience of people in the twentieth century, so there is a responsibility on archaeologists to facilitate understanding. As archaeological approaches to the investigation of monastic sites have broadened, there is in any case a much wider range of information to be conveyed. In addition, archaeologists have come to realise that publication of research demands more than an academic report, essential though that is. Publication of information in a popular form is also part of the archaeologist's responsibility. It is as demanding, both intellectually and creatively, as the production of research reports. The forms which such popular accounts may take range from books and brochures, to exhibitions and audio-visual productions. The remainder of this chapter consists of a number of examples of good practice from a variety of sites throughout the British Isles.

Beaulieu Abbey, Hampshire

The Cistercian abbey of Beaulieu, founded in 1204, was dissolved in 1538, and the site was sold to Thomas Wriothesley, who also acquired Titchfield Abbey. It descended from him to the Montagu family, the present owners. Three major elements of the monastery survive virtually intact, the refectory (which was converted for use as a parish church), a gatehouse with its chapel, and the two-storey west range. This originally housed the lay brothers' dormitory on the upper floor, over a vaulted undercroft. The monastic remains were first opened to visitors in 1906, and in 1952 Palace House (which incorporated the remains of the inner gatehouse) was opened (Montagu 1967). In 1977 an exhibition on monastic life was established in the refectory to interpret the remains of Beaulieu Abbey, as an adjunct to the National Motor Museum and Palace House. It was one of the first modern interpretive exhibitions designed to explain the significance of monastic remains to visitors. Amongst the models used in the exhibition is a fine representation of the abbey's tithe barn at Beaulieu St Leonard's. The site is laid out to show the outline of the the great abbey church and the infirmary and its chapel. A building identified as a fulling mill and weaving shed has been excavated recently (Allen 1990).

Bede Monastery Museum, Jarrow, Tyne and Wear

The establishment of the Bede Monastery Museum was a result of the excavations directed by Rosemary Cramp on the site of the seventh-century monastery where the Venerable Bede lived and wrote *The History of the English Church and People*. The excavations revealed the remains of buildings to the south of the present church, which became part of the Benedictine monastery that was refounded in 1074. A great range of objects relating to the daily life of the Northumbrian monks was found, as well as components of the buildings, including coloured glass from the windows. Such was the importance of the site and the significance of the objects that it was decided to establish a site museum. One of the sponsors was the *Sunday Times*, which had already become involved in archaeology through its support in 1968 for the exhibition at Fishbourne Roman Palace – a project which had a considerable influence on the way in which sites were presented to the public (Hudson 1987, 35–8). Jarrow Hall, the near-derelict former rectory standing close to the monastery, was restored as a museum. The displays incorporate finds from the excavation, including the Saxon glass, carved stonework and writing implements. A superb model of the site and an audio-visual presentation about the life of the monks assist visitors in picturing Jarrow monastery in its heyday.

Holycross Abbey, County Tipperary

The restoration of the buildings of Holycross Abbey has been described above. The continuing work has enabled visitors to watch stonemasons carrying out the highly skilled tasks of cutting moulded stones and building masonry structures. Booklets describe the rescue of the buildings, and also the recovery of medieval bells now hanging in the tower.

Jedburgh Abbey, Borders

David I of Scotland founded Jedburgh for Augustinian canons in 1138, partly as an act of piety and partly as an assertion of the Scottish Crown's authority in the Borders (Fawcett 1988). The proximity of the border, 8 miles (12 km.) to the south, exposed the abbey to English attacks. Those in 1523, 1544 and 1545 were particularly devastating, and the abbey never fully recovered. The church, however, continued in use until 1875, with makeshift structures created successively beneath the tower and in the nave, ensuring its survival – although today it is roofless.

During the 1980s, Jedburgh Abbey was the subject of a campaign of excavation, followed by the implementation of an interpretive scheme. It is now a model of how a range of techniques can be brought to bear to make a monastic site intelligible to its visitors. Members of the public are prepared for their tour in the visitor centre, where they can watch a video presentation, are able to see excavated finds, and can examine an excellent model. This shows the conjectural appearance of the buildings in 1500, and is positioned in front of a large viewing window overlooking the site. The visitor can therefore directly compare the surviving remains with the buildings represented on the model. The comparison is facilitated by the layout of the monastery, which was terraced into the slope leading down to the River Jed, and can therefore be taken in from the viewpoint on the south (figure 98). Emerging from the centre, the visitor follows a self-guided tour of the site alongside the east range, into the church with its beautiful Transitional nave, the cloister, the west range, the abbot's residence and the mill stream. At key points there are viewpoints with panels of illustrations and explanatory text. The cloister has been planted with herbs and other appropriate flowers and shrubs in an attractive layout. The site interpretation is supported by an illustrated guide-book (Fawcett 1988).

Norton Priory, Cheshire

The excavation of the site and the creation of a museum at Norton Priory was an initiative of Runcorn Development Corporation which was engaged in the creation of a New Town in the 1970s. The project was started in

Figure 98. Interpretation of the monastic remains, Jedburgh Priory, Borders. The building in the distance is the visitor centre with a large window overlooking the site. In the foreground is one of the series of interpretation panels.
    Photograph by Patrick Greene.

1971 as a means of providing the new community with historic roots in the form of a medieval site (the evolution of the project is described in Greene 1975, 1983 and 1989b). At first it was intended simply to display the excavated walls and foundations as landscaped features. As the excavation progressed, however, the need for a site museum became apparent. There were large numbers of finds such as mosaic-tile floors, carved sandstone grave-slabs, a tile kiln, a bell mould, and fine carved stonework which required the protection of a building for their display. There was also the need to provide an introduction for visitors to the site, using the results of archaeological research to explain details of medieval monastic life and crafts, and also Norton's post-Dissolution history. In addition it was essential that facilities for the storage and conservation of archaeological material were provided, as well as accommodation for educational activities.

    There are consequently a range of interpretive techniques in use at Norton Priory Museum. The heart of the display is a large model of the monastic buildings showing their possible appearance in the early sixteenth century. The construction of the model was based on information provided by the excavation for the layout and dates of buildings, together with details from excavated stonework such as corbels and window mouldings, and comparison with monastic remains of similar dates elsewhere. The model is a great help to visitors in making the excavated walls intelligible in terms of standing buildings. Its production also provided an excellent research framework in which to bring together an extensive body of information on the form and date of each element of the monastery. Another model demonstrates the constructional techniques used by medieval masons (figure 34). A video provides visitors with an account of the process of discovery and conservation of the site. The exhibition covers such topics as the work of medieval masons, tile making, food and drink, and death and burial.

A viewing gallery, built over the standing remains of the west range undercroft, allows visitors to look down on the excavated site, thereby getting a much better appreciation of the plan of the buildings than is possible at ground level. Site panels are a further means of interpretation, providing information on monastic life in the various parts of the priory, supported by reconstruction drawings. The museum also deals with post-Dissolution history through exhibitions, the restored woodland gardens, and in the Georgian walled garden and ice-house that have been rescued from dereliction and returned to use.

Rievaulx Abbey, Yorkshire

The Cistercian abbey at Rievaulx in West Yorkshire is one of the monastic sites for which excellent educational materials have been prepared by English Heritage. Schools visiting the site are able to book an education room as a base for using the site for teaching projects. One of these, supported by a video programme, has structures as its theme and encourages children to think about the buildings in terms of the way in which they were built. Medieval technology, and the mathematics of weight and strength, are conveyed through experiments that primary school children can carry out for themselves. It is an example of the way in which objectives that form part of the National Curriculum can be tackled in an innovative manner. Another enterprising means of interpreting the site is through a 'family pack' containing a variety of activities for visiting family groups. A similar publication has been produced for Battle Abbey.

York, St Mary's Abbey

The site of the Benedictine St Mary's Abbey, near the centre of York, has been available to the public within botanic gardens four hectares in area since the nineteenth century. The remains of the abbey church are fragmentary, although nonetheless impressive, survivals of one of the richest English monasteries. They are the setting for performances of the York Mystery Plays. Much of the abbey's precinct wall still exists, with one of the gatehouses. The guesthouse, with a stone ground floor and timber-framed upper storey, stands to the west of the church. However, until recently the thousands of visitors to Museum Gardens had no means of appreciating the significance of the site's medieval origins. The Yorkshire Museum, which was built in 1827–30 as the museum of the Yorkshire Philosophical Society, occupies the site of the east range of the abbey (figure 16). In 1988 the

Figure 99. The reconstructed entrance to the late-twelfth-century chapter house of St Mary's Abbey, York. The original blocks of masonry are of a slightly darker hue than the replica blocks.
Photograph supplied by the Yorkshire Museum.

museum capitalised upon its location by opening a new exhibition which provides a history of St Mary's Abbey, and which displays objects found on the site. The most important of these are a series of life-size figures of Apostles and Prophets which once stood in two tiers within the chapter house (Wilson 1983). Recent scientific research has shown that they were once vividly coloured. Moses' face was bright pink, with blood-red lips and gold hair, and his tunic was blue with white and blue detail. There are also glazed floor-tiles, stained glass, and the bronze mortar from the abbey infirmary.

As visitors descend to the basement, they pass a window overlooking the remains of the late-thirteenth-century church. They then find themselves in the vestibule of the chapter house, above which the lecture theatre of the museum was built in 1911–13. The ornate late-twelfth-century entrance to the chapter house has been partially reconstructed on its original site. It forms a dramatic and unexpected feature of the exhibition (figure 99). It was in the chapter house that the famous dispute occurred in 1132 which led to the walk-out by the monks who favoured a more austere observation of the Benedictine Rule, and who founded Fountains Abbey. The displays in the Yorkshire Museum are of high quality, and an excellent guide book provides information on the entire monastic complex (Wilson and Burton 1988).

Tintern Abbey, Gwent

As the most-visited monastic house in the care of Cadw, with around 100,000 people attracted to it each year, Tintern has been at the forefront of the interpretation programme for the Welsh monasteries. The complexity of the remains, and the impressive extent to which they survive (see Chapter 4), made it a site where interpretation was particularly necessary. There are three principal means by which visitors are provided with information. A series of site panels and a completely redesigned guide book are complementary methods (Robinson 1989). The writing of the text and the specially prepared illustrations (for example, figures 36 and 38) are of the highest quality in both the guide book (Robinson 1986, revised 1990) and the site panels which were subsequently installed. A third method used at Tintern is the recorded tour using Sony Walkman tape-players. The visitor is provided with a stream of information, with instructions on a route to follow around the site. The use of stereo in a programme such as 'Tintern Abbey by Moonlight' provides layers of information through the clever use of sound. All these methods of interpretation require high levels of archaeological and historical research to produce authoritative information, and also production of materials of the best quality. Popular, accessible interpretation is not an easy option. Nor can it stand still. Further research modified views on the form of the superstructure of the church, necessitating the revision of the guidebook (Robinson 1990).

Whithorn Priory, Dumfries and Galloway

The excavation of Whithorn Priory, the Christian site in longest continuous use in the British Isles (see Chapter 7), has provided an excellent opportunity for interpretation, not only of the site itself, but also of the archaeological process of investigation (Hill 1988). The visitor centre on the main street has an introductory audio-visual show which uses superb photographic images. Visitors then tour an exhibition which traces the history of the site from the time of Ninian in the fifth century. A third element of the visit is the little museum operated by Historic Scotland, containing a remarkable collection of early Christian memorial stones and Norse standing crosses. The highlight of the tour is the excavation itself, where one of the archaeological team takes visitors around the dig and describes the latest discoveries. There is then the opportunity to see the site of the Premonstratensian priory-cathedral, and its vaulted crypts. Income from visitors through admission and tour fees, profits from the well-stocked shop, and donations help to fund the excavation (figure 79).

Other sites to visit

The following monastic sites are a selection designed to reflect the diversity of size, order and geographical location. They do not necessarily have spectacular standing remains, but all have features that illustrate aspects of the archaeology of monasteries.

Beeston Priory, Norfolk

The priory of St Mary in the Meadow at Beeston is an example of the type of small monastery built for a handful of inmates that was a characteristic of East Anglian foundations by members of the lesser gentry (figure 40). It belonged to the Order of Peterstone, a group of four small Augustinian priories that may have come together because of their size. Beeston had five canons. Excavation and presentation of the remains has been carried out under the auspices of Norfolk County Council (Heywood 1989).

Bordesley Abbey, Redditch, Hereford and Worcestershire

The annual excavation at the Cistercian abbey takes place each summer, and special viewing days for the public are arranged. At other times the consolidated remains of the church may seem very modest for a site that has such a high reputation in the field of monastic archaeology. However, it is the very complexity of the archaeology that has determined the speed at which buildings can be uncovered. The extensive nature of the earthworks that cover the Arrow Valley can be explored on a footpath system that leads through the country park. The footpaths can be reached from the car park for the Needle Museum, a water-powered mill that is also worth visiting.

Buckfast Abbey, Devon

Buckfast Abbey was an Anglo-Saxon monastery refounded after the Conquest as a Savignac house in 1137. Parts of the medieval buildings survive, but the site is famous for the construction of a new monastery in the 1920s and 1930s by Benedictine monks, originally from France. Visitors are welcome, and get some impression of the practice of monastic life. Bee-keeping and the manufacture of tonic wine are specialities.

Fountains Abbey, North Yorkshire

The importance of Fountains Abbey to monastic archaeology and history will be clear from the other chapters in this book. As a place to visit it never disappoints. So many details of the monastic buildings can be explored, as well as the landscaped valley of the River Skell which forms part of the parkland of Studley Royal. Previously, however, its potential for the general visitor had been limited by the very complexity of the remains of the abbey. Now the National Trust has embarked upon a project to build a visitor centre that will prepare people for their visits by providing background information and orientation.

Glastonbury Abbey, Somerset

Glastonbury's fame in the medieval period partly rested on its (mainly bogus) Arthurian associations, and today the visitor to the town will not escape the commercialised aura of Avalon. However, the abbey site itself remains impressive, although little of the church and claustral buildings escaped

estruction at the Dissolution. The most complete element of the church is
ne exquisite chapel of St Mary (figure 92), built at the western end in Tran-
itional style following a disastrous fire in 1184. This unusual location is
hought to mark the site of the original pre-Conquest church. The remainder
.f the enormous church, which neared 200 m. in length, is fragmentary. A
ense of the qualities of the buildings that no longer exist is, however,
.rovided by one that has survived. The abbot's kitchen, built in the second
.alf of the fourteenth century, combines utility with great beauty. Other
.uildings in the area should form part of the visit. The Somerset Country
.ife Museum is housed in one of the abbey's tithe barns (figure 59). In the
.own are the court-house (known as the Tribunal) and an inn (the George).
.t Mere, the abbot's fish house can be visited.

Gloucester Cathedral

Gloucester is one of the most complete monasteries in the British Isles. The
.resent church of the Benedictine St Peter's Abbey was begun by Abbot Serlo
n 1089; it has a crypt beneath its eastern end. The church underwent many
.dditions, including a lady chapel. The ornate wooden choir stalls survive.
.ne of the shrines that attracted pilgrims was the tomb of Edward II, built
.y his son Edward III. Donations by pilgrims helped finance building
.ampaigns, including the fan-vaulted cloister walks erected in the fifteenth
.entury. The carrels (work spaces for the monks) can still be seen in the
.outh cloister-walk, as can the long wash-basin in the north walk. There is
.a Romanesque chapter house, an almonry, a gatehouse and precinct walls.

Kells Priory, Co. Kilkenny

Augustinian canons from Bodmin in Cornwall were brought to Ireland to
found Kells Priory in 1193. The church, although subject to a number of
rebuildings, is similar to many other Augustinian churches elsewhere in the
British Isles, having a single aisle to the nave, and a large chapel to the north
of the chancel. To the south of the church there are substantial remains of
the claustral buildings. The most remarkable feature of Kells, however, is its
defences. One enclosure, with walls, turrets and a gatehouse largely intact,
surrounds the church and cloister. Adjoining it on the south is another
walled enclosure with five tower-houses spaced at intervals along its
perimeter. Two further towers are attached to the church, at the west end
of the aisle and on the south side of the chancel. The function of the
southern enclosed area is unknown, but it is conceivable that it was designed
to be a defended town. The overall walled area is 2 hectares (5 acres) in
extent.

Lacock Abbey, Wiltshire

This house of Augustinian nuns was founded in 1232, and after the Dissolution the buildings were converted into a country house (see Chapter 8). The
way in which the adaptation took place, and the subsequent modifications
to the house, can be seen. The cloister and chapter house are particularly

beautiful. The brewhouse, with its cauldrons, vats and cooling trays, i situated on the outer courtyard. It is a post-Dissolution feature, but must b little different to monastic brewhouses. By walking round the exterior of th house to the back, it is possible to see how the wall of the nave of the churcl was used as the outer wall of the house. There is a museum devoted to th work of the pioneer of photography, William Fox Talbot, also run by th National Trust.

Llanthony Priory, Gwent

The Augustinian priory at Llanthony was founded at a remote valley in th Black Mountains, originally as a hermitage. After attacks by the Welsh, th canons moved to a site outside Gloucester, which was given the name Llan thony Secunda. The original site became a cell of its daughter, but it buildings have survived to a greater degree. The gatehouse has beer converted into a barn. The church, which shows considerable signs o subsidence (figure 44), has a pair of towers at the west end, an aisled nave and a crossing tower. Part of the west range (originally the store with prior' accommodation on the upper floor) has become a hotel, with a pub in the undercroft particularly popular with ramblers. Work has recently taken place to restore the buildings of Llanthony Secunda, some of which were incor- porated in a farm, and also the priory tithe barn.

Mount Grace Priory, North Yorkshire (figures 11, 12, 49)

The Carthusian priory of Mount Grace is owned by the National Trust and administered by English Heritage. The layout of a Carthusian monastery can be understood easily from the extensive surviving remains. One of the two- storey cells that line the great cloister has been reconstructed and furnished. It can therefore be seen that the term 'cell' is something of a misnomer, for these were well appointed dwellings, every one with a small garden, which allowed each monk to live a life of solitary contemplation, work and prayer with the minimum of distractions. The arrangements for the supply of water and for the sanitation of each cell can be seen. The church and chapter house form the eastern side of the cloister. Service buildings such as the bakehouse and brewhouse stand near the entrance gatehouse. The guesthouse still survives, incorporated within a post-Dissolution house. There is an excellent new guide book (Coppack 1991).

Portchester Priory, Hampshire

Portchester is worth a visit to see a practically unaltered twelfth-century church, despite the fact that it is the only monastic building on the site. The church has a simple, unaisled cruciform plan, with a tower over the crossing. The south transept has been demolished and the chancel altered. The blocked doors to the cloister-walks can be seen, as well as the fine Romanes- que west door. The latrine shoots, cut through the Roman fort wall, mark the position of the east range. The priory was placed in the south-east corner of the Roman fort, having been founded in 1133 by William Pont d'Arch whose castle occupied the north-west corner. It was this proximity that proved too much for the canons. They moved across Portsdown Hill to Southwick. It is now the parish church of Portchester, and the fort and castle form an English Heritage guardianship site.

Quin Franciscan Friary, Co. Clare

The history of Quin Friary is complex, which accounts for the extraordinary appearance of the site. A church which was burned down in 1278 was replaced by a castle in the form of a square with massive rounded towers at the corners. The Irish sacked the castle in about 1285, and in due course the site again reverted to religious use with a church built on top of the ruins. In 1433 the Franciscans were brought to Quin. The church was remodelled, consisting of a simple chancel, nave and south aisle. The cloister, as with most Irish friaries, was placed to the north of the church. The three ranges and the cloister-walk survive in a substantially complete form. Three of the castle's rounded bastions still exist, giving the friary a martial appearance. There are earthworks of a village surrounding the site.

Sweetheart Abbey, Dumfries and Galloway

The name given to Sweetheart is a reference to its origins. It was founded by Dervorgilla, the widow of John Balliol, four years after his death in 1273. She was buried in the chancel of the Cistercian church in 1290, with the casket of ivory bound with silver in which she had placed her husband's heart, and which she had kept close to her in life. The fragments of Dervorgilla's tomb were reassembled in the 1930s. Although the church now lacks a roof, it is otherwise in very complete condition. The way in which the church and claustral ranges were built can be seen particularly well from the chapter house. The dark red sandstone ashlar facing blocks contrast in colour with the light-coloured granite boulders used in the wall cores (figure 29). Another impressive feature of Sweetheart is the precinct wall constructed of massive granite boulders. Within the village of New Abbey is the corn mill that is probably the successor of the monastic mill, and a fish-pond can be seen near the river. The abbey and mill are both in the care of Historic Scotland.

Westminster Abbey, London

Because it is now a place of burial for the famous, and a major tourist attraction that is often uncomfortably crowded, the importance of Westminster Abbey as a medieval monastery can be overlooked. The Benedictine abbey church built by Edward the Confessor was dedicated on 28 December 1065, the day before Edward died. It was the most advanced Romanesque building in England. In subsequent rebuildings, Westminster was particularly influential in areas such as decoration and figure sculpture. The blank arcading along the nave-aisle outer walls, although cut by many later memorials, has a great deal of interesting carving of heads, beasts and foliage. The chapel of Henry VII at the eastern end of the church has some of the finest fan vaulting, built to crown the space dedicated to the burial place of the king. The cloister is relatively quiet, and gives access to the magnificent polygonal chapter house with its superb tiled floor and wall paintings. There is a good exhibition about the abbey's history in the dormitory undercroft. The abbey is best visited soon after it opens in the morning. It fills up quickly once the changing of the guard has finished at Buckingham Palace and the coaches arrive.

Postscript: The future of monastic archaeology

The advances that have been made during the past quarter-century in the use of archaeology for investigating medieval monasticism have been considerable. It might be thought, therefore, that less scope existed for future archaeological research. In fact, there remain many topics where further investigation would be justified. In 1987 the Society for Medieval Archaeology published its recommendations to English Heritage on priorities in the allocation of grants for medieval projects (Hinton 1987). Although the Society was careful to emphasise the limited nature of the consultation, the views expressed on monastic archaeology are worth examining here.

A fundamental element in the Society's submission was to urge the adoption of policies that 'lead to the furtherance of our knowledge and understanding of the entire landscape', and that any excavation should be considered as a detailed investigation of a small part of the landscape. Sites which are likely to contribute to a reconstruction of the total environment of their period were regarded as particularly worthy of study, and the existence of extensive documentary information about a site could enhance its value. Excavation should allow the formulation of ideas about the processes that caused the archaeological record to be established, and not mere classification. It was recognised that the full potential of sites is hard to establish without excavation; the unexpected is an inevitable element of archaeology.

In making recommendations about religious sites, the Society recognised the way in which religion permeated the whole of medieval society, and that understanding its material remains is a high priority. The arrangement of the claustral buildings of pre-Conquest monasteries is of great interest in view of the discoveries at Jarrow and Monkwearmouth. Every opportunity should be taken to investigate major pre-Conquest churches and their subsidiary buildings. In the case of post-Conquest monasteries, further projects to investigate the church and cloister buildings should not have high priority. Stress should be placed on the investigation of non-claustral areas, examining in particular their impact on the society and economy of the surrounding region, and the investments made in agriculture and industry. Less well-known buildings such as granges, urban friaries, colleges and hospitals should be investigated as opportunities arise. The potential of cemeteries for providing information about human behaviour, demography and biology was stressed.

The Society's recommendations provide a sound basis for future work in monastic archaeology. Research designs that ask new questions of the evidence, or utilise innovative analytical methods, can expand the range of monastic archaeology (Mytum 1989). The following topics are my suggestions for future research.

Regional variation

There are considerable differences in the extent to which monastic sites have been the subject of detailed study in different parts of the British Isles. For example, although a number of early Christian monastic sites in Ireland have been excavated to a high standard, few later monasteries have been the subject of detailed, extensive investigation. Given the richness of the remains of Irish monasteries, the potential is enormous. Of particular interest are the contrasts that exist amongst the development of monasteries in Ireland Scotland, England and Wales. Differing political and economic circumstances produced different patterns of monasticism in the four countries Within each country, further differences exist between regions. The work of scholars such as Roger Stalley on the buildings of the Cistercians in Ireland (Stalley 1987), D.H. Williams on the Cistercians in Wales (Williams 1970 and 1990, for example), and David Robinson on the geography of Augustinian settlement in England and Wales (Robinson 1980) demonstrate the potential.

Intensive excavation

The expense of archaeological excavation prohibits the excavation of all but a few sites on a large scale. Where it has been carried out, as for example at Bordesley (Hirst, Walsh and Wright 1983), Norton (Greene 1989) and Whithorn (Hill 1990), the contribution to the study of monasticism is enormous. The sheer scale of monastic sites means that to obtain a full picture of their development is a daunting challenge. The frequency with which Bordesley has been cited in this book is an indication of how greatly the excavation has expanded understanding of, for example, the liturgical arrangements of the choir, the use of water power by the abbey mill, and even the way in which the church was demolished. The experience built up by an archaeological team dealing with an individual monastic site over a number of years brings its own rewards in terms of both the development of skills required by the conditions on that particular site, and the insights produced by the sustained intellectual appraisal of evidence drawn from a wide range of archaeological and historical sources. A further benefit is the recovery of material in quantities that allow analysis on a statistically valid sample size. An example is the study of human remains. Most reports on skeletons from monastic excavations deal with no more than a score of individuals, buried at a variety of dates. As samples from which general conclusions can be drawn, they are worthless. At Whithorn, in contrast, about 1,600 burials of lay people have been excavated from areas to the east of the church and south of the monastery. The phasing of the graveyard, and the identification of specific areas used for special groups of the population, will allow demographic trends to be ascertained. The comparison of life expectancy of similar groups in the population in different parts of the British Isles is a fascinating prospect for future research. Monastic sites have the potential for providing three distinct classes: the monks themselves; benefactor families, and lesser lay people.

It would be a realistic objective for a long-term research excavation to be started once in each decade. The choice in each case should be a site that is likely to produce information of a very different nature to that already available from large excavations. Such candidates might include, for example, a nunnery or an Irish rural friary. It should have extensive remains known from aerial photography or geophysical survey, and preferably good documentation as well. The research design would include the church, claustral ranges, outer courtyard and precinct.

A temporary site

A prime candidate for excavation is the site of a monastery that is known to have been occupied for a short period of time. There are many examples of monasteries where the inmates decided to move to a better site after a few years (see Chapter 3). The excavation of such a site would be likely to reveal a great deal about the methods of laying out the site, the order in which buildings were erected in masonry, the speed of work, and the temporary quarters of both monks and building workers. The advantage of investigating such topics on a site that was occupied for, say, twenty years would be the lack of disturbance from later occupation, and the relatively simple stratigraphy that would enable rapid progress on a large-scale excavation. There would be the added benefit of the recovery of artefacts such as pottery and stonework from a closely defined time-frame that could be used for dating comparable material from other sites.

Investigation of previously-excavated sites

Small-scale excavation of sites that were subject to clearance or partial excavation in the past can add considerably to knowledge of their archaeology. Often it is the need to undertake remedial work to a guardianship site that prompts such investigation. For example, subsidence of flooring in the nave of Gisborough Priory necessitated excavation. As well as discovering the cause of the problem (a burial vault), a great range of other information was derived from a small area measuring 25 m. by 26 m. (Heslop forthcoming). Discoveries included Saxon occupation features beneath a layer of medieval plough soil. On this were built the foundations of a temporary building – possibly an early church. This in turn was overlain by a Norman church, which was completely replaced by a new church in the thirteenth century (figures 31 and 32). Other discoveries in the excavation were lead water pipes, a bell casting pit, and the scorching of masonry probably associated with a fire in 1289; fragments of a shattered bell and broken grave-slabs testified to the extent of destruction. Rebuilding in the fourteenth century included new arcades, a new floor of sandstone slabs, incorporating a burial vault containing six skeletons. It was this that had led to the subsidence that necessitated such an unexpectedly productive excavation.

Figure 100. Computer-generated model of the appearance of the interior of the nave of the church, Furness Abbey, Cumbria.

Illustration supplied by Lancaster University Archaeological Unit, created (using PDMS and EVS software) in association with North Cheshire College and British Nuclear Fuels plc.

Standing masonry

The way in which the analysis of the standing remains of Furness Abbey have been the subject of a programme of recording and interpretation was described in Chapter 2. There is a strong case for applying these principles on every monastic site with standing masonry, for the accelerated deterioration caused by acid rain and other pollutants makes recording, and preventative conservation, a high priority.

The use of information technology

Furness Abbey provides an example of how detailed recording of standing structures can be assisted by the use of computer-based technology, particularly in the resolution of the inevitable lens distortion in photogrammetry to produce accurate line drawings. The accumulation of measured data can be taken further, however, by the application of computer graphics and data visualisation to produce reconstruction models (Delooze and Wood 1991) (figure 100). The technology, which has been developed to assist in

the design and management of complex chemical plant and engineered structures, can be adapted to play a part in archaeology. Further development
would allow the production of an interactive videodisc, allowing visitors to
a site to interrogate the model, and with animation to move around it,
'seeing' the buildings as the monks did – at least through the intermediary
of the archaeologist.

Another application with considerable potential is the recording of
mouldings from masonry buildings. The corpus being assembled by Dr
Richard Morris at Warwick University using a computer database presents
the opportunity for recognising the work of individual masons, or building
teams, on different sites. The recording of masons' marks and the introduction of standardised recording techniques in other areas – for example,
medieval floor tiles (Stopford 1990) – have similar potential.

The precinct

The richness of the archaeological record in the outer courtyard areas at
Thornholme Priory illustrates the enormous potential of archaeology to
investigate the economy of a monastic house. The surveying of precincts, in
the form of surviving earthworks, traces appearing on air photographs as at
Shouldham (figures 13 and 14), or by means of geophysical methods, is
essential in order to define the extent of monastic sites. There is a strong case
for reviewing the protected area of every scheduled monastic site in the light
of such survey work, and extending protection to the important but
vulnerable precinct in its entirety.

Manors and granges

The limitations of knowledge of monastic estates were described in Chapter
6. The investigation of sites such as South Witham in Lincolnshire (Mayes
forthcoming) and Roystone in Derbyshire (Hodges 1991), both in terms of
excavation and survey, demonstrates the considerable contribution to the
knowledge of monastic economy that can result. Such studies should not be
carried out in a piecemeal fashion, for it is the study of all aspects of a
chosen monastery's use of its resources that will be of real value. As well as
grange sites and field systems, such studies should take account of wool-
houses, cattle enclosures, barns, mills, drove roads, bridges, and all the other
components of a complex economic unit. Similarly, there is a strong case for
the detailed investigation of extractive industries such as quarrying, the
exploitation of deposits of metal ores, and coal mining. The excavation of
a 'bell-pit' coal or iron-ore mine with its surroundings could yield valuable
information on the technology of mining, although it would be a difficult
exercise to undertake.

The future

This postscript has indicated a number of areas in which the archaeology of medieval monasteries can develop. It is not an exhaustive survey of the potential; it is certain that in the future new approaches will be developed and new questions will be asked of the material. The vast field of medieval monasticism will provide exciting challenges for research and dissemination of information to a wide public. Monasticism transcended political boundaries of the medieval world, and its study in the future will benefit from a genuinely international approach.

Glossary

Ambulatory. A 'walking space' for liturgical processions, or to enable pilgrims to approach a shrine without intruding on services in the church.

Apse. A semi-circular recess, or (most frequently in a monastic context) the semi-circular or polygonal termination of the chancel, transept chapels or chapter house.

Augmentations Office. Organisation set up by the state to survey, manage and dispose of monastic property acquired by the Crown as a result of the Dissolution.

Canons. Secular canons were ordained brethren attached to a religious foundation. Regular canons were ordained brethren living in a religious house under a Rule (usually that of St Augustine of Hippo); they included Augustinians, Premonstratensians and Gilbertines.

Canonesses. Nuns following the rule of St Augustine, but who unlike their male counterparts could not be ordained and therefore required a male chaplain to celebrate the holy offices.

Cartulary. The collection of charters which every monastic house built up over the years, in which all its properties and privileges were recorded.

Cellarer. One of the offices to which a monk or canon of every religious house was appointed. He was responsible for the management of the monastic lands and the provisioning of the house.

Charterhouse. The popular name for a Carthusian priory.

Chevet. An elaborate form of the apsed eastern end of a church with radiating chapels and ambulatory, often built to enable an important shrine to be housed, for example at Hailes and Vale Royal.

Clerestory. Windows in the walls of the nave of a church, above the aisle roof.

Collation. A reading, usually from the writings of Cassian, given every day in the cloister after supper. Collation seats have been identified in a number of cloister walks where the abbot could sit during the reading.

Commandery. A religious house (often in the form of a grange) owned by the Knights of St John of Jerusalem.

Commendator. A layman appointed to the title of abbot and often (as in

Scotland from the fifteenth century) acquiring the income of the abbey.

Corrodians. Lay people with whom a monastery made agreements, usually to provide accommodation and food and drink, in return for an advance payment. Some corrodians were pensioners which the Crown prevailed upon religious houses to accept. Corrodians often turned out to be a drain on the monastery's resources.

Demesne. Land owned and administered directly by a monastery rather than being leased or rented out.

Dorter. A term sometimes used as an alternative to dormitory.

Friar. Member of one of the orders that spread rapidly throughout Europe in the thirteenth century, characterised by evangelical activities and a mendicant (i.e. relying on alms) life-style.

Glebe-land. Land that was attached to the rectory of a church, and which therefore benefited a monastery that had appropriated the church (i.e. had gained the right to appoint a vicar as the priest).

Lavatorium. Name often given to the wash-basin placed in the cloister-walk near the refectory, or projecting into the cloister.

Lay brothers and sisters. Members of religious orders who had accepted the monastic rule without being required to observe the seven services of the monastic day. They were therefore available for manual work on behalf of the monastery.

Monks. Members of a community living under the rule of St Benedict or one of its variants, observing the requirements of religious life, and having made vows of poverty, chastity and obedience.

Nuns. The female equivalent of monks, living according to the rule of St Benedict, but with the difference that they were unable to be ordained as priests. Nunneries therefore required a chaplain, or in the case of double houses such as some Gilbertine foundations, the canons could act as celebrants.

Observances. Regulations that developed to govern religious life in areas not covered by the rule of the order.

Piscina. Basin, usually set in the south wall of the chancel or chapel near the altar, where the communion vessels were washed following the celebration of the Eucharist.

Precentor. An office filled by one of the brethren who was responsible for the conduct of the divine offices, choir training, etc.

Preceptory. A religious house belonging to the Knights Templar; sometimes the church had a nave built to a circular plan in imitation of the Temple of Solomon.

Quoins. Ashlar blocks at the corners and other angles of a building.

Reredorter. Name sometimes given to the monastic latrines attached to the dormitory.

Sacristy. Room (or sometimes merely a cupboard) attached to the church in which communion vessels and altar furnishings were kept, cared for by one of the brethren who had been appointed sacrist, who was also responsible for the maintenance of the church and often for accounting for income from spiritualities as well.

Soffit. The underside of an arch, vault or lintel.

Spandrel. The surface between two arches.

Triforium. Band of arcading, sometimes incorporating a passage, above the main arcade and below the clerestory in a church.

Visitation. A regular, formal inspection that a religious house was subject to (unless it had gained exemption) carried out by the abbot of another house, or the local bishop depending on the order to which the house belonged. Visitation records are an invaluable source of information on numbers of religious, finance, the state of buildings, and the morale and morals of individual houses.

Voussoirs. Wedge shaped stones that, when assembled, formed an arch or vault.

Bibliography

Addyman, P.V. and Black, V.E. 1984. *Archaeological Papers from York*. York, York Archaeological Trust.

Andrews, F.B. 1901. *The Benedictine Abbey of SS Mary, Peter, and Paul, at Pershore, Worcestershire*. Birmingham, Midland Educational Co.

Armitage, P.L. and West, B. 1985. 'Faunal evidence from a late-medieval garden well of the Greyfriars, London' *Trans. London and Middlesex Archaeol. Soc.* 36, 107–36.

Ashmore, O. 1962. 'The Whalley Abbey bursar's account for 1520' *Trans. Hist. Soc. Lancashire and Cheshire* 114, 49–72.

Astill, G. 1989. 'Monastic research designs: Bordesley Abbey and the Arrow Valley' in Gilchrist and Mytum (eds.) 1989.

Aston, Margaret 1973. 'English ruins and English history: the Dissolution and the sense of the past' *J. Warburg and Courtauld Institutes* 36, 231–55.

Aston, Mick 1988. *Medieval Fish, Fisheries and Fishponds*. British Archaeol. Rep. 182, Oxford.

Ayloffe, J. 1786. 'An account of the body of King Edward the First, as it appeared on opening his tomb in the year 1774' *Archaeologia* 3, 1786, 376–413.

Bann, S. 1988. 'Views of the past' in Fyfe, G. and Law, J. *Picturing Power: visual depictions and social relations*. Sociological Review Monograph 35, London, Routledge.

Barker, P. 1982. *Techniques of Archaeological Excavation*. London, Batsford.

Batselier, P. 1981. *Saint Benedict: Father of Western Civilization*. New York, Alpine Fine Arts.

Beard, D. 1986. 'The infirmary of Bermondsey Abbey' *London Archaeologist 5*, no. 7, 186–91.

Beard, D. and Phillpotts, C. 1991. 'The religious life and the worldly life: London's monasteries and towns' *Current Archaeology* 124, 177–181.

Bentham, J. 1771. *The History and Antiquities of the Conventual and Cathedral Church at Ely*. Cambridge.

Beresford, M.W. and St Joseph, J.K.S. 1979. *Medieval England: an aerial survey*. Cambridge, Cambridge University Press.

Biddle, B. and Biddle, M. 1986. 'St Albans' *Current Archaeology* 101, 178–83.

Black, G. 1976. 'Excavations in the sub-vault of the misericord of Westminster Abbey, February to May, 1975' *Trans. London and Middlesex Archaeol. Soc.* 27, 1976.

Blair, J., Lankester, P. and West, J. 1980. 'A Transitional cloister arcade at Haughmond Abbey, Shropshire' *Med. Archaeol.* 24, 1980, 210–13.

Blair, J. 1990. *Saint Frideswide's Monastery at Oxford*. Gloucester, Alan Sutton.

Bond, C.J. 1973. 'The estates of Evesham Abbey: a preliminary survey of their medieval topography' *Vale of Evesham Hist. Soc. Research Papers* 4, 1973, 1–61.

Bond, C.J. 1975. 'The medieval topography of the Evesham estates: a supplement' *Vale of Evesham Hist. Soc. Research Papers* 5, 1975, 51–9.

Bond, C.J. 1979. 'The reconstruction of the medieval landscape: the estates of Abingdon Abbey' *Landscape History* 1, 59–75.

Bond, C.J. 1989. 'Water management in the rural monastery' in Gilchrist and Mytum (eds.) 1989, 83–111.

Bradley, J. and Manning, C. 'Excavations at Duiske Abbey, Graiguenamanagh, Co. Kilkenny' *Proc. Royal Irish Academy* 81c, 1981, 397–426.

Brakspear, H. 1901a. 'The church of Hailes Abbey' *Archaeol. J.* 58, 1901, 350–8.

Brakspear, H. 1901b. 'Lacock Abbey, Wiltshire' *Archaeologia* 57, 125–158.

Brakspear, H. 1911. 'Lead panels' *Proc. Soc. Antiquaries* 23, 366–369.

Brakspear, H. 1934. *Tintern Abbey* guidebook. London, HMSO.

Brakspear, H. 1905. *Waverley Abbey*. Lewes, Surrey Archaeol. Soc.

Brooke, C. 1982. *Monasteries of the World*. Ware, Omega Books.

Brooke, C. 1986. 'St Bernard, the patrons and monastic planning' in Norton and Park 1986, 11–23.

Brown, R.A. 1981. 'The Battle of Hastings' *Proceedings of the Battle Conference 1980*, 1–21.

Brown, W. and St John Hope, W.H. 1905. 'Mount Grace Abbey' *Yorkshire Archaeol. J.* 18, 252–309.

Brownbill, J. 1914. *The ledger-book of Vale Royal Abbey*. Lancashire and Cheshire Rec. Soc. 68.

Bucher, F. 1957. *Notre-Dame de Bonmont und die ersten Zisterzienserabteien der Schweiz*. Bern.

Buck, S. and Buck, N. 1774. *Antiquities*. London.

Burne, R.V.H. 1962. *The Monks of Chester*. London, SPCK.

Burrows, T. 1985. 'The geography of monastic property in medieval England: a case study of Nostell and Bridlington, Yorkshire' *Yorkshire Archaeol. J.* 57, 1985, 79–86.

Butler, L.A.S. 1976a. 'Valle Crucis Abbey: an excavation in 1970' *Archaeologia Cambrensis* 125, 80–126.

Butler, L.A.S. 1976. *Neath Abbey*. London, HMSO.

Butler, L.A.S. 1982a. 'The Cistercians in England and Wales: a survey of recent archaeological work 1960-1980', in M.P. Lillich, ed., *Studies in Cistercian Art and Architecture* 1, 88–101.

Butler, L.A.S. 1982b. 'The Cistercians in Wales: factors in the choice of sites' in B. Chauvin (ed.) *Melanges Anselme Dimier. Architecture Cistercienne* 3, Arbois, Pupillin, 35–8.

Butler, L.A.S. 1984. 'The houses of the mendicant orders in Britain: recent archaeological work' in Addyman and Black 1984, 123–136.

Caroe, W.D. 1929. 'The Canterbury Cathedral water tower' *Canterbury Papers* 1, Friends of Canterbury Cathedral.

Christie, P.M. and Coad, J.G. 1980. 'Excavations at Denny Abbey' *Archaeol. J.* 137, 138–279.

Clark, A. 1990. *Seeing Beneath the Soil: prospecting methods in archaeology*. London, Batsford.

Clarke, H. 1990a. *Medieval Dublin: the making of a metropolis*. Dublin, Irish Academic Press.

Clarke, H. 1990b. *Medieval Dublin: the living city*. Dublin, Irish Academic Press.

Clifton-Taylor, A. 1967. *The Cathedrals of England*. London, Thames and Hudson.

Coppack, G. 1986. 'Some descriptions of Rievaulx Abbey in 1538-9: the disposition of a major Cistercian precinct in the early sixteenth century' *J. British Archaeol. Assoc.* 139, 100–33.

Coppack, G. 1986b. 'The excavation of an outer court building, perhaps the woolhouse, at Fountains Abbey, North Yorkshire' *Medieval Archaeol.* 30, 46–87.

Coppack, G. 1989. 'Thornholme Priory: the development of a monastic outer court' in Gilchrist and Mytum 1989, 185–222.

Coppack, G. 1990. *Abbeys and Priories*. London, Batsford/English Heritage.

Coppack, G. 1991. *Mount Grace Priory*. London, English Heritage.

Cotton, C. 1938. 'The burning and repair of Canterbury Cathedral' *Canterbury Papers* 3, Friends of Canterbury Cathedral.

Courtney, P. 1981. 'Monastic granges of Leicestershire' *Trans. Leicestershire Archaeol. and Hist. Soc. 56.*

Courtney, P. 1989. 'Excavations in the outer precinct of Tintern Abbey' *Med. Archaeol.* 33, 1989, 99–143.

Cowan, I.B. and Easson, D.E. 1976. *Medieval Religious Houses*, Scotland. London, Longman.

Cox, D.C. 1990. 'The building, destruction, and excavation of Evesham Abbey: a documentary history' *Trans. Worcestershire Archaeol. Soc.* 12, 123–46.

Craster, O.F. 1956. *Tintern Abbey, Monmouthshire.* London, HMSO.

Croft, R.A. and Mynard, D.C. 1986. 'A late-13th century grisaille window panel from Bradwell Abbey, Milton Keynes, Bucks' *Medieval Archaeol.* 30, 1986, 106–111.

Crossley, F.H. 1949. *The English Abbey.* London, Batsford.

Cruden, S. 1986. *Scottish Medieval Churches.* Edinburgh, John Donald.

Currie, C.K. 1989. 'The role of fishponds in the monastic economy' in Gilchrist and Mytum 1989, 147–72.

Daniels, R. 1986. 'The excavation of the church of the Franciscans, Hartlepool, Cleveland' *Archaeol. J.* 143, 260–304.

Delooze, K. and Wood, J. 1991. 'Furness Abbey survey project – the application of computer graphics and data visualisation to reconstruction modelling of an historic monument' in Lockyear, K. and Rahtz, S. *Computer Applications and Quantitative Methods in Archaeology.* Oxford, British Archaeol. Rep. international series 565, 141–8.

Dixon, P. 1985. 'Jedburgh Friary and the Border Burghs' *Current Archaeol.* 97, 59–61.

Dobson, B. 1984. 'Mendicant ideal and practice in late medieval York' in Addyman and Black 1984, 109–22.

Donkin, R.A. 1978. *The Cistercians: Studies in the medieval Geography of England and Wales.* Toronto. Pontifical Institute of Medieval Studies.

Drury, P.J. and Pratt, G.D. 1975. 'A late thirteenth- and early fourteenth-century tile factory at Danbury, Essex' *Med. Archaeol.* 19, 92–164.

Dugdale, W. 1: 1655; 2: 1661; 3: 1673. *Monasticon Anglicanum.* London.

Duncan, H.B. and Wrathmell, S. 1986. 'Bell moulds from Kirkstall Abbey, West Yorkshire' *J. Hist. Metallurgy* 20, 33–5.

Dunning, G.C. 1952. 'A lead ingot at Rievaulx Abbey' *Antiquaries J.* 32, 199–202.

Eames, E.S. 1980. *Catalogue of Medieval Lead Glazed Earthenware Tiles.* London, British Museum.

Eames, E.S. and Fanning, T. 1989. *Irish Medieval Floor Tiles.* Dublin, Royal Irish Academy.

Edwards, D.A. 1989. 'Norfolk churches, air photography and the summer of 1989' *Bull. CBA Churches Committee* 26.

Edwards, D.A. and Wade-Martins, P. 1987. *Norfolk From the Air.* Norwich, Norfolk Museums Service.

Elliott, A.L. 'The Abbey of St Thomas the Martyr' in Clarke 1990b, 62–76.

Evans, D.H. 1980. 'Excavations at Llanthony Priory 1978' *Monmouthshire Antiquary* 4.

Evans, D.H. 1983. 'Further excavation and fieldwork at Llanthony Priory, Gwent' *Monmouthshire Antiquary* 5, 1–61.

Evans, D.H. 1987. *Valle Crucis Abbey.* Cardiff, Cadw.

Evans, J. 1956. *A History of the Society of Antiquaries.* London, Society of Antiquaries.

Everson, P. 1989. 'Rural monasteries within the secular landscape' in Gilchrist and Mytum 1989, 141–5.

Fanning, T. 1976. 'Clontuskert' *Royal Irish Academy Proc.* 76c, 97–169.

Faull, M.L. and Moorhouse, S. 1981. *West Yorkshire: an archaeological survey to AD 1500.* 4 vols., Wakefield.

Fawcett, R. 1988. *Jedburgh Abbey.* Edinburgh, HMSO.

Fergusson, P. 1983. 'The first architecture of the Cistercians in England' *J. British Archaeol. Assoc.* 136, 74–86.

Fergusson, P. 1984. *The Architecture of Solitude.* Princeton, Princeton University Press.

Fernie, E. 1987. 'A reconstruction of Edward's Abbey at Westminster' in Stratford, N. 1987, 63–7.

Fowler, J.T. 1903. *The Rites of Durham.* Durham, Surtees Soc., 107.

Franklin, J.A. 1989. 'Bridlington Priory: an Augustinian church and cloister in the twelfth century' *Medieval Art and Architecture of the East Riding of Yorkshire* 44–61, London, British Archaeol. Assoc.

Garton, T. 1987. 'The Transitional sculpture of Jedburgh Abbey' in Stratford, N. 1987, 69–81.

Geddes, J. 1983. 'Recently discovered Romanesque sculpture in south-east England' in Thompson, F.H. *Studies in Medieval Sculpture.* London, Soc. of Antiquaries Occ. Paper (N.S.) 3.

Geddes, J. 1986. 'Cistercian metalwork in England' in Norton and Park 1986, 256–65.

Gilchrist, R. 1989. 'The archaeology of English medieval nunneries: a research design' in Gilchrist and Mytum 1989, 251–60.

Gilchrist, R. and Mytum, H. (eds.) 1989. *The Archaeology of Rural Monasteries.* British Archaeol. Rep. British Ser. 203, Oxford.

Gilyard-Beer, R. and Coppack, G. 1986. 'Excavations at Fountains Abbey, North Yorkshire, 1979–80: the early development of the monastery' *Archaeologia* 108, 147–88.

Girouard, M. 1978. *Life in the English Country House.* New Haven and London, Yale University Press.

Godfrey, W.H. 1952. 'English cloister lavatories as independent structures' *Archaeol J.* 106, 91–7.

Gough, R. 1768. *Anecdotes of British Topography.* London.

Gough, R. 1786–96 (5 vols.). *Sepulchral Monuments in Great Britain.* London.

Gough, R. 1792. 'The mosaic pavement in the Prior's Chapel at Ely' *Archaeologia* 10, 151–5.

Graham, A.H. 1986. 'The Old Malthouse, Abbotsbury, Dorset: the medieval water-mill of the Benedictine Abbey' *Proc. Dorset Nat. Hist. and Archaeol. Soc.* 108, 103–25.

Graham, R. and Braun, H. 1940. 'Excavations on the site of Sempringham Priory' *J. British Archaeol. Assoc.* 5, 73–101.

Graham, R. and Gilyard-Beer, R. 1966. *Monk Bretton Priory.* London, HMSO.

Grainger, I. and Hawkins, D. 1988. 'Excavations at the Royal Mint site 1986–1988' *London Archaeologist* 5, no. 16, 429–36.

Green, C. and Whittingham, A.B. 1968. 'Excavations at Walsingham Priory, Norfolk, 1961' *Archaeological J.* 125, 255–90.

Greene, J.P. 1975. 'Norton Priory, history for a New Town' *Museums J.* 75, September 1975, 75–7.

Greene, J.P. 1979. 'The elevation of Norton Priory, Cheshire, to the status of Mitred Abbey' *Trans. Hist. Soc. Lancashire and Cheshire* 128, 97–112.

Greene, J.P. 1983. 'The new museum at Norton Priory, Cheshire' *Museums J.* 82, March 1983, 219–22.

Greene, J.P. 1989a. *Norton Priory: the archaeology of a medieval religious house.* Cambridge, Cambridge University Press.

Greene, J.P. 1989b. 'Methods of interpretation of monastic sites' in Gilchrist and Mytum 1989, 313–25.

Greene, J.P. and Johnson, B. 1978. 'An experimental tile kiln at Norton Priory, Cheshire' *Medieval Ceramics* 2, 30–41.

Greene, K. 1990. *Archaeology: an introduction.* London, Batsford.

Grose, F. 1794–5. *The Antiquities of Ireland.* 2 vols. 1794 and 1795, London, S. Hooper.

Gwynn, A. and Hadcock, R.N. 1970. *Medieval Religious Houses, Ireland.* London, Longman.

Hahn, H. 1957. *Die fruhe Kirchenbaukunst der Zisterzienser: Untersuchungen zur Baugeschichte von Kloster Eberbach im Rheingau unt ihren europaischen Analogien im 12. Jahrhundert.* Berlin.

Halsey, R. 1986. 'The earliest architecture of the Cistercians' in Norton and Park 1986, 65–85.

Harbottle, R.B. and Fraser, R. 1987. 'Black Friars, Newcastle upon Tyne, after the Dissolution of the Monasteries' *Archaeologia Aeliana* 5th ser. 15, 23–150.

Hare, J.N. 1985. *Battle Abbey: the eastern range and the excavations of 1978-80.* London, Historic Buildings and Monuments Commission for England.

Harris, E.C. 1979. *Principles of Archaeological Stratigraphy.* London, Academic Press.

Harrison, E.E. 1991. 'The history of Charterhouse and its buildings' *Trans. Ancient Monuments Soc.* 35, 1–28.

Harvey, J. 1972. *The Medieval Architect.* London, Wayland.

Hassall, T.G. 1972. 'Excavations at Oxford 1969, second interim report' *Oxoniensia* 35, 5–18.

Hassall, T.G. 1973. 'Excavations at Oxford 1970, third interim report' *Oxoniensia* 36, 1–14.

Hassall, T.G., Halpin, C.E. and Mellor, M. 1991. 'Excavations in St Ebbe's, Oxford, 1967–1976: part 1: Late Saxon and Medieval domestic occupation and tenements, and the Medieval Greyfriars' *Oxoniensia* 54, 1991, 71–278.

Hayes, J. 'Prior Wibert's waterworks' *Canterbury Chronicle* 71, 1977, 17–26, Friends of Canterbury Cathedral.

Heslop, D.H. 1987. 'Gisborough Priory: initial excavation of the priory church 1985' *Yorkshire Archaeol. J.* 59, 175–8.

Heslop, D.H. forthcoming. 'Excavation within the church at the Augustinian Priory of Gisborough, 1985-6'.

Hewett, C.A. 1985. *English Cathedral and Monastic Carpentry.* Chichester, Phillimore.

Hewitt, H.J. 1967. *Cheshire Under the Three Edwards.* Chester, Cheshire Community Council.

Heywood, S. 1989. 'The Priory of St Mary in the Meadow of the Order of Peterstone, Beeston next the Sea, Norfolk' *Norfolk Archaeology* 40, pt. 3, 226–59.

Hibbert, F.A. 1910. *The Dissolution of the Monasteries of Staffordshire.*

Hicks, M. and Tatton-Brown, T. 1991. 'St Gregory's Priory, Canterbury' *Current Archaeol.* 123, 100–6.

Hill, P.H. 1988. 'Whithorn' *Current Archaeol.* 110, 85–91.

Hill, P.H. 1991. *Whithorn 3: excavations at Whithorn Priory 1988-90.* Whithorn, Whithorn Trust.

Hinton, D.A. 1987. 'Archaeology and the Middle Ages' *Medieval Archaeology* 31, 1–12.

Hirst, S.M., Walsh, D.A. and Wright, S.M. 1983. *Bordesley Abbey II*. Oxford, British Archaeological Reports 111.

Hodder, M.A. 1991. 'Excavations at Sandwell Priory and Hall, 1982–88' *Trans. S. Staffordshire Archaeol. and Hist. Soc.* 31.

Hodges, R. 1991. *Wall-to-Wall History: the story of Roystone Grange*. London, Duckworth.

Hodges, R., Poulter, M. and Wildgoose, M. 1982. 'The medieval grange at Roystone Grange' *Derbyshire Archaeol. J.* 102, 88–100.

Hope, W.H. St J. 1901. 'Watton Priory, Yorkshire' *East Riding Antiq. Soc.* 8, 70–107.

Hope, W.H. St J. 1903. 'London Charterhouse and its old water supply' *Archaeologia* 58, 293–312.

Hope, W.H. St J. 1908. 'The round church of the Knights Templar of Temple Bruer' *Archaeologia* 61, 177–98.

Horn, W. and Born, E. 1965. *The Barns of the Abbey of Beaulieu and its Granges of Great Coxwell and Beaulieu St Leonards*. Berkeley, University of California Press.

Hudson, K. 1987. *Museums of Influence*. Cambridge, Cambridge University Press.

Jackson, V. 1990. 'The inception of the Dodder water supply' in Clarke 1990a, 129–41.

James, M.R. 1925. *Abbeys*. London, GWR.

James, T. 1978. 'A survey of the fishponds, watercourses and other earthworks at the site of Whitland Abbey and iron forge' *Carmarthenshire Antiquary* 14, 71–8.

Jones, A.K.G. 1976. 'The fish bones' in Black 1976.

Jones, A.K.G. 1989. 'The survival of fish remains at monastic sites' in Gilchrist and Mytum 1989, 173–84.

Keene, D. 1985. *Survey of Medieval Winchester*. Oxford, Clarendon Press.

Kemp, R. 1984. 'A fish-keeper's store at Byland Abbey' *Ryedale Historian* 12, 44–51.

Kemp, R. 1987. 'Anglian York – the missing link' *Current Archaeol.* 104, 259–63.

Kenyon, J.R. 1990. *Medieval Fortifications*. Leicester, Leicester University Press.

Klein, P. and Roe, A. 1988. *The Carmelite Friary, Corve Street, Ludlow: its history and excavation*. Birmingham.

Knowles, D. 1948–59 (3 vols.). *Religious Orders in England*. Cambridge, Cambridge University Press.

Knowles, D. 1976. *Bare Ruined Choirs*. Cambridge, Cambridge University Press.

Knowles, D. and Hadcock, R.N. 1971. *Religious Houses of England and Wales*. London, Longman.

Knowles, D. and St Joseph, J.K.S. 1952. *Monastic Sites from the Air*. Cambridge, Cambridge University Press.

Lamb, H.H. 1966. *The Changing Climate*. London, Methuen.

Lambrick, G. and Woods, H. 1976. 'Excavations on the second site of the Dominican Priory, Oxford' *Oxoniensia* 41, 168–231.

Lambrick, G. 1985. 'Further excavations on the second site of the Dominican Priory, Oxford' *Oxoniensia* 50, 131–208.

Lawless, G.P. 1987. *Augustine of Hippo and his Monastic Rule*. Oxford, Clarendon Press.

Leask, H. 1958–60. *Irish Churches and Monastic Buildings*. Dundalk, Dundalgan Press.

Leland, J. 1550. (published 1710–12). *Itinerary*. London.

MacGiolla Phadraig, B. 'Fourteenth century life in a Dublin monastery' in Clarke 1990b.

Mackie, R.L. and Cruden, S. 1954. *Arbroath Abbey*. Edinburgh, HMSO.

McAvoy, F. 1989. 'Sempringham Priory, Lincolnshire', *Work of the Central Excavation Unit*, London, English Heritage.

McDonnell, J. and Harrison, S.A. 1978. 'Monastic earthworks south of Byland Abbey' *Ryedale Historian* 9, 56.

McNeil, R. 1983. 'Two twelfth-century Wich Houses in Nantwich, Cheshire' *Med. Archaeol.* 27, 40–88.

McNeil, R. and Turner, R.C. 1990. 'An architectural and topographical survey of Vale Royal Abbey' *J. Chester Archaeol. Soc.* 70, 51–79.

Mayes, P. forthcoming. *The Templar Preceptory at South Witham, Lincolnshire.*

Mellor, J.T. and Pearce, T. 1981 *The Austin Friars, Leicester*. London, CBA Research Report 35.

Moffat, B. 1986. 'The environment of Battle Abbey estates in medieval times: a re-evaluation using pollen and sediments' *Landscape History* 8, 77–93.

Montagu of Beaulieu 1967. *The Gilt and the Gingerbread*. London, Michael Joseph.

Moorhouse, S. 1972. 'Finds from the excavations in the refectory at the Dominican Friary, Boston' *Lincolnshire Hist. and Archaeol. J.* 7, 21–53.

Moorhouse, S. 1986. 'A medieval monastic farm on Levisham Moor, North Yorkshire' *CBA Forum* 1986, 8–12.

Moorhouse, S. 1989. 'Monastic estates: their composition and development' in Gilchrist and Mytum 1989, 29–81.

Moorhouse, S. 1990. 'The quarrying of stone roofing slates and rubble in West Yorkshire during the Middle Ages' in Parsons 1990, 126–45.

Mytum, H.C. 1979. 'Excavations at Polesworth' *Trans. Birmingham and Warwickshire Archaeol. Soc.* 89, 79–90.

Norton, C. and Park, D. 1986. *Cistercian Art and Architecture of the British Isles*. Cambridge University Press.

Ormrod, W.M. 1985. 'Burials and benefactors: an aspect of monastic patronage in thirteenth-century England' in *England in the thirteenth century*. Grantham, Harlaxton College.

Ottaway, P. 1981. 'Sites review: Castle Garage' *Interim* 8, no. 3, 14–19, York Archaeol. Trust.

Park, D. 1986. 'Cistercian wall painting and panel painting' in Norton and Park 1986, 181–210.

Parsons, D. 1990. *Stone Quarrying and Building in England AD 43–1525*. Chichester, Phillimore.

Peers, C.R. 1927. 'Finchale Priory' *Archaeol. Aeliana* 4th ser. 4, 193–220.

Phillips, D. 1985. *The Cathedral of Archbishop Thomas of Bayeux: excavations at York Minster, vol. 2*. London, HMSO.

Platt, C. 1969. *The Monastic Grange in Medieval England*. London, Macmillan.

Platt, C. 1984a. *Medieval England from the Air*. London, George Philip.

Platt, C. 1984b. *The Abbeys and Priories of Medieval England*. London, Secker and Warburg.

Ponsford, M.W. 1975. *The Grey Friars in Bristol*. Bristol, Bristol City Museum.

Poulton, R. and Woods, H. 1984. *Excavations on the site of the Dominican Friary at Guildford*. Surrey Archaeol. Soc., Guildford.

Poulton, R. 1988. *Archaeological Investigation of the Site of Chertsey Abbey*. Res. Vol. of Surrey Archaeol. Soc. 11, Guildford.

Pugin, A.W. and Le Keux, J. 1827. *Specimens of the Architectural Antiquities of Normandy*. London, J. Britton.

Pugin, A.W. and Willson, E.J. 1821–31 (2 vols.). *Specimens of Gothic Architecture*. London, M.A. Nattali.

Rackham, O., Blair, W.J. and Munby, J.T. 1978. 'The thirteenth-century roofs and floors of the Blackfriars Priory at Gloucester' *Medieval Archaeol.* 22, 105–22.

Rahtz, P. and Hirst, S.M. 1976. *Bordesley Abbey*. British Archaeological Reports 23, Oxford.

Richardson, J.S. and Hume, J. 1987. *Sweetheart Abbey*. Edinburgh, HMSO.

Richardson, J.S. and Wood, M. *The Abbey of Dryburgh*. Edinburgh, HMSO.

Richardson, W. and Churton, E. 1843 (2 vols.). *The Monastic Ruins of Yorkshire*. York, Robert Sunter.

Rickman, T. 1819. *An Attempt to Discriminate the Styles of English Architecture*. Oxford, J.H. Parker.

Roberts, C.A., Lee, F. and Bintliff, J. 1989. *Burial Archaeology: current research, methods and developments*. Oxford, British Archaeological Reports 211.

Robinson, D.M. 1980. *The Geography of Augustinian Settlement in Medieval England and Wales*. Oxford, British Archaeological Reports 80.

Robinson, D.M. 1986. *Tintern Abbey*. Cardiff, Cadw.

Robinson, D.M. 1989. 'The introduction of new guidebooks at Welsh sites: experiences at Tintern and Valle Crucis' in Gilchrist and Mytum 1989, 327–38.

Robinson, D.M. 1990. *Tintern Abbey*. Cardiff, Cadw.

Robinson, J.M. 1979. *The Wyatts: an architectural dynasty*. Oxford, Oxford University Press.

Rodwell, R. 1981. *The Archaeology of the English Church*. London, Batsford.

Ronan, M.V. 1990. 'St Patrick's staff and Christ Church' in Clarke 1990b, 123–31.

Ross, F. 1882. *The Ruined Abbeys of Britain*. London, William Mackenzie.

Schofield, J. 1984. *The Building of London from the Conquest to the Great Fire*. London, British Museum Publications.

Shackley, M.L. 1981. *Environmental Archaeology*. London, George Allen and Unwin.

Shackley, M.L., Hayne, J. and Wainwright, N. 1988. 'Environmental analysis of medieval fishpond deposits at Owston Abbey, Leicestershire' in Aston, M. 1988, 301–8.

Sherlock, D. 1976. 'Discoveries at Horsham St Faith Priory' *Norfolk Archaeology* 36, part 3.

Sherlock, D. and Woods, H. 1988. *St Augustine's Abbey: report on excavations 1960–78*. Kent Archaeol. Soc., Maidstone.

Soulsby, I. 1983. *The Towns of Medieval Wales*. Chichester, Phillimore.

Southouse, T. 1671. *Monasticon Favershamiense*. London.

Speed, J. 1614. *Theatre of the Empire of Great Britain*. London.

Spencer, B. 1990. *Salisbury and South Wiltshire Museum Medieval Catalogue: Part 2. Pilgrim Souvenirs and Secular Badges*. Salisbury.

Stalley, R.A. 1980. 'Mellifont Abbey, a study of its architectural history' *Proc. Royal Irish Academy* 80c, 263–354.

Stalley, R.A. 1987. *The Cistercian Monasteries of Ireland*. New Haven, Yale University Press.

Steane, J.M. 1971. 'The medieval fishponds of Northamptonshire' *Northants Past and Present* 4, 299–310.

Stocker, D.A. 1984. 'The remains of the Franciscan Friary in Lincoln; a reassessment' in Addyman and Black 1984, 137–44.

Stones, J. 1989. *Three Scottish Carmelite Friaries*. Edinburgh, Soc. of Antiquaries.

Stopford, J. 1990. *Recording Medieval Floor Tiles*. London, CBA.

Stratford, N. 1987. *Romanesque and Gothic: essays for George Zarnecki*. Woodbridge, Boydell Press.

Stukeley, W. 1725. *Itinerarium Curiosum*. London, Baker and Leigh.

Stukeley, W. 1770. 'An account of Lesnes Abby' *Archaeologia* 1, 49–53.

Tabraham, C.G. 1984. 'Excavations at Kelso Abbey' *Proc. Soc. Antiquaries of Scotland*, 365–404.

Tatton-Brown, T. 1983. 'The precinct's water supply' *Canterbury Cathedral Chronicle* 77, 45–52.

Taylor, C. 1973. *The Cambridgeshire Landscape*. London, Hodder and Stoughton.

Taylor, C. 1979. *Roads and Tracks of Britain*. Guildford, Dent.

Thawley, C.R. 1981. 'The mammal, bird, and fish bones' in Mellor and Pearce 1981, 173–5.

Thompson, F.H. 1962. 'Excavations at the Cistercian Abbey of Vale Royal, Cheshire, 1958' *Antiquaries J.* 42, 183–207.

Thompson, F.H. 1983. *Studies in Medieval Sculpture*. London, Soc. of Antiquaries.

Thompson, M.W. 1981. *Ruins: their preservation and display*. London, British Museum.

Thompson, M.W. 1986. 'Associated castles and monasteries in the Middle Ages: a tentative list' *Archaeol. J.* 143, 305–21.

Walsh, D.N. 1979. 'A rebuilt cloister at Bordesley Abbey' *J. British Archaeol. Assoc.* 132, 42–9.

Walsh, D.N. 1980. 'Measurement and proportion at Bordesley Abbey' *Gesta* 19, 109–13.

Watkin, H.R. 1914. 'Use of Norse standards of measurement by the Normans as exemplified by the structure of Torre Abbey' *Trans. Devon Assoc.* 46, 326–45.

Weatherill, J. 1954. 'Rievaulx Abbey' *Yorkshire Archaeol. J.* 151, 333–54.

Weever, J. 1631. *Ancient Funerall Monuments*. London.

Wellbeloved, C. 1829. *Account of the Abbey of St Mary, York*. York, Yorkshire Philosophical Society.

Whitaker, T.D. 1801. *A History of the original Parish of Whalley and honour of Clitheroe in the Counties of Lancaster and York*. Blackburn.

Whitaker, T.D. 1823. *An History of Richmondshire in the North Riding of the County of York*. London.

Wildgoose, M. 1987. 'Roystone Grange' *Current Archaeol.* 105, 303–7.

Williams, D.H. 1990. *Atlas of Cistercian Lands in Wales*. Cardiff, University of Wales Press.

Williams, J.H. 1978. 'Excavations at Greyfriars, Northampton, 1972' *Northamptonshire Archaeol.* 13, 96–160.

Willis, R. 1868. 'The architectural history of the conventual buildings of the Monastery of Christ Church in Canterbury' *Archaeologia Cantiana* 7, 1868, 158–83.

Wilson, A.N. 1989. *The Laird of Abbotsford*. Oxford, Oxford University Press.

Wilson, C. 1983. 'The original setting of the Apostle and Prophet figures from St Mary's Abbey, York' in Thompson 1983, 100–21

Wilson, C. and Burton, J. 1988. *St Mary's Abbey, York*. York, The Yorkshire Museum.

Wood, J. 1991. 'Furness Abbey – recent archaeological work 1989–90' *Archaeology North* 1, June 1991.

Wood, J. forthcoming. *Furness Abbey – Survey and Archaeological Interpretation*. English Heritage Archaeological Report Series.

Woodfield, C. 1981. 'Finds from the Free Grammar School at the Whitefriars, Coventry, c.1545–c.1557/8' *Post Medieval Archaeology* 15, 81–159.

Woods, H. and Lambrick, G. 1976. 'Excavations on the second site of the Dominican Priory, Oxford' *Oxoniensia* 41, 168–231.

Woodward, S. 1836. 'An account of some discoveries made in excavating the foundations of Wymondham Abbey' *Archaeologia* 26, 287–99.

Wrathmell, S. 1987. *Kirkstall Abbey. The Guest House*. Wakefield, West Yorkshire Archaeology Service.

Wrathmell, S. and Moorhouse, S. *Kirkstall Abbey 1 – The 1950–64 excavations: a reassessment*. Wakefield, West Yorkshire Archaeology Service.

Index